Making Do and Hanging On

Growing Up in Apple Country
Through the Great Depression

by

Bruce L. Foxworthy

For Pat
Best wishes
Bruce Foxworthy

authorHOUSE®

AuthorHouse™
1663 Liberty Drive, Suite 200
Bloomington, IN 47403
www.authorhouse.com
Phone: 1-800-839-8640

This book is a work of non-fiction. Unless otherwise noted, the author and the publisher make no explicit guarantees as to the accuracy of the information contained in this book and in some cases, names of people and places have been altered to protect their privacy.

First published by AuthorHouse   12/11/2008

ISBN: 978-1-4343-9918-2 (e)
ISBN: 978-1-4343-9917-5 (sc)

Library of Congress Control Number: 2008906407

Printed in the United States of America
Bloomington, Indiana

This book is printed on acid-free paper.

Dedication

I dedicate these memoirs to my beloved family, including those acquired by the great good fortune of rediscovering and marrying my first and always love, Cleo Buckley, a "town girl" from Entiat.

1925

Imagine, if you can, a United States of only 115 million people, little more than a third of today's population, with most folks living on farms or in small towns. Imagine a time when most rural homes lacked electricity, running water, and indoor toilets; a time when horse and mule teams outnumbered trucks or tractors. Imagine life without a refrigerator, washing machine, central heating or air-conditioning; without color photographs, copy machines, television, computers or the Internet. That was the life into which I was born, in 1925.

I arrived for only the waning hours of my birth year, but 1925 had been quite a year. Calvin Coolidge was our President, and Charles Dawes our Vice President. Overseas, Adolf Hitler and Benito Mussolini were gaining power in Germany and Italy respectively, in moves that would progress ultimately to World War II. The British could still boast that the sun never set on the British Empire, in reference to their far-flung land possessions and colonies. The United States, in its self-declared role as protector of the Western Hemisphere, sent troops to Panama in 1925 "to protect U.S. interests"—mainly business interests and the Panama Canal.

Technology advanced rapidly in automobiles, aircraft, and communications. Motion pictures—"movies"—vied increasingly with Vaudeville, stage plays, and church sermons in shaping the public's attitudes and interests. Every town of any size had at least one movie theater, ranging from converted livery stables to glamorous showplaces that rivaled princely palaces. The only seeming requirement was electrical power to run the carbon-arc projector lights.

Charlie Chaplin, Harold Lloyd and Buster Keaton starred as comedy performers in the black-and-white, silent movies, which, in all but the very small-town theaters, were accompanied by live piano or organ "mood music." Romantic movie heartthrobs included Greta Garbo, Clara Bow, John Barrymore, and the great Rudolf Valentino, whose girlish voice prevented his conversion to the "talkie" movies that were on the way. Mack Sennett's Keystone Kops had introduced the slapstick comedy carried forward by later comedy teams. Western adventures, with dashing stars such as Tom Mix, Buck Jones, and Hoot Gibson, were favorite movies for young boys.

For home entertainment, many folks had wind-up phonographs. The sound came from grooves in black shellac disks turning under steel needle points pressed down by heavy "tone arms." The sound was strictly acoustical; carefully designed wooden sound ducts, or "speakers" provided the only amplification. Radios, powered by cumbersome batteries, were also becoming common, and the ultimate home-entertainment system was a combination phonograph and radio, "with ample space within the cabinet for batteries."

In 1925, the newest songs included *"Sweet Georgia Brown," "If You Knew Susie like I Know Susie,"* and the more romantic *"Moonlight and Roses."* The latest dance rage was the "Charleston."

Prohibition against alcohol had been the law of the land since the federal Volstead Act took effect in January, 1920. Prohibition caused thousands upon thousands of otherwise law-abiding Americans to become criminals under the Volstead Act. I was to learn that some of my own extended family defied the law by making, and even selling, home brew during the "dry" years.

The year 1925, like later years of the 1920s, was a time of relative prosperity. Census records show the average income for 1925 of $2,240, which bought goods at prices such as 9 cents for a loaf of bread, a gallon of milk for 56 cents, and gasoline for 12 cents per gallon. Coffee sold in Wenatchee, Washington, at 43 cents and sirloin beef steak at 22 cents per pound. That December, extra-fancy Delicious apples sold in the range of $3.21 to $4.00 per bushel box.

Optimism and investments in the future grew to unprecedented highs. A boom in installment buying—"a dollar down and a dollar a week"—let Americans have instantly what they might have waited years for in earlier decades. "Betting on the come," a gambler might say. One developer promoted "Houses with land for $6,000, one percent down, one percent a month" with first and second mortgages.

The pervasive optimism and the ease of installment buying led to a malignant growth of consumer debt and speculation in risky "get-rich-quick" schemes. The country was setting itself up for the financial crash of 1929. But even the few who foresaw that economic train wreck could not imagine the casualty toll.

CONTENTS

PREFACE

The Great Depression dominated conditions during my boyhood. Folks who did not live through that period, between 1929 and 1939, can scarcely imagine the full force and impact of the depression. It caused enormous hardship for tens of millions of Americans and spread to the rest of the world. A large percentage of our nation's banks, businesses, and farms failed during that time, causing massive unemployment which quickly translated into widespread poverty and suffering. The depression was a cruel crucible that tested and tempered those who survived it.

These memoirs are the product of my recollections, beginning in 1927, reinforced and expanded by accounts from family members and contemporaries, as well as by researched documents and photographs. The memoirs center on the time of my family's residence in the Entiat Valley, in the eastern foothills of the Cascade Range of central Washington State, a region noted for its productive orchards and the high quality of its fruit.

Just as the routines of daily life are punctuated by special events, the following descriptive reminiscences are interspersed with anecdotal stories and vignettes about the life and times I survived. The descriptive narration is factual to the best of my memory and research. The inserted stories, too, are faithful to the times and based on fact, but some have been shaped to fill gaps, or to create a more engaging tale, or to protect the guilty (often myself). To identify these vignettes for the reader, their titles are shown in italics. In these stories, a few names have been changed, for example, to avoid embarrassment to some fellow mischief-makers. If any of the latter read the stories and think they recognize untenable things about themselves, I shall hide behind the usual disclaimers and perhaps insist that their memories are faultier than mine.

For the Entiat Valley, the depression resulted in sharp declines in demands and prices for apples and pears—the main local commodities—followed by rapid exhaustion of family savings and the slide into widespread subsistence living. Despite unprecedented governmental spending on job creation and aid for farms and businesses, hardships dragged on in our valley as in the rest of the country, and economic recovery did not take hold until the beginning of World War II.

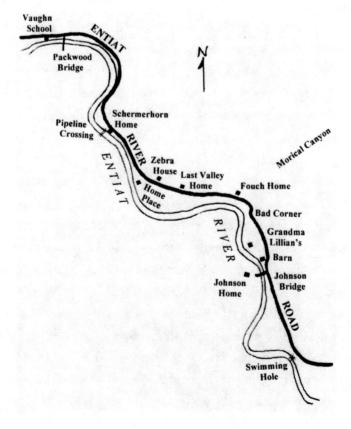

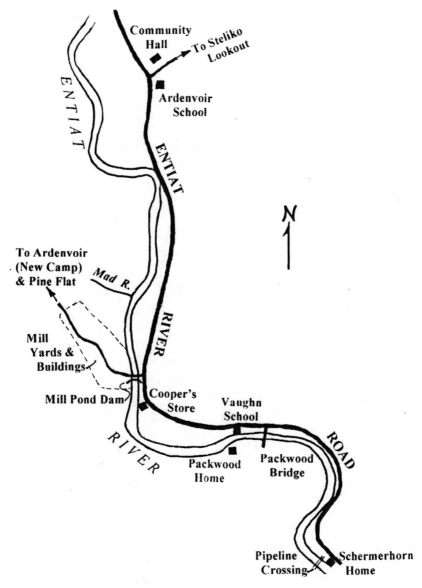

*(above) Sketch map showing selected features in the middle
Entiat Valley, northern part, in the 1930s*

*(left) Sketch map showing selected features in the middle
Entiat Valley, southern part, in the 1930s*

DEPARTURE AND ARRIVAL

"Tell me, Bruce," the grizzled recruiting officer asked, "What's your reason for joining the Navy?"

From across his scarred, wooden desk, I answered honestly. "To stay out of the Army."

I watched the recruiter's index fingers type "PATRIOTIC" onto my enlistment form. The loud strikes of the Royal typewriter's keys seemed the only sounds in the world. In a chair to my left, my pacifist mother wiped her eyes on a small handkerchief.

The recruiting office was in Wenatchee, county seat of Chelan County, the most central of Central Washington and thirty road miles from where I'd grown up. The time was December 1943, a few weeks before my eighteenth birthday, when I would be eligible for the World War II military draft. The U.S. armed forces were in bloody struggles in both Europe and the Pacific region, and the prospect of my being drafted into the Army ground forces finally convinced Mother to sign my Navy enlistment papers.

I was five-foot-six and a solid 145 pounds. Just right, I thought, for a Navy fighter-plane's cockpit or the cramped quarters of a submarine. Alas, the flawed vision in one eye prevented either future. My enlistment came with no promises, just uncertainties.

The recruiter gave me a railroad pass to Spokane, dated a few days hence, along with my orders to report for duty. "You'll be met at the Spokane station and taken to the receiving center there," he said. "Welcome to the Navy, and good luck."

Mother said little while I drove back home. Once, I saw her crying quietly while she stared out the car window.

All too soon, my departure time came. The evening of December 28, after a good home-cooked supper, Dad and Mom drove me and my sweetheart, Cleo, to the Great Northern Railroad depot in Wenatchee to await the night train from Seattle to Spokane. The depot closed at night during wartime, so we had no place to wait except in Mom's 1935 Chevy.

The train was very late. Time hung as heavy as the wet snow falling around us in the parking lot. All of us had long-since run out of small talk. Periodically, Dad would start the car to run the windshield wipers and the heater, then kill the engine to save precious gasoline. The snow turned the brown car white, and the windows steamed over to exclude the outside world. In the front seat, my folks faced forward, Dad in stoic silence, Mom with frequent sniffles. In the back, Cleo and I cuddled under a lap robe and declared our love in whispers.

At about 1:30 a.m., the train's headlight appeared far up the track and its whistle sounded. In the three minutes it took the train to reach the depot, there were multiple hugs and kisses, and a firm handshake from my Dad.

"Now you be a good boy," Mom admonished, "and stay out of trouble, and don't start smoking.

"And write!" Mom called after me as I trotted toward the station platform carrying my small valise in one hand and a lump the size of an apple box in my throat.

*   *   *

Spokane, Washington, where I was sworn into the Navy, is also where I was born. My arrival to this world came in a crowded bedroom of a small, frame house at 526 South Thor Street, in what was then the eastern edge of the city.

"He's not strong," the doctor said, "but with good care he should do fine."

My grandmother Edna, herself the mother of two sons, was not so sure. She reportedly shook her head and muttered, "That boy will never amount to much." Those words must have come to Mamma's mind many times through the years while she and Dad struggled to do their best for me.

Mamma was attended by her mother, Edna Bedient, and by Dr. John E. Hoyt. The date was December 30, 1925, of an apparently unremarkable winter. As you will see further on, Dad was a frugal opportunist, and he was sometimes accused of attempting to produce the first baby of 1926. In those days, parents of the New Year's first arrival often received a valuable array of gifts. I missed that notoriety by twenty-seven hours.

As far as I know, my birth had no particular complications, but in those days, nice women did not openly discuss human reproduction.

After a "lying-in" period, my father bundled Mamma and me into their black Model T Ford touring car and headed westward across the Big Bend plateau toward the Entiat River valley. The drive was more than 160 miles, mostly along U.S. Highway 2, which was largely paved by then. We passed through a few scattered farming towns, but most of our route crossed rolling, bleak expanses of basalt scabland and dry-land wheat fields from Spokane to Waterville.

West of Waterville, we descended the steep and twisting Pine Canyon road connecting the plateau with the floodplain of the Columbia River, roughly two thousand feet lower. At that time, the Pine Canyon road, switch-backing between steep canyon walls, was a real test of automotive machinery. That down-hill passage would have been a special challenge to the transmission bands and mechanical brakes of the Model T.

Pine Canyon's mouth opens onto the village of Orondo. From there we traveled four miles northward, and across the free-flowing Columbia River on a small wooden ferry, to the town of Entiat.

The last leg of the trip was 8 1/2 miles up the Entiat River valley on a graveled road to the small apple ranch of my widowed paternal grandmother, Lillian Foxworthy.

That wintertime trip certainly was no crossing of Donner Pass by covered wagon, but it must have been demanding nonetheless: a noisy touring car with only fabric roof and leaky side curtains to keep out the wind; no car heater, just blankets for warmth; long stretches of desolation between towns; and average driving speeds of forty miles per hour or less.

"Entiat" is from an Indian word meaning "rapid waters." My home for the next eighteen years was the steep-sided, pine-sprinkled Entiat Valley, carved into the eastern foothills of the Cascade Range by glaciers and "rapid waters." The southeast-trending valley of the Entiat River lies about midway between the better known valleys occupied by Lake Chelan, to the north, and the Wenatchee River, to the south. All three water bodies drain into the massive Columbia River. The Entiat Valley is about fifty-five miles long from its head at the basin of Entiat Glacier to its mouth at the town of Entiat. Its upper part is heavily forested, and its lower dozen miles or so have historically contained very productive fruit orchards.

THE NURTURERS

DAD AND MOTHER

My father, Gerald LaVerne Foxworthy, was born in Barron, Wisconsin, on July 5, 1901, to Bruce Lynn Foxworthy and Lillian Arvada Foxworthy. Dad used to joke that after one Wisconsin winter he convinced his folks to move west to a milder climate. They reached the original Entiat town site in 1902, when Dad was just a toddler. From there the family moved several times, progressively up the Entiat Valley, but Dad did most of his growing up on "the old Foxworthy place," 8 1/2 miles up valley from the town, with his only sibling, my Aunt Achsa.

My father was short and wiry, with curly light-brown hair, wild eyebrows and a quick grin that showed a gold front tooth acquired as a result of playing amateur ice hockey.

Dad had experienced some bad teen years. He carried the scars of severe acne, which must have been terrible for a gregarious fellow like Dad. But much worse, the untimely death of Grandpa Bruce in 1920 left Dad, at age eighteen, the man of the small family. And in between came great disappointment about his schooling, which had to end just past the grade-school level.

Dad and his sister Achsa got most of their education through the eighth grade at the Gaines School, about three miles down valley from their home. However, the nearest high school, at Entiat, was 8 1/2 miles from the ranch, more than two hours each way by foot or horseback. There was no school bus then, and no way Dad could attend Entiat High unless he got lodgings in town, impossible for the family at that time.

In contrast, by the time Aunt Achsa finished eighth grade, enough neighbors were driving to the high school that she could arrange rides with them, and she graduated from Entiat High in the spring of 1926.

Dad, after taking the few freshman-level courses he could at Gaines school and then swallowing the disappointment of not being able to attend high school, moved to a boarding house in Wenatchee and got a job as a messenger in the Commercial Bank and Trust Company. He liked the work and earned promotion to a position as clerk, but the fates conspired to end his banking career. First, a balky car backfired while he was cranking it and broke Dad's right arm, and then his father's death forced his permanent return home to work the family orchard.

Dad always regretted the stifling of his education, and took at least one correspondence course, in electro-mechanics. I know because, as a child, I found his texts and workbooks in the attic and tried to make sense of them as soon as I could read.

My mother, Alma Lulu (Bedient) Foxworthy, was born August 28, 1905, at Cheney, Washington, to Edna (Zesiger) Bedient and Albert Bedient. Her school years were spent in Palouse, Wash., where she graduated from high school in 1923. She had four siblings—two brothers and two sisters—the youngest of whom died as a child. Her family later lived in Spokane and Oroville, Washington, before settling in the Entiat area.

Mother was five feet of plump, brown-haired sweetness, with dark crescents under her eyes and a naturally down-turned mouth. Those features probably gave her a sultry look when Dad met her, but in later years they imparted a sad, though sympathetic, appearance.

Mother was bright and literate, and I owe whatever grammar skills I have to her use of proper English in our home. Like most others in my family, and most neighbors too, Mamma tried to live by the Ten Commandments and the Golden Rule. She was devoutly religious, and always had her Bible nearby.

She lived with her family in Oroville, Washington, when, at age nineteen, she learned of work opportunities in the apple harvest and went to work sorting apples at Keystone Ranch in the lower Entiat Valley. I never heard where Mother, by all accounts a very proper young lady, stayed during this time. I also don't know how Dad met her there—perhaps he was trucking apples to that packing shed. Aunt Achsa said that Dad had been squiring around a lovely school marm, as teachers were often called, but the teacher faded into obscurity after Gerald and Alma got acquainted. They married in a simple civil ceremony in Omak, December 23, 1924.

Alma and Gerald Foxworthy, wedding picture, 1924

GRANDPARENTS

Grandma Lillian ("Mom") Foxworthy, was born Lillian Arvada Denman at Inwood, Indiana, November 18, 1878. She told me most of what I know about her side of the family but little about her own background in the Midwest, except that most of her Denman relatives were in Indiana. Nor do I know much about her education, although it probably stopped at grammar school; girls then were seldom prepared for any role other than housewife and mother.

I was told by a Denman genealogist that Denman ancestors have been in America since the 1700s, and that two of them fought in the Revolutionary War. Therefore, if my descendants care about such things, they could qualify as Daughters (or Sons) of the American Revolution.

Grandma Lillian said the Denmans were Scotch-Irish and Dutch.

My knowledge about Grandpa Bruce is similarly sketchy. He was born May 3, 1875 at Bloomfield, Indiana, and probably grew up on a farm nearby. I don't know how he met Grandma Lillian or when the couple moved to Barron, Wisconsin, where Dad was born. They were married on May 5, 1898, at Shelburn, Indiana.

Grandpa Bruce had two brothers, Bright and Dwight, and a sister Hope. Bright stayed in Barron, Wisconsin. Hope and Dwight moved to Fitzgerald, Georgia. Only Grandpa Bruce brought his family west.

My Foxworthy grandparents and baby Gerald arrived at the original Entiat town site in 1902, after traveling west by train to Wenatchee. In those days, a family could rent half or all of a box car and live in it with their belongings during the trip. At Wenatchee, my grandparents transferred their goods to a paddle-wheel steamboat, which took them the twenty miles up the Columbia River to the old Entiat Landing, near the mouth of the Entiat River. They chose the Entiat Valley for their future because friends from Wisconsin, a family named Fletcher, were already established four miles up the valley and had sent back encouraging letters about local opportunities.

Dad's folks and baby Gerald arrived at Entiat with only the things they could bring on the train and steamboat, and without a place to stay. At first, Grandma ran a restaurant in the old town's hotel, probably in exchange for the family's lodging. Grandpa took whatever work he could find, mainly orchard work and road-building with a team of horses. I don't know about all their later living arrangements, but in 1908, when my aunt Achsa (Laura Achsa) was born, they lived in a small cabin in the lower end of Mills Canyon, 3 ½ miles up valley from Entiat town. A succession of other moves followed, including a stay in a cabin owned by the Fletchers, the purchase in 1913 of a house and roughly 1 ½ acres of land in Roaring Creek Canyon, and even a stay in a cellar-house of a family named Bortz. That cellar house was the last place they lived before they finally had accumulated the money for "Grandma Lillian's place," my first residence in the valley.

Grandma Lillian and Grandpa Bruce Foxworthy, young Gerald (Dad), and unhappy looking Aunt Achsa

I never knew my Grandfather Bruce, except in sepia daguerreotypes and other old photos. He died in 1920 of Bright's disease, a kidney ailment. He and other Foxworthys are buried in Entiat Valley Cemetery, four miles up valley from the town. I remember the shock when, as a boy, I first saw my own name, "Bruce L. Foxworthy," on Grandpa's tombstone. I had not known how close my name was to his, differing only in middle names with the same initial.

The Foxworthy name is English, but I have not made the family connection to England.

On my Mother's side, I know even less about the family. I do know that grandpa Albert Bedient was trained as a printer and typesetter, and worked at that trade before the depression. From their long-term home in Palouse, Wash., the Bedient family moved several times—to Oroville, to Spokane, and finally to the Entiat area, where Mamma's relatives survived (but didn't exactly prosper) at various jobs in fruit orchards and packing sheds, at cutting timber in the upper Entiat basin, and at various jobs in lumber mills.

The Bedient name, too, is English.

Grandma Edna Bedient was Swiss, a daughter of Swiss immigrants named Zesiger. She had four siblings: a sister and brother, my Great Aunt Bess and Great Uncle Ben who lived nearby with their spouses, plus two other brothers who settled in western Washington.

Grandpa and Grandma Bedient had five children, four of whom survived childhood. In addition to my mother were my Aunt Verna (or "Dee Dee", later shortened to "Deed"), and my uncles Dick and Max. Max was an "afterthought" child, only five years older than I. He assumed the role of big brother to me, and was a large part of my early life. Another girl, born after Aunt Verna and before Uncle Max, died in the influenza epidemic of 1918. I never heard her called anything but "poor Bessie."

EXTENDED FAMILY

I was blessed not only with loving parents and grandparents but also with extended family, most of whom, during my growing-up years, lived close by:

- Aunt Achsa (Laura Achsa) Foxworthy (after marrying Frank T. Cook in 1933, she went by Achsa Foxworthy Cook). They had no children then, but were especially influential in my life, not only because they usually lived nearby, but also because they were unfailingly kind and understanding. Aunt Achsa worked in business offices and later packed apples and pears in local packing sheds. Uncle Frank worked mostly at local lumber mills.

- Aunt Verna (Deed) Lanoue and her husband, Jess Lanoue; parents of Gary (ten years younger than I) and Gail (twelve years younger). Uncle Jess worked in the woods as a tree faller. Aunt Verna packed fruit in valley packing sheds, often with Mamma and Aunt Achsa. I stayed with the Lanoues often, and learned doggerel poems from Aunt Deed.

- Uncle Dick Bedient and his wife Dorothy; parents of Virgil (about one year younger than I) and Jean (about three years younger). Uncle Dick worked as sawyer at the C. A. Harris & Son lumber mill in our valley, and later as millwright at a mill at Manson, Washington, where I visited the family in summers.

- Great Aunt Bess (Zesiger) Frakes and her husband, Richard (Dick) Frakes. They had no children, but were kind and patient with me when I occasionally stayed with them. Uncle Dick had been an expert rifleman in the Marine Corps during World War I, but wouldn't talk to me about the war.

- Great Uncle Ben Zesiger and his wife Isabel. Their one child, Mary Louise, was three years older than I and rather disdainful of a boy my age. As early as I can remember, Uncle Ben owned a Shell service station beside the main street of Entiat. He added a beer counter in the station at the end of Prohibition. He let me work the big toggle handles that forced gasoline up into the glass reservoirs atop his gravity-fed gasoline pumps.

- Uncle Max Earl Bedient, only five years older than I, but to me a sophisticated man of the world. I stayed often with my Bedient grandparents and, therefore, with Max. He and I had space to roam by ourselves in those times and places, and we did occasionally exceed the boundaries of good sense: swimming in risky places, making unprotected campfires, hunting rattlesnakes, shooting our slingshots at questionable targets, and other mischief that shall go unmentioned.

GRANDMA LILLIAN'S

My first home in the Entiat Valley was at Grandma Lillian's. At the time of my arrival, she had been widowed for about five years. A few years prior to the death of my grandfather, Bruce L. Foxworthy (middle name Lynn instead of my LaVerne), the family had purchased about four acres of land with a producing apple orchard. This little ranch included a small frame house, a nearby cellar house, and a barn. Only the house had paint, a weathered white, and even its wide back porch matched the bare, weathered brown of the other buildings, including the outhouse.

Grandma's orchard was divided by the Entiat River Road, at that time unpaved but fairly well maintained by county road graders. The upper orchard perched on a narrow slope ending at a road cut about fifteen feet high. The lower orchard and the buildings spread over a flatter, gravely terrace of the Entiat River, nowhere more than ten feet above the river's springtime flood stage. The river skirted the entire lower property (flowing southeasterly here), and the sound of rushing water permeated my early life.

Hilltop view in central Entiat Valley, showing most of Grandma Lillian's place. Cellar house is left of house and woodshed (sunlit roof). Sharp bend in road, right-center, is site of The Car Collector. Above that is barn of neighbor Earl P. Fouch. Our home-place orchard shows in left distance as indistinct band in front of darker trees. Grandma's barn is out of view, lower right.

Though tiny by today's standards, Grandma Lillian's house seemed sturdy and well-made. It had three rooms—kitchen, living room and bedroom—high ceilings, and a shingled roof. In the fashion of the time, the upper walls and ceiling were lath-and-plaster, and the lower walls vertical-board wainscoting, painted light-grey, as I remember. A kitchen door opened onto the roofed back porch and, in the packed-dirt backyard just beyond, to the water pump. A front door from the living room opened onto a little patch of lawn on the side of the house toward the valley road, some hundred yards distant beyond a strip of orchard.

The bedroom held two feather-beds, used by Grandma and Aunt Achsa, a chest of drawers, a dressing table with mirror and, of course, chamber pots under the beds. Adults could scarcely squeeze between the beds, and had to sit on a bed to use the dressing table. As a youngster, I had many a nap in that tiny bedroom.

The kitchen, at the other end of the little house, was typical for the time and place: wood-fired cooking range, linoleum-topped work counter with cupboards above and below, and a small, rectangular table that could be dragged away from a wall at mealtime to seat the family in round-backed, wooden chairs. The water supply sat atop the counter in a bucket with dipper, and disposal of waste water was accomplished by carrying its container out to the back porch and throwing it onto the back yard.

The living room, too, was crowded. Besides the heater stove and small box for its wood supply, the room held a daybed (my father's bed in his youth), a small side table, and two straight-back chairs. A larger table had been moved out to the back porch to make room for the family's tall, dark-veneered Victrola phonograph and Aunt Achsa's upright piano.

Aunt Achsa displaying me on her 1925 Model T Ford coupe.

19

Achsa loved music, and had me singing beside her on the piano bench before I could possibly have understood the words I parroted. One of our favorite duets was *Ramona*.

Although Grandma's house had formerly served her family of four, it was too small to hold my grandmother, eighteen-year-old Achsa, and Dad's new family. Therefore, the first two winters of my life, Grandma and Aunt Achsa made the sacrifice of moving across the back yard into the cellar house while my folks and I occupied Grandma's house. When the weather warmed during those first two years of my life, my folks and I traded places with my aunt and grandma, moving them back into their house and us into the cellar house. My first memories date from our cellar-house sojourn.

THE CELLAR HOUSE

The cellar house spanned a convenient steepening of the slope between the back yard of Grandma Lillian's house and the riverbank. It was a rough wooden structure some twenty feet long with a "daylight" cellar below the river end of the building. The door of the upper level opened onto Grandma's back yard. A trapdoor in the floor provided access to a crude wooden stair that descended into the cellar. The dirt-floored cellar had its own glass-paned door facing the river.

For its intended purposes—dry storage for equipment and orchard supplies in the upper part, food storage below—the cellar house was adequate. However, for human habitation it left something to be desired. The sides and the floor of the upper story were of rough fir lumber with plenty of knotholes and cracks between the boards. Even with the addition of a wood-fired kitchen stove and cardboard tacked inside the walls to baffle the wind, the cellar house was rough living. Its only advantage was its nearness to the outhouse for wintertime nature calls. During warm weather, however, that proximity was a disadvantage because of outhouse flies and smells.

My very earliest memory is of lying face-down on that floor peering down between the cracks, especially when the musty smelling, dirt-floored cellar below was illuminated by the afternoon sun shining through the dirty, cobwebbed glass of the cellar door. I was accused of stuffing small objects through those floor cracks to fall into the dirt of what we would now call the crawl space, or into the cellar itself. By my own reflections, I was guilty.

THE GARNET RING

Oh, I almost forgot again, Alma thought, smiling.

She always smiled when she thought of her engagement ring, a thin gold band adorned by the single, deep-red stone held in delicate golden fingers. Gerald had wanted to buy her a diamond, or at least her ruby birthstone. But because they needed so many things, she had suggested a less-expensive garnet instead. It would look almost like a ruby, she told him, and even though garnets don't wear well, she would always remember to take it off when she was doing rough work. Besides, she couldn't love it more if it were the Star of India, because it came from him and symbolized their love.

Alma slipped the garnet ring from her finger, leaving the narrow, plain wedding band. She placed the ring on the upended, curtained wooden apple box that held the chamber pot beside their bed. Her hand rested briefly on her bible, always on that improvised bed stand unless she was reading it.

God has been good to us, she thought. *They were afraid the baby might not live because he was so frail. He seems fine now, praise the Lord.*

She smiled over at the boy, lying on his stomach looking down through a crack between the worn, grey floorboards.

He spends a lot of time there. At least it keeps him away from the hot stove while I'm busy.

The sound of bubbling water drew her attention to the oblong copper boiler resting on the small, black cook stove with its crackling wood fire. With her paring knife, she cut strips from a bar of brown lye-soap, letting the pieces fall into the steaming boiler. The pungent smell of the soap filled the oppressively hot room, masking the normal smells: muskiness rising from the underlying dirt cellar, and urine odor from the diaper can and the dirty-clothes box next to the boy's crib.

From a heaping dishpan of diapers and other baby clothes that she had previously rinsed in buckets outside the door, she added these pieces to the steaming water, stirring them in with a length of bleached broomstick. She glanced at the boy. He was still staring down through a crack in the floor.

Alma paused to pick up the hem of her faded yellow apron and wipe sweat from her face. She waved both hands at a fly buzzing around her head, causing the stick she was still holding to strike one of the old, brown rafters above the stove. The noise caused the boy to raise his head and look at her. Their eyes met as he watched for a while, as if trying to relate the strange sound to what she was doing. Finally, he turned his attention back to the crack.

"I'll be so glad when you're out of diapers, Brucie Bug," Alma said aloud.

The boy crawled over to his mother and grasped the hem of her dress. "Uh, uh," he urged.

"No, honey. Mamma can't pick you up right now."

"Uh, uh, UH!" he grunted, trying to pull himself up by her leg and skirt.

She shifted the stick to her left hand and stooped to grasp him under one arm, raising him to stand against her. She stooped again to feel his diaper.

"You're okay, and Mamma's busy now. You go away from this hot stove. Go rock in your little chair."

The boy dropped to a sitting position and looked up at her. When she didn't relent, he crawled slowly toward the edge of the small room.

She stopped stirring and poking at the clothes in the boiling water, and opened the door of the glowing firebox to add a stick of wood.

The child began to cry, in a way that got her attention. She came toward him, wiping her hands on her apron.

"What's wrong, honey?" she asked the boy, who was now sitting on the floor.

In reply, he patted the crack with his right palm, still howling.

In only a moment, she understood. Shifting the boy a few feet away, she knelt down and looked through the crack.

She saw a spoon he had been playing with; then, more faintly, his cellu-loid teething ring.

"Mamma can't get your toys down there, honey. Maybe Daddy can reach them from the cellar when he gets in. Don't put anything else down the cracks. Bad, bad!"

Something about the boy's renewed howling sent a shiver of apprehen-sion through her. She recalled seeing him standing beside the bed stand. She jumped up and stepped toward the bed. The crying stopped.

"My ring's gone!" Turning to the boy, she asked breathlessly, "Did you have Mamma's ring? What did you do with Mamma's ring? Show me what you did with Mamma's ring."

Solemnly, the boy crawled over and patted the crack again.

"Oh, baby," she sobbed, dropping to the floor beside him and sweeping him up against her breast. "What have you done? What have you done?"

*　　*　　*

Despite hours spent in moving shelves of canned fruit, and digging and sifting soil beneath the floor, the garnet ring was never found. And in the hard-time years that followed, it never was replaced.

CHICKENS IN THE YARD

Most families in the valley had chickens. The eggs were a staple for breakfast and for cooking, and chicken was the cheapest meat available other than wild fish and game. (Grandma Lillian's chicken-and-dumplings dish was fabulous.)

Farm chickens don't require much care, just dry places to roost and lay eggs, and a little "egg mash" and cracked wheat. Otherwise, the chickens just roam around, making clucking sounds and eating bugs and grass. If you want chicks, of course, you also need a rooster, Nature's dawn alarm clock.

Chickens in the yard do present certain hazards, especially for little kids. Chickens don't like to be grabbed and held, which is a natural tendency of children. The rooster and the older hens try to establish the child rather low in the pecking order, by means of real, painful pecking. Also, chickens poop a lot, and youngsters are not good at avoiding these deposits. My second-earliest memory involves this latter hazard.

The day was warm, and I was padding around the packed dirt of the back yard wearing just a diaper. I apparently wandered into the chickens' favorite dump site, and suddenly realized that I had stinky, gushy chicken poop on my feet. I did what I considered to be sensible. I sat down and tried to wipe the do-do off with my hands. Reportedly, I not only sat in more of it but, in trying to wipe the disgusting stuff from my feet and then my hands, I was pretty well covered from chest to toe by the time I howled my frustration to my mother.

Instead of treating my plight with the expected tender sympathy, however, Mamma dragged me to the water pump and doused me with torrents of shockingly frigid water while she washed me roughly and scolded me for getting into the chicken poop.

Since then, I have felt that the only good chicken is a dead—and preferably roasted—chicken. And I have made it a lifelong practice to avoid further contact with chicken poop.

The author, in yard near the cellar house, getting bath from Grandma Lillian's pump.

THE HOME PLACE—
EARLY YEARS

The second home I remember was less than a mile upriver from Grandma Lillian's. My folks and I lived the longest together there, and it is the place my thoughts flash back to when I think of "home."

The home place comprised about ten acres of apple orchard and undeveloped terrace land between the Entiat Valley Road and the river. Our small, white-painted frame house sat among mature apple trees near the upstream end of the property. Someone said the house was moved there from another site by truck—a story that I first discounted as being one of the fables that grownups tell us kids. But I think I always knew we weren't its first occupants, because I don't remember the digging of the well we had near the south side of our house, nor the planting of our small lawn in front.

It was in that front yard that I learned to respect apple trees.

DON'T PEE ON APPLE TREES

One seemingly pleasant day before I started school, while I was playing on my hands and knees on the front lawn, I felt a call of Nature. Because I had been imbued with the need for modesty, I knee-walked over to a nearby large apple tree to screen myself from the house. Still kneeling, I relieved myself against the base of the tree trunk. I was vigorously shaking off the last drops, in the manner of my male relatives, when suddenly Daddy appeared behind me. He jerked me to my feet with one hand while he whipped off his belt with the other. Roaring, "Don't do that!" he gave me two or three lashes with the leather, then dropped me to the grass and stomped off.

I no doubt bawled my head off and ran to Mamma, who, as I recall, seemed sympathetic to my story but just said, "Mind your father."

That lesson stayed with me for sure. I doubt that I ever peed on another apple tree, even after I figured out Dad's mistaken reason for punishing me that day.

*   *   *

Our home was respectable for the times—four small rooms with white lath-and-plaster walls, and French windows that swung open to a small porch and lawn in the front. But it was crowded and primitive by today's standards. We had no plumbing, no electricity, no telephone—no such wire or pipe connections to the outside world. In fact, in all our Entiat Valley homes, we never had running water, much less an indoor toilet. Our heat came from wood stoves—the cook stove in the kitchen and a tall, ornate wood heater in the living room. The two bedrooms were unheated. Any extra heat for our beds on cold nights came in the form of hot-water bottles, or heated sadirons wrapped in towels, tucked in to preheat the flannel sheets and left in to warm our feet.

Our only "running water" poured from the spout of an old pitcher pump at the well a few steps outside the kitchen door. That pump required priming each time it was used—in the winter with steaming teakettle water.

Wood for our stoves was mostly "slab wood" from the nearby Harris mill—chunks of the bark-covered, rounded slabs from the first cuts of the huge band saws to square off the logs. Slab wood was given free to all the mill employees, and sold for very little to other valley residents. Slab wood from the mill's yellow pine was not bad to handle, but I disliked the slab wood from fir trees, which was especially messy and slivery.

When Dad had time to join one of the family "wood parties," he and the other men would drive his truck out into the national forest and locate a downed tree, saw it into moveable lengths, and haul home the tree sections for further sawing and splitting into clean firewood.

The Harris mill also provided us with another special kind of wood. Because most of the mill's production comprised the lumber pieces, called "box shook," for wooden apple and pear boxes, one byproduct was the semi-smooth lumber trimmings. I loved the truckloads of box wood that Dad brought home. Not only did the box wood make my chore of splitting kindling a clean, pleasant task, but it provided a treasure of smooth wood for imaginative building projects. Many a miniature sled, boat and airplane were fashioned by my friends and me from box wood, nailed together with 5½-penny box nails scrounged from sawdust piles where the neighbors made their apple boxes.

For several years at the home place, our nighttime light was from the weak, yellow flames of smelly kerosene lamps. Only about 1934, years after the power lines first ran past our home, could the folks afford to have the power service extended to our house. Dad and an uncle wired the house, with white ceramic knobs and tubes to insulate the primitive two-wire system in the attic. We never progressed beyond having single bare light bulbs, in pull-chain sockets, dangling from the ceiling of each room. But the light they produced was dazzling compared to kerosene lamps.

As with most farmhouses of the time, the heart of things was Mamma's kitchen, even though that room was barely large enough for the essentials. The kitchen held a black-and-nickel wood range complete with warming oven; a small table covered with green-checked oilcloth, where we ate when we weren't expecting company; and a linoleum-topped work counter where sat canisters, the bread box, and a white, chipped-enamel water bucket with its dipper. Above and below the counter were Mamma's storage shelves. They were not enclosed by neat wooden doors, but instead were screened by brightly flowered curtains which swept aside easily for reaching dishes, pots and dishpans, or boxes of oatmeal and the carefully rationed sugar, cocoa and coffee. Our grey enameled wash basin and a soap dish sat handy atop our small, varnished-walnut ice box just inside the kitchen door. The linoleum of the kitchen floor was different than the countertop.

The kitchen range was where Daddy popped his popcorn, in a large covered skillet that he shuffled vigorously across the cast-iron stovetop heated by flames roaring in the firebox underneath. I remember clearly how the stove resounded as he jerked the pan back and forth across the uneven stove lids to stir the kernels. That sound never failed to bring the cats running to the French doors to be let in. They loved the popcorn for its salt and butter, and later as bat-toys.

But that was when we *had* popcorn. One of my most cherished memories about my father resulted from a lack of that treat.

POPCORN ODYSSEY

My dad loved popcorn. He especially loved a big bowl of buttered, salted popcorn with a couple of Staymen-Winesap apples while listening in the evenings to "Amos n' Andy" and "Lum n' Abner" on our old Grebe radio.

Usually, someone in the family grew enough popcorn to supply us through the winter. The winter when I was six, however, we ran out of popcorn during a long, snowy spell.

With outdoor work stifled by the heavy snow, Daddy had nothing to do but fret about his inactivity and the lack of popcorn. And when we gathered in the evening to hear those magical voices from the radio, it was not the same, as Daddy said, without the popcorn.

Cooper's Store, about a mile up the graveled valley road, carried popcorn, so I guess some families could afford to buy it. But we weren't among those lucky few. We, like many of our neighbors during the Great Depression, were living on home-canned food, apples and potatoes from the cellar, and venison, looking forward to next year's garden produce. Cash was almost nonexistent; most local commerce was by barter or credit until the next sale of apples—provided there was an apple crop and buyers for the fruit.

So there was poor Daddy, stuck in the little house with Mamma and me, dead broke and staring at the piling-up snow, wrinkling his brow and muttering in the throes of popcorn withdrawal.

But all that changed one morning when he came to breakfast smiling and said to me, "Son, how would you like to take your sled out today?"

I thought we were going coasting, and I could hardly wait while Mamma put so many clothes on me that I waddled penguin-style. Daddy waited outside with my short Flexible Flyer sled, onto which he had fastened a wooden apple box.

We trudged out to the valley road, which had become a white trench between snow banks higher than my stocking cap. The roadway was packed down, but the steadily falling snow kept everything clean with a

31

white fluffiness that muffled all noise. As I recall, the road was ours alone, and the only sounds we heard were our steamy breathing and the squeaky crunch of snow under our boots. Just my dad and I—he pulling the sled by its rope and I hurrying along beside him. When I got tired, he let me ride in the apple box atop the sled.

I knew by then we weren't going coasting. When Daddy told me which neighbors we were going to visit, the distance seemed far to me, but it was really less than two miles down valley from home. I wondered briefly why we hadn't taken the car—a 1928 Pontiac—but I guessed it was because we couldn't afford the gas. I was very familiar with "we can't afford it." It was even given as the reason why I didn't have a little brother or sister.

Daddy also told me the purpose of our visit. Months before, he had helped this family by loaning them ten cents. The loan had been in real money, not the cheaper "tin money" used at the local Cooper's store and comprising much of the coinage then circulating in the valley. Dad learned that the family had acquired some tin money, and he was willing to take repayment in that. It was part of a plan, he said with a wink.

Fortunately, the neighbor didn't quibble about settling the loan. I'm sure he also saw the advantage of repaying Dad with the scrip coins, which normally were discounted at least ten percent at any nearby store except Cooper's, the proverbial "company store" for the valley's Harris mill. We were soon on the road again toward home.

Daddy was now whistling and talkative. I rode in the apple box with my knees pushed up, enjoying his good mood. At one point, he took out the two repaid "nickels" and showed them to me.

"Son," he said with snowflakes on his lashes, "this nickel is for us, and this nickel is for popcorn." In my childish faith, I almost expected Daddy to make the transformation on the spot. But then he put the metal disks back carefully into a pocket, and I remained puzzled about his meaning.

I didn't ask, of course. Our relationship was strictly at his pleasure, on his terms. Dad was a stern father and expected more of me than I could sometimes deliver. He was not above corporal punishment, either. As a result, I kept a wary distance and walked softly around him.

But now he was in a good mood, and I could relax.

When we got home, Daddy was all smiles, and soon Mamma was, too, when he gave her one of the nickels. I think back with amazement at how that small amount of money brightened my folks. Surely those two coins—not even genuine—could have meant little to our future. Yet, they must have seemed to my folks like a spark of hope during those dismal days when the very economic framework of the nation had betrayed them.

Mamma fixed lunch for us, and then Daddy and I were off again, this time pulling the sled up valley. When we arrived at Cooper's store, I assumed that we would buy popcorn and return home.

"Two plugs of Horseshoe chewing tobacco, please," Dad said, snapping his nickel onto the counter.

What was he thinking? Daddy didn't chew, nor did he smoke or drink. Imagine wasting a whole nickel on chaw! That nickel could have bought one of the quarter-pound Love Nest candy bars perched so enticingly on a nearby shelf!

But I held my tongue.

The next shock came when we left the store and headed up river instead of down toward home. This time I did summon the courage to ask where we were going. I was much relieved when Dad smiled and ruffled my stocking cap.

"Why, we're going to get that popcorn, Son," he said.

He trudged up valley for about three miles along the monotonously white, empty road while I rode in the sled box most of the way. Finally, we turned into a snow-fenced driveway.

"Is the popcorn here, Daddy?" I asked.

"Yes it is. See all those cornstalks in the field, poking up through the snow? They had a big crop last fall."

"Will they sell us some, Daddy?"

"We didn't come to buy, Son. We came to swap. Mr. Lyle chews tobacco—a filthy habit that gives men a strong craving for the stuff. I figure he's been out of chaw about as long as everyone's been out of cash."

Daddy grinned. "He'll trade his popcorn, Son. The only question is, how much?"

We were welcomed to the white-shrouded, smoke-wreathed farmhouse like long-lost relatives.

I liked the matronly Mrs. Lyle immediately. She fussed over me, helping to unbundle me, giving me cookies and milk at a table close to the warm kitchen stove, and later showing me a litter of kittens she was keeping in from the cold.

In the meantime, Daddy and Mr. Lyle visited in the parlor. I heard little of their talk, but it must have continued for a couple of hours. I didn't realize that, behind the pleasant palaver, some serious bargaining was going on. All I remember was being tired and fidgety, and bored with the stereopticon pictures that Mrs. Lyle had set out for me.

But I knew enough to stay quiet and not disturb the grownups. I think I fell asleep.

Next I remember the jovial mood, and Mrs. Lyle helping me into my bulky clothes. Outside, I was surprised to see the sled box holding a big gunny sack that was chock full of unshelled corn cobs. The men shook hands before we left. Mr. Lyle had a wad of chaw inside his cheek.

I later learned how adroit my dad was at dickering, but that afternoon I was not impressed that he had parlayed a tin nickel into enough popcorn to last us many months. All I thought about was walking those long miles back home because the sled was full.

But Daddy soon saw how tired I was, and he swung me up and carried me on his shoulders while he pulled the sled. And he talked to me; not just about the big bowls of popcorn we would have, with plenty of apples. Daddy talked of many things while he trudged back home along that quiet, snowy road in the deepening twilight, with me huddled over his head and the laden sled tugging behind.

And I got to talk as well.

*　　*　　*

The author, summer before the Popcorn Odyssey.

In the winter of the popcorn odyssey, the snow went on and on. In my childish memory it was the most ever. It had long since obliterated Mamma's dahlia bed, and it finally climbed up the trunks of the apple trees to the crotches of the big, starkly bare limbs. As the snow deepened and slid off the roof, it formed white breastworks that rose to almost meet the downward growing icicles. Our cozy house seemed to shrink around us, and the outside chores became a welcome break. Bringing in the firewood was my job; shoveling out the path past the woodshed to the outhouse was one of Daddy's. We all worked the noisy hand pump to get bucket after bucket of water for baths and washing.

But chores occupied only a few hours of the long snowy days and longer nights. The old Grebe radio helped to fill the evenings, but we used it sparingly. Daddy said we had to save the batteries for really important times. I understood that need the same way I accepted the need to conserve food and take good care of everything else, like my hand-me-down coat and mittens.

That winter may also have been one of the times we ran low on coffee, another of Daddy's addictions.

Whenever Mamma decided that the supply of coffee was getting low, she would grind less coffee for the percolator. At first this meant only fewer cups of coffee for her and Daddy to share at breakfasts and suppers. Then the coffee got weaker and weaker. When such rationing progressed to what Daddy ruefully called "tea coffee," Mamma would switch to drinking hot water with her meals. She would pour the weak percolator brew into Daddy's cup and then fill her own from the steaming teakettle, adding the same sugar and milk they both normally used in coffee. As an acknowledgment of Mamma's sacrifice, I think, Daddy would then decide he'd been using too much sugar, and he would forego the sweetener until more coffee somehow appeared and he and Mamma could both enjoy their drink of savory luxury.

*   *   *

I don't remember whether confinement and shortages that winter caused unusual friction between my parents. But whenever voices got loud and angry, I tried to disappear.

In warmer weather, I retreated to my corner bedroom, sometimes to the floor behind my bed, or to my favorite apple tree out front where I could perch among the foliage and observe a kitchen window and both doors. In cold weather the refuge was my "cave"—under the round oak dining table which usually sat tight against the back wall of the living room. Small for my age, I fitted nicely in the space behind the massive pedestal. The wooden runners that supported the heavy table top and enabled it to expand for company formed a wonderful secret shelf where I stored small things that helped me to pretend.

I seldom knew what caused the occasional domestic dust-ups, but the situation was serious whenever I became "The Boy," as in "Not in front of The Boy!" My folks never came to blows, however, and never really argued long. I learned that Mamma simply refused to sustain an argument. During any flare-up Mamma soon began to cry, and then Daddy would stomp outside. From whichever sanctuary I occupied, I listened for sounds that would tell me what Daddy did next. For some reason, I always felt relieved when I heard the sound of wood-chopping. Mamma's greatest solace was her Bible.

*   *   *

Getting electricity at the home place lightened one of Mamma's most arduous chores—doing our laundry. My folks were finally able to get an electric iron and an electric washing machine, an "Easy" brand. The washer was second-hand, of course, for Daddy seldom bought anything like that brand new. The Easy replaced an older gasoline-powered Thor washer. Mamma hated the little gas engine, which had to be started with a pull-rope and was as contrary as a cow. Still, the Thor surely beat boiling the white clothes in our boiler tub and hand-scrubbing the rest on a wash-board, as Mamma had to do earlier.

The Easy washer had a round, copper-clad tub on a roll-around frame which held the electric motor, and drive gears for the washer's agitator, underneath the tub. Bolted onto one side of the tub was a sturdy, vertical tube topped by the "wringer," a metal frame holding two spring-loaded, white-rubber rollers, also powered by the electric motor. The wringer rollers, tight enough to crush unprotected buttons and indiscriminate about squeezing wet clothes or fingers, had safety features consisting of a reverse lever and an emergency release of roller pressure.

The washer tub's big, pot-type lid was just heavy enough to stay in place while the washer swished and tumbled the clothes. The base of the tub had a drain faucet that fit our garden hose. That washer was the jewel of Mamma's laundry equipment.

Washing machines of the time were designed for use with two large wash tubs on stands next to the machine. The washing machine held hot, soapy wash water, heated in our oblong, copper boiler tub atop the wood-fired kitchen range. We filled our two galvanized wash tubs with cold water for rinsing—clear water in the first rinse, and water with "bluing" added in the final rinse, when we could afford the bottle of "Mrs. Stewart's Concentrated Liquid Bluing."

After the clothes sloshed around in the machine's hot water for a time decided by Mamma, she took them from the washer tub—fishing the steaming pieces out with a length of broomstick—and fed each piece through the powered wringer rolls, which she had pivoted around so the squeezed-out clothes fell into the first rinse tub. She immediately put the next load of dirty clothes into the washing machine. While the machine washed the second load, Mamma put the first batch through the rinsing steps: After she sloshed them up and down thoroughly in the first rinse tub, she unlocked the wringer frame and pivoted it around to feed the clothes into the final, blue rinse. And after that final rinse, she again shifted the wringer to feed the clean, damp clothes into wooden apple boxes. During breaks in the washing and rinsing routine, Mamma hung the wet wash on our three-wire clotheslines, which stretched between "T"-shaped end posts about twenty feet apart in our yard. As the clotheslines sagged under the weight of wet laundry, we propped them up with tree props from the orchard.

Mamma set aside the washed garments she intended to starch. After the other clothes were on the line, she carefully dipped the selected clothes in a dishpan holding a weak solution of starch before hand-wringing them and hanging them separately.

The washing had to be done in strict order: white clothes first, then colored and heavier things, and last the dirtiest and darkest, like overalls and household rags. We used the same water throughout the washing. As Mamma put the laundry through the steps, the hot water in the machine cooled, water in the first rinse tub grew soapy and grey, and the blue water became diluted and pale.

Mamma wasted little of the laundry water, every ounce of which had been laboriously pumped from our well. We dumped the water from the rinse tubs onto the vegetable or flower gardens, and Mamma used the soapy water from the machine to scrub floors.

Monday was the traditional wash day. When that had to be changed because of travel, or because a Monday was too stormy, Mamma complained that her "whole week was out of whack." Stormy weather not

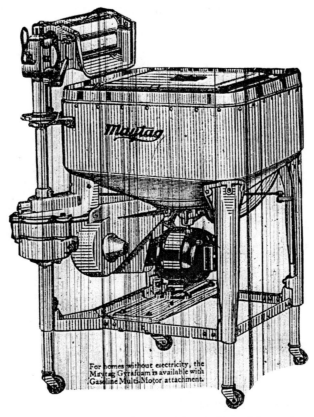

For homes without electricity, the Maytag Gyrafoam is available with Gasoline Multi-Motor attachment.

Advertisement for washing machine similar to Mamma's first. Hers was powered by a gasoline engine.

only hampered the drying of the clothes, but also impeded the washing itself, for that had to be done in the open, outside our tiny house. Mamma's laundry site was the side yard, under an apple tree for shade, and near the water pump and the clotheslines. A long extension cord brought electrical power from the house out to the washing machine.

Most of the time in our semiarid climate, the clothes dried quickly on the clotheslines and carried a pleasant, fresh smell. In cold weather, the clothes "freeze-dried" on the lines, sometimes brought in stiff as boards but requiring little time inside the warm house to soften and dispel residual dampness. When a rain shower came while clothes were on the line, Mamma, and whoever was there to help, stopped everything else and scrambled to get the clothes in from the rain.

When I think of wash days at the home place, I can almost smell steamy air and the blended fragrances of boiling starch water and ham-flavored beans. Because a hot fire had to be kept going in the kitchen stove to heat wash water, wash day was a day for cooking navy beans. On wash days we had the beans for the midday meal (then called "dinner") and also for supper. At dinner, we ate the beans with cornbread, and at supper with fried potatoes. A vegetable from the cellar or from the garden rounded out each meal.

Some of our neighbor ladies seemed to compete to be the first to get their wash out on the line each Monday. Mamma just laughed at them, saying they were prideful and pride was a sin. Mamma said she was "happy just to get the wash done."

If Mondays were wash days, Tuesdays were ironing days. Mamma didn't iron towels, socks, sheets or blankets, but she ironed just about all our other laundry. "Wrinkle-free" fabrics didn't exist—all clothing wrinkled. Wrinkle-free in those days meant freshly ironed.

Clothes are best ironed when damp, and every household owned a water bottle with some kind of sprinkling cap on it. The garment was spread out, sprinkled with water, rolled up to distribute the dampness evenly, and that roll stacked with other rolls to await ironing.

Sometimes, if a light shower came while the wash was drying on the clotheslines, Nature helped with the sprinkling. At such times, Mamma first rushed to take in the clothes she didn't iron, leaving those to be ironed until last. With luck, the last armloads from the lines would be sprinkled just lightly. This led to our use of a phrase which now evokes only vacant stares: If caught briefly in a shower, we might say we got "sprinkled just right for ironing."

Mamma also cherished her electric iron for the drudgery it saved her. My first memories of Mamma ironing envision her standing at her folding wooden ironing board a few steps from the hot wood stove, ironing a while and then stepping over to the stove to unlatch one heavy "sadiron" and latch onto another heating on the stove top. The "D-shaped" handle never left her right hand as she pulled the handle's trigger to unclasp each cooling iron and clamp onto a hot one. She kept three of these heavy sadirons always sitting on the back of the stove top.

Ironing then was a fast-moving work of art. Mamma's right hand slid the heavy iron quickly over as much garment as possible before the iron cooled, while her left hand deftly positioned and smoothed the cloth ahead of the iron. If she "ironed in" a wrinkle, she just kept going, only later re-sprinkling the spot and ironing it out with a fresh, hot iron. Part of the ironing art was always knowing the approximate temperature of the sadiron, determined by the way it "spat" when touched with a saliva-moistened finger. Mamma's newer, constant-temperature electric iron allowed her to work away from the blistering-hot stove and afforded her much greater flexibility in the ways and the fabrics she could iron.

With either electric iron or sadirons, starched garments were among the trickiest to iron, because starch scorches much quicker than the fabric itself. In fact, odors of hot fabric and scorched starch dominated the ironing-day smells. I don't remember everything Mamma starched, but she always starched my school shirts. I'll never forget how my collars, when they got a little frayed and Mamma got liberal with the starch, sawed at my scrawny neck.

ORCHARD LIFE

SEASONS OF WORK

Apple prices in the 1920s were generally adequate to support the family orchards in our valley. Even so, success of the smaller orchards such as ours required hard work from the whole family. I cannot remember when I first climbed up into an apple tree to "help Daddy."

The year's work started in late winter while the tree sap was down, with the pruning and shaping of the trees. Daddy usually did that without help, using "loppers" (pruning shears) and long pole pruners, working from the snowy ground. Sometimes a high tree, or removal of a heavy limb, required a ladder, set carefully in the snow, or climbing the tree to use a saw. After pruning came the back-straining task of picking up the brush and carrying it to open spaces for burning. Picking brush was one of my first jobs, working alongside Mamma.

Next began the spraying, a seemingly endless process to keep at bay the codling moths and other pests that could make the difference between "extra fancy" apples and culls. Again, Dad usually did this by himself, using a spray machine mounted on an old wagon chassis with wide steel wheels.

He pulled it behind a tractor that also had steel wheels (the rear ones cleated for traction). The wagon chassis carried a big wooden tank, shaped like half a barrel, to hold the spray mixture, plus the spray pump and pump engine, which was a two-cycle, "one-lung" gasoline engine.

To begin the spraying operation, Dad towed the sprayer to a low place where he could fill it by gravity flow with irrigation-ditch water, at which time he mixed in the "spray dope." The engine that powered the spray pump also turned paddles within the tank to keep the solution mixed. After filling the tank, Dad towed the sprayer to the first "set" and shut off the tractor. He then cranked up the spray-pump motor (they were notoriously balky) and dragged the high-pressure rubber spray hose out to its full length. After Dad had sprayed all the trees he could reach in one direction, he had to drag the heavy hose back toward the sprayer and then off in another direction. When all trees in one set were covered, he dragged the hose back and coiled it on its hangers on the sprayer, cranked up the tractor and drove to the next set, diverting to refill the sprayer as needed.

It was monotonous, tiring work, to say nothing of the unpleasantness of getting soaked with spray solution. Dragging the hose for hours, along with the unnatural position of pointing the spray nozzle up into trees, made for aching shoulders and backs. Other than Mamma's hearty lunch at the house, and maybe a brief after-lunch nap on the kitchen linoleum (there because his clothes were soaked), the moves between sets and the refills of the tank were Dad's only "rests" during the long days of spraying.

At dusk, after he could no longer see to spray, Dad trudged back to the house, stripped off his spray-soaked clothing down to his long johns, and washed his hands and face. Mamma hung up his work clothes to dry as much as possible before the next day, and then we sat down to eat. Dad ate well for a small man, even in damp long johns.

The first spray in the spring, a mixture of powdered lime and sulfur, coated everything (including the person spraying) a lovely bright yellow, and stank of rotten eggs. This was the only spray, I think, for which Dad wore goggles, and maybe a bandanna over his nose and mouth. A later spray combined pine-tar soap (shredded with a knife before mixing) and black, oily liquid nicotine (nicotinic acid) which came in five-gallon cans. The last several sprays of the season, continued right up to picking time, applied lead arsenate, which gave the apples a light, powdery coating. Black, ugly skull-and-crossbones symbols on the cans of nicotine and the paper bags of arsenate warned even us kids of their deadly threat. Spray ingredients were handled with great care, not so much for worker safety but because they were expensive. It is a wonder any of us survived a few spray seasons, much less a lifetime of the exposure.

Along with the frequent spraying, a big orchard job was thinning the fruit. Thinning started when the green apples (or pears, apricots or peaches) were about the size of marbles, and sometimes dragged on until the apples had grown to golf-ball size. The objectives were simple: break up clusters, leaving only the best single fruit per stem spur; and snap off all deformed, scarred, wormy or scaly fruit.

Mamma instructed me in thinning, in between her household chores. Dad always was too busy. She thinned trees closest to the house, standing on the ground or on our shortest ladders (eight-foot wooden, tripod ladders) which allowed her to reach up into the middle of the trees. Dad or hired men came along and "topped" her trees in their thinning sweep through the whole orchard.

At first I crawled up inside the trees beside Mamma while she showed me which fruit to sacrifice and how to snap off the stems. Later she taught me to use ladders—how to maneuver them carefully between the vulnerable branches, how to balance them upright, then set the ladder's slender, hinged tongue and stomp the ladder's feet securely into the soft soil. Our ladders ranged from eight to sixteen feet in height, the latter needed to reach the twenty-foot-high limbs common in those days. I always felt proud when, as I grew, I could control the next longer ladder and guide it into a tree by myself.

Thinning usually was not bad work, but pretty boring after selection of the sacrificial fruit became so automatic that it no longer required thought. Thinning extended through some of the hottest days of the year;

we welcomed any summer showers to cool us off and perhaps force a break from the boring work.

The only really bad fruit to thin is the peach. No matter what one wears that is tolerable in the summer heat, the fuzz from peaches finally gets through to the skin and starts the itching. Once you have given in and begun to scratch, the problem intensifies, until you are thinning half- time and scratching half-time. I always thought peach fuzz would be an appropriate torture to induce enemy spies to reveal their secrets.

As the ripening fruit grew heavy, sagging branches required propping so they would not break. Our props were wooden poles of just about any kind strong and light enough for the purpose, ranging from 2x4s notched at one end to "lodge-pole" saplings with a hook fashioned at the top. In length, props ranged from about six to twelve feet, some perhaps longer. Every orchard had one or more prop piles at strategic places, ready for those crucial weeks before the harvest.

Propping was tiring work, not only from carrying the props out among the trees but also from heaving the props up under the laden tree branches. It was not nearly as hard on the back, however, as the dragging weight of picking bags during harvest, or the springtime task of picking up brush.

The annual spraying cycle extended into propping time, and props became the bane of the sprayers. The long spray hoses had to be dragged carefully around the props, lest a prop get tripped down and cause a heavily laden tree branch to break. If curses had been flames, many a prop would have ignited during the last spray of the season.

Mamma occasionally worked alongside Dad at picking times, for as long as her shoulders and back could stand the heavy pull from the harness of the canvas picking bags. Aunt Achsa also worked some with Dad at Grandma Lillian's but, even so, Dad was hard-pressed to keep up the work at both orchards. We always needed hired men during the height of the picking as well as the thinning.

The most beautiful times in a fruit orchard are in springtime when the trees bloom and in the fall when the fruit is ripe. At these times, one is treated not only to visual beauty but also to heady fragrances that are never forgotten: first the rich promise of the blossoms and finally the fulfilling bounty of sweet fruit ripe in the warm sun.

IRRIGATION

In the semiarid climate of the Entiat Valley, growing fruit and most other things depends absolutely on irrigation. Lacking electrical power and the efficient pumps of today, the early ranchers had to get the water by gravity flow through ditches, flumes, and pipelines that diverted water from the Entiat River. These gravity-flow lifelines were possible because the gradient of the river is much steeper than is needed to maintain ditch flow to the bordering orchards, even orchards extending relatively high on the valley sides. Some of those irrigation systems carried enough water to be called "canals" in some cultures. But if it had dirt sides and carried water, we called it a ditch, whether a large trench that carried water for miles or a tiny rill that trickled between tree rows.

The ditches, flumes and pipelines were financed, built and maintained cooperatively by the ranchers who used the water. When someone bought existing ranches, as my family did, the new owners also bought into the expense and labor of maintaining the ditch that served their land. I never heard of state water rights in those days—just "ditch shares." Each contributing rancher along the ditch got to use the water for specified days, and woe to the person who "got confused" and took water out of turn. I personally know of two rather serious ditch-bank fights resulting from "extra" watering.

Orchards received water from the main ditches by diversions into small, parallel ditches, or rills, that trickled the water downhill between the rows of trees. Horse-drawn (later tractor-drawn) cultivators initially carved the rills, which thereafter were repaired with shovel or hoe. "Header ditches," which tapped into the main ditches at spaced "head gates," fed different sections of the rills. Water was seldom available to irrigate an entire section of orchard at one time, so the watering was rotated by means of mud "dams" to shut off some of the rills at their upper ends. "Changing water" was a job of the irrigator, often kids like me. Another, more demanding job was regulating the water so it trickled the full length of the rills but didn't waste much as "tail water." Whenever the lower end of a rill was dry or carried too much water, the irrigator had to note which rills needed adjusting, and then trudge back to the top to fix the flows. On some days "chasing water" was a fulltime job, leaving no time for periodic cooling dips in the river, which I counted on to make the job less onerous. Sometimes I resorted to soaking my shirt in ditch water and putting it back on to keep cool.

Small animals were the curse of my days as an irrigator. When I could not "push" water through a rill to its end, the reason usually was a gopher hole that diverted the flow underground. After the extra chore of walking the individual rill to find the problem, I was not in an environmentally forgiving mood. I took delight in using my shovel handle to jam the little drain hole full of dirt so the flow would resume in the rill, all the time hoping that I might be crushing the rodent underneath. The latter never happened, of course, for the gopher would have long-since abandoned the flooded part of its tunnel.

The gopher problem got so bad that some orchardists bought scads of traps and paid kids a bounty for all the gophers they could catch. My uncle Max made pocket money trapping gophers at Keystone Ranch, in the lower valley. I think the bounty was a half-penny per gopher, but a penny then was something valuable.

Another bane of irrigators was the rattlesnake. These "buzz worms" thrive in semiarid conditions, but they much prefer to be near water for their own cooling and for small prey that are attracted to the water. Imagine, then, what a perfect environment for the snake is the orchard, with its summer weeds, its trickling water, and the abundance of mice and gophers. We didn't realize the predatory benefits of the rattlesnakes—just that they startled the crap out of us. Killing any rattler we saw was considered a civic obligation, and we happily chopped them into pieces with our shovel or hoe. Dangerous as the rattlers were said to be, I know of only two persons bitten in the valley, and both of them survived. Fortunately, we left the bull snakes and garter snakes alone, or our rodent problems would have been even worse.

Many parts of the valley had two levels of ditch-and-flume systems, serving higher and lower orchards. Such was the case at Grandma Lillian's. Her upper orchard was the end place served by the Fouch Ditch, named after our neighbor who had been the motivator for construction of that ditch system. Any surplus water, or "tail water," from the upper orchard was intercepted by a larger ditch-and-flume system just above the main road. That larger system supplied Grandma's lower orchard and her yard. It also happened to be the same irrigation system that supplied our home place less than a mile upstream. At the home place, that main ditch ran all along the upper side of the property, just below the Entiat Valley Road.

The Fouch Ditch, not available for our use at the home place, ran past on the hillside above the road, and extended upstream around a rocky point by means of a wooden flume perched on timber scaffolding. It was relatively short and was one of the newer ditches in the valley.

Daddy helped build the Fouch Ditch, trenching the soil along the side-hill contour using a "slip" bucket—a narrow scoop with handles, resembling a construction wheelbarrow minus the undercarriage and front wheel. The slip was drawn by a single, slow-walking horse, reined by Dad as he also guided the slip. By pressure on the handles, Dad would control the depth of the slip's bite and, at regular intervals, twist the slip and hoist mightily on the handles to dump the dirt. That loose dirt, dumped on the downhill side of the trench, formed the water-retaining ditch bank.

SELLING THE FRUIT

I began learning about apple prices in the fall of 1931, the year I started first grade. That's when I also started learning about the curse of expenses.

One evening Daddy sat reading the paper in our living room when he suddenly put the paper down, shook his head with a frown and said to Mamma, "Hard to believe, just two years ago Delicious extra-fancies were selling for over three dollars a box. This year, by the time ours get ripe we'll be lucky to get much more than a dollar a box—if anyone buys them."

I surely didn't get the full meaning of Daddy's comment, for even a dollar seemed big money to me then. But for the first time I related money to my image of a box of newly picked apples sitting out in the orchard. Even then I got it wrong, of course; the prices Daddy read in the paper were not for a box of loose "orchard run" apples, but for a packed box of the top-grade fruit ready for shipment.

"Why won't people buy our apples, Daddy?"

"Oh, we hope they will, Son. But the whole country's in a bad depression. Lots and lots of people have lost their jobs, and they just don't have money to buy apples."

"Many families don't even have money for bread," Mamma put in, "or milk and oatmeal for their kids."

Lack of oatmeal seemed no great hardship to me, but I knew better than to say so.

"But wouldn't a dollar for a boxful be enough?" I asked instead.

Daddy twisted in his chair to face me. He was going to be serious, so I'd better pay attention.

"Yes, Son. A dollar for every box of apples from our orchard would be a good price, if we got to keep the whole dollar for ourselves. But you see, out of that dollar, or whatever price we get, we have to pay expenses. We've already spent a lot of money for spray dope this year, and we had to pay Eddie while he helped me thin, and soon we'll have to pay some men to help pick the apples. And I'll have to buy gas to haul our apples to the warehouse...."

I'm sure Daddy went on to list all the growers' expenses after the apples reached the warehouse: the basic handling and storage charges, the grading and packing charges, the pre-cooling of the packed fruit before loading it into refrigerated boxcars, and finally the sales commissions. I'm also sure I understood little or none of this.

"Every time we have to pay out money for the apple crop," Daddy was saying, "it's called an expense. All those expenses will count up to more than half a dollar a box. So our return—money we get back to live on—won't be very much."

"But we'll be fine," Mamma put in quickly, exchanging a look with Daddy.

"Yes, we'll get by," he echoed.

Thus reassured, I forgot about the economics of apple ranching until some days later, when I couldn't wait to get home from school to tell Mamma what I'd heard.

"Bobby says his folks are going to pack their own apples this year! To save expenses. In the shed above their ice house!"

Mamma did not seem excited by my news. Neither did Daddy when he got home from hauling with his truck.

"Well," Daddy said, "they've got a small crop this year, so I guess they can handle it by themselves. Rollo still has his old grader in their shed...." He let the statement hang.

"Can we pack our own apples, Daddy? Can we?"

He shook his head. "I'm afraid not, Son. We have way more crop than we could possibly pack ourselves. We'll just have to finish out the year as cheap as possible, and haul our apples to the packing shed like always, and take the best deals the co-op can get for us—and hope we don't go deeper into debt."

And that is the basic plan my folks followed as long as we were in orcharding. Dad hauled our apples to the cooperatively owned Entiat Warehouse, one of three large packing sheds and fruit warehouses located in Entiat, next to the Great Northern Railroad tracks. Each of the three not only graded and packed the growers' fruit, but also could store it in either refrigerated or "common" storage, buy and sell the fruit or broker its sale, and load the packed boxes into refrigerated railway cars for shipping. All these services, of course, came with costs. We suffered these expenses along with the other growers and had only one small advantage in the horticultural crap-shoot; our crop consisted largely of the Delicious variety, and when any market for apples existed, the call most often was for Delicious.

While the prices and demands for the apples had fallen precipitously, most expenses had not. Labor costs were the only notable exceptions, because of the unprecedented job losses in other industries and the resultant abundance of job seekers. Costs for shipping to major markets in eastern cities remained high and generally inflexible. Freight charges for refrigerated railway cars from central Washington to markets east of the Missouri River were murderous—as much as or even more than half the selling price of the fruit at the eastern auctions. Such high shipping costs, of course, disadvantaged Northwest fruit growers in competition with growers in Michigan, New York, Virginia, and elsewhere in the East.

Dad discerned another disadvantage for Entiat Valley growers. Quite often, apple prices tended to ratchet down as the harvest progressed. Because our valley's apples ripened later than others—in the Yakima, Washington, region or in Virginia, for example—Dad felt that we usually were not able to sell at the most favorable prices. In keeping with his belief that selling early was best, his motto was "sell 'em right off the end of the grader"—that is, as soon as they were packed, rather than putting the packed boxes into refrigerated storage and gambling that better prices in the future would more than offset the storage and handling costs.

Our valley growers, most with small-to-middle-size orchards, strove to counter the low returns any way they could. They traded work, shared equipment, and bartered goods. They hired each other before they hired outsiders, and paid kids like me for work formerly done by hired men. Many worked outside jobs to "support the orchard" as did my folks, with Mamma

53

packing apples and Dad using his truck for hired hauling. Anything to get through to the next year, until the recovery promised in President F. D. Roosevelt's radio "Fireside Chats" would surely take hold.

Some small growers gambled on packing their own fruit—dusting off old sorting tables and World War I era grading machines, enlisting family and friends to work, and trusting that their packed fruit would be worth something in the end. Sometimes it was. When it was not worth the shipping cost, for example, the grower had little choice but to pry open the wooden boxes and dump the fruit. Nobody knows how many tons of good but unprofitable fruit left the valley via the Entiat River during the depression.

Other growers concentrated their efforts only on the most popular varieties of their fruit. Some varieties rotted on the trees simply because bringing them to market was to go deeper in debt. The sacrificial fruit included the so-called summer apples which did not ship well—varieties such as Red June, Yellow Transparent, Striped Astrakhan—and some "winter" varieties such as Ben Davis and Winter Banana. To avoid the cost of obligatory spraying for pest control, orchardists cut down or pulled out most such varieties, effectively eliminating them from future markets. Growers also were encouraged to pull out trees that produced poorly colored, "C-grade" apples, which became a drug on the market.

Mr. and Mrs. Henry Walker, neighbors of my Grandma Lillian, operated a small apple orchard which, in the 1920s, would have provided them a decent living. During the bad times, however, they had to resort to working murderous hours, packing their own apples, seldom hiring help, and diversifying into selling flowers and garden vegetables.

Closer neighbors, Mr. and Mrs. Earl Fouch, weathered the depression by trucking their crop each fall to a leased warehouse in Bakersfield, California, from where they distributed their apples throughout the winter before returning to their ranch in early spring to repeat the orcharding cycle.

My folks, too, tried direct selling. In 1933 and 1934, they augmented returns from the warehouse sales by peddling the remaining apples from the back of Dad's truck (see "Peddling Apples").

Probably the most successful of the valley's growers through the depression were the bigger outfits that had packing sheds large enough and modern enough to take sizeable crops through all the steps from receiving the loose apples to shipping the packed boxes to established buyers. The two largest of these in the valley were the Keystone ranch, roughly two miles up the Entiat Valley from its mouth, and the Pine Tree ranch, about four miles up valley. My family had close ties to both ranches. The Keystone is where my folks met and where Mamma's parents later lived and worked for several years. At the Pine Tree ranch, owned by the J.K. McArthur family, my mother, Aunt Achsa and Aunt Verna packed apples each fall through most of the depression and into the years of World War II (see "Income—Any Income").

Weak demands for apples persisted until the beginning of World War II. I learned much later that demands might have been even lower had not the International Apple Shippers' Association come up with a scheme, designed specifically to move Northwest apples, which turned thousands of unemployed big-city dwellers into apple sellers. It began in 1930 and worked like this: Every morning an individual could buy, on credit, a box of large apples at a shipping warehouse in his city, spend the day selling them on the street for a nickel apiece, then return to the warehouse to pay off his debt and walk away with a profit of more than a dollar. "Buy an apple a day and eat the depression away!" the Association proclaimed in advertisements, and for a time the downtown sidewalks of most major cities in the country blossomed with apple sellers. New York City alone reportedly had six thousand of them.

Despite all my folk's hard work and Dad's strategies, despite having the popular Delicious variety to sell, and even with the boost of the unknown apple sellers in the East, our family orchards never turned an actual profit after 1930.

Even through the bad years for apple sales, however, Dad remained philosophical and as upbeat as possible.

"You have to be a dad-burned optimist," he maintained, "or you can't be an apple rancher."

HIRED HELP

During the busy times in the orchards, beginning with the thinning, Dad needed to hire help. And from 1930 for as long as Dad ran an orchard, plenty of workers were available owing to historic events that occurred far from our valley.

The first of these began in late October of 1929, when America's stock markets and other financial institutions collapsed following years of widespread, unregulated, wildly speculative investing. The collapse happened not in a single "black" day, as commonly believed, but in what has been described as "eight days of Armageddon." During the worst day, investors and brokers watched the collective wealth disappear at an incredible rate of $2 billion an hour—equivalent to perhaps $20 billion an hour in today's dollars. This financial collapse led progressively to widespread failure of banks and businesses and the closing of major industrial plants. The Great Depression settled over the country (and the world) like a black shroud. Millions lost their jobs. In the worst times, one out of four American workers was out of work. Many remained unemployed for years.

And as if the Depression were not bad enough, a series of droughts, beginning in the early 1930s, along with windstorms that blew away inches of topsoil, ravished vast farming areas in the southern part of the Midwest, which became known as the Dust Bowl. Many thousands of families left their ruined farms and migrated westward seeking work—any kind of work.

Every day or so during the open seasons in our valley, out-of-work men walked the valley road from orchard to orchard, seeking jobs. These transient job seekers were not bums. Most were upright citizens, penniless through no fault of their own. Many were married men who left families behind while they desperately sought an honest way to make a living. Mamma got tears in her eyes listening to the plights of some. But at any time we could only afford to hire one or two men—three at most—sometimes just for a few days.

These job seekers were all Caucasian men, many of them refugees from the Dust Bowl. As I recall, we never saw a black man, a Hispanic, or an Indian seeking work. In fact, Indians were the only "minorities" I knew about in those days.

Some of these job-seeking men would have worked for bed and board, even though the "bed" meant a thin mattress in our barn loft. But good old Dad insisted on paying them *something*, no matter if he couldn't afford much. Usually, the only cash he had at those times was government "seed money" advanced against the autumn apple sales.

The hired men took their meals with Dad in the kitchen, after which Mamma ate with me. Mamma also did their clothes on washday, an embarrassing time for one fellow who had to stay naked in the barn loft while Mamma scrubbed and rinsed his only clothes, then dried them on the clothesline.

My folks also hired girls to help Mamma with chores such as the summer canning and to ride herd on me while she worked elsewhere. But those girls never seemed to stay long. I heard that maybe Mamma was difficult to work for. Also, the girls had to live close enough to get to and from our place on their own. We had only a bed-davenport for overnight female guests, and could offer them little privacy in our tiny house.

I don't remember every hired man. One was Mel, my "riding instructor" (see "Orchard Cowboy"). Another hired man whom I remember much better was Archie Bond.

Archie showed up one spring day, clean-shaven and neat despite some travel dust, with a compact bedroll hanging from a strap over one shoulder. He told us he was from Nebraska, seeking "any kind of honest work." He had come west by train, he said, and stopped at every place in the nine-mile walk up valley from the rail yard in Entiat. None of the other places, he said, had wanted to hire a "flatlander" with no orchard experience.

"If you don't have a job open, can I please chop wood or something for a meal? I haven't eaten in a while."

Well, this melted my tender-hearted Mom, and she got busy cooking up a whopping meal. "We'll talk about wood-chopping later," she said.

While she happily watched him eat every scrap and then mop his plate with bread, Mamma asked, "Are you a Christian?" And when he quoted a favorite Bible verse in response, Archie was as good as hired.

Archie was about five-nine in height, twenty-something, thin but well-muscled. Sandy hair framed his tanned, square-jawed face. His easy nature produced frequent smiles showing even, white teeth.

Archie settled into the barn loft, which he insisted on sweeping out and scrubbing down first. He also took out the two thin mattresses from the loft, hung them on the clothesline "to sterilize in the sun," and beat the sin out of them with a broomstick to get rid of dust and any small occupants. This gave our first indication of Archie's exceptional cleanliness and neatness.

Archie was, in fact, the cleanest person I ever knew for those times. He bathed daily, as weather allowed, plunging naked into the glacier-fed river at a place where he was hidden from the house, soaping down, then flopping in again to rinse, and rubbing down briskly with his towel. He carried extra underwear and socks, which he changed and washed out between Mamma's Monday washdays. He shaved every morning, in cold water with an old, worn safety razor. Such daily ablutions were unheard of in our family, especially the daily shaving.

In contrast, most folks I knew averaged weekly baths—more often in the summer, including swimming, and perhaps less often in winter. Sweaty men and fastidious folks might have sponge baths and shampoos in between, but the Saturday-night bath was the recognized standard for families who, like us, had no bathing facilities except washtubs or the river. Consequently, people smelled, with their own distinctive odors, even when those odors might include an element of lady's perfume. However, we didn't know, until the advertisers got to us in the 1930s through the magazines and radio, that body odor ("B.O." they called it), was such a sin. Archie Bond was the only man I knew who seldom smelled of anything but soap or honest sweat.

Archie proved to be a quick learner and an efficient orchard hand. He worked for us for three summers, both at the home place and at Grandma

Lillian's. His arrival each spring was a happy occasion, and his departure in the fall, after the last box of apples had been picked, a time of sadness. He would have come for a fourth season, I suppose, if Dad's cousins from Indiana hadn't asked to come that summer and stayed with us instead.

Archie drew little of his earnings during his stays with us—just enough for soap, toothpaste and the like. At departure time each fall, he had Daddy mail a check for his accumulated wages to his home in Nebraska, less a few dollars for Archie's essentials on the trip. He always wrote to tell us of his safe arrival.

A wonderful mentor, Archie helped guide me through my middle grade-school years. He was the only person, except my uncle Max, with whom I could safely and openly discuss any subject. Moreover, information from Archie, in contrast with that from Max, was invariably honest, authoritative and, as Mamma said of Archie, wholesome. I marveled at the depth of Archie's wisdom, and can only attribute it to his prolific reading.

He taught me more about sanitation and personal hygiene than did my folks or teachers, and the information not only proved to be true, but ahead of the times.

"The two greatest sanitizers we have are the sun's rays and the oxygen in the air," he told me while he hung his just-washed underwear on Mamma's clothesline. "Always wash your hands after going to the toilet," he advised another time, while we shared the two-holer outhouse. "And dry your hands in the air and sun instead of with a towel that others have used."

While I shared Archie's river baths, he gave me clinical answers to my questions about male genitals, girls and other things that kids in my circle would never dare to discuss with their parents. Again, all of Archie's information proved, ultimately, to be sound.

Archie fascinated me with tales of traveling, and just surviving, during those depression years, when no social "safety nets" existed for the able-bodied single man. His yearly "train travel" actually was "riding the rails," or in boxcars, with other transients.

"Most of the hobos aren't criminals or deadbeats," he told me, "just guys out of work or down on their luck. They share whatever food they have, and also share information about where and when to catch or drop out of a boxcar, where a guy might get a handout—things like that. It's best to find a couple other guys to travel with, so you can take turns sleeping and watching out for thugs."

"What are thugs, Archie?"

"They're guys who rob and beat the 'bos, stealing what few goods they have, sometimes getting them thrown in jail. Some of the thugs are railroad bulls. Their job, I guess, is to keep folks from riding the trains without paying. Some of the bulls are good people, and even turn their backs when they see hobos catch a ride. But others are downright mean and cruel—just like some people everywhere.

"Anyway," Archie added, "I don't want you to ever, *ever* try hitching rides in boxcars...you hear?"

Only then did I realize that Archie wasn't riding the rails by choice but out of hardship.

But Archie did not tell me the worst of what he must have seen: of ragged, hollow-cheeked families riding the boxcars aimlessly because they had no other shelter, dropping off only to wash in streams and forage for food. Or of the many "Hoovervilles" he must have passed—tin-and-tarpaper shantytowns packed with desperate folks living in abject poverty and blaming the President after whom they named their colonies of shacks. I did not learn about these terrible aspects of those times until years later while reading about the depression in retrospect.

Archie told me how to eat on the cheap. He recounted the first time he came west in the boxcars, starting with five dimes and a small glass jar of peanut butter.

"If you keep yourself clean, you can go into restaurants, but not if you look like a bum. I choose a place where coffee is five cents and they have cream and sugar on the counter. I order a cup of coffee and load it up with the cream and sugar. Then I take out my peanut-butter jar. With my coffee spoon, I dig out a rounded spoonful of peanut butter—just one—and lick that while I sip my coffee. Even if the place doesn't give free coffee refills, that'll keep me going for the day. And I've only spent a nickel."

I must have looked skeptical, for Archie grinned and added, "People tend to eat too much. Why, just one of those apples out there on your daddy's trees can keep a man going for another day."

Archie admitted, in fact, to swiping the occasional fruit and garden vegetable in his travels. "I never stole a chicken, though, or anything big, like some of the 'bos do."

I had known, as long as I could remember, that we could not afford many things that others had. Archie's tales, however, were my awakening to just how bad conditions were elsewhere, and how lucky I was to always have shelter and never go to bed hungry.

Many times, I've wondered where Archie Bond finally landed and how my old friend and mentor fared. Of two things I'm sure: He lived his life as a good man and, barring some sort of tragedy, he survived the cruel times of the Great Depression.

PLANTING TREES BUT GROWING ROCKS

When we moved to the home place, our orchard comprised a grove of mature apple trees near the house, but the downstream "tail" of our teardrop-shaped land was undeveloped river terrace. Over the next few years, while I was in the middle grades of school, Dad planted some forty additional apple trees.

Working alone, or with occasional help from Mamma or a hired man, Dad dug the planting holes in the gravely terrace deposits. He patiently dug hole after hole with pick, shovel and sweat. The holes seemed overly large to me for the little sticks he planted.

"There's not much soil here, Son," Daddy explained. "It's mostly clean river sand and rocks. We have to dig out all the rocks and haul in good, rich dirt to fill the holes. That'll make the baby trees grow up big and give us good apples."

As Daddy dug and planted, dug and planted, large piles of cobbles and boulders accumulated down the rows of new plantings. With his usual wit, he referred to his toil as "planting trees but growing rocks."

I assumed that these rock piles would be permanent features of our new orchard. But one day Daddy declared that he was going to build a "stone boat" to remove the orchard rocks.

A stone boat, I thought. *It must be some kind of barge to ferry the rocks down river. How exciting!*

Days later, Daddy announced, "Well, the stone boat's finished."

I could hardly wait to have him show me. *Will it be pointed at the front,* I wondered, *like the picture of the Ark in Mamma's bible book? Will I be able to ride on it?*

Daddy walked me out to his pile of salvaged lumber and pointed. "There she is."

I tried not to show disappointment—Daddy seemed so proud. But he hadn't made a boat at all, just a raft. An ugly raft!

Dad had cut down a small fir tree from a grove at the upstream end of our land and split a section of the log down the middle. He had spread the two halves, curved sides down, and spiked planks across them. The thing looked awfully heavy.

"Will it float, Daddy?"

Daddy laughed so hard that he had to sit down on the lumber pile.

After finishing his laugh and wiping his eyes on his ever-present red bandana, Daddy explained that it was not really a water boat, but a kind of sledge to be dragged over the dirt to haul rocks out of the new orchard. He showed me the steel rings he had bolted to the front.

"Now," he declared, "all we need is the horse to pull it."

A horse! Oh, happy day! The prospect of having a horse more than made up for my disappointment with the "boat." My enthusiasm waned only slightly when Daddy said we would rent the horse from a neighbor instead of getting one of our own.

ORCHARD COWBOY

Like most young boys of those times, I fantasized about cowboy life and riding horses like I saw in movies starring Tom Mix, Hoot Gibson, and Buck Jones. My Uncle Max and I turned everything possible into imaginary horses during our play. One favorite was my long-suffering Grandma Edna's clothes-drying rack. That wooden rack, when folded together, was just the right height and width to be a perfect imaginary steed. Max and I finally, and literally, shook the rack to pieces "galloping" and "bucking" on that poor "horse." The drying rack had to be put down, but our fixation

The Orchard Cowboy, in the back doorway at the home place.
Mamma's kitchen range shows in the background.

with horses survived. So when Daddy told me, the summer when I was eight, that we were getting a horse to move rocks out of the orchard, I went into rapture.

We already had a small barn, built across the driveway from our house by Daddy and my uncles using salvaged lumber and straightened nails. Any hired men or other male visitors slept in the hay loft, and our Guernsey cow Peggy had a stall on the dirt floor of the barn. To accommodate the horse, my folks cleared extra space alongside Peggy.

When Daddy brought the brown mare home, my bubble of euphoria burst. Instead of an alert, sleek palomino or quarter horse, as in the movies, he led in this sleepy-eyed, broad-beamed middleweight.

"Her name's 'Dolly,'" Daddy said.

Dolly? I wanted a "Dasher," or a "Charger," or a "Flash." "Dolly" was a *terrible* name, especially for this horse. She surely was no beauty. Her brown hide bore darker harness mars, and she was slightly swaybacked. Her big hooves clomped the ground in something between a plod and an amble. Even her tail looked lazy, swishing at occasional flies.

Still, she *was* a real, live horse, and she seemed gentle enough. I could hardly wait to get on her back, but my folks would not allow that until Daddy worked her for awhile.

With Dolly came a set of harness, and I thought Daddy was the smartest man on Earth to take that mess of leather and metal and wood and know how to put it on the horse, and then hook it up so it would drag the stone boat he'd built for rock removal. I didn't realize then that Daddy's dad had been a part-time teamster, and that horses had been the "tractors" of Dad's boyhood.

Daddy and a dark-haired hired man named Mel spent days loading rocks onto the horse-drawn stone boat and skidding the loads to the edge of the river bank, where they dumped the rocks. By the end of each day, both men and horse needed rest, and my pleas for a horseback ride were shushed. On Sunday, however, my folks finally relented, and Daddy asked Mel to put a bridle on Dolly and oversee my first attempt at horseman-ship.

Dolly came without a saddle, so I rode bareback. Her back was so broad and my legs so short that I balanced there in the splits position, with absolutely no way to grip the animal's sides. Mel held the bridle and paraded us back and forth near the house so my folks could watch, then handed me the reins and left me free to ride along a fringe of open land between our orchard and the river bank.

I began by walking the horse, practicing reining and commands of "whoa" and "giddup." Mel shouted his advice and encouragement. Everything was fantastic! At last I was on a real horse, in total control.

But of course I got greedy. I wanted action. I wanted *speed*!

I began kicking Dolly's ribs and urging "Giddup! Giddup!" My steed finally broke into a reluctant trot. I liked that a lot, even though I bounced all over the broad back. "Giddup, Dolly!" I shouted, kicking harder. The trot became more vigorous, as did my bouncing.

"I doubt that she'll run for you," Mel called. But I kicked again.

Just then, Dolly made a sharp left turn that almost dumped me, and trotted under a low limb of the nearest apple tree. It scraped me off and dropped me to the ground that quick. Mel arrived to help, laughing so hard he could barely lift me. My traitorous steed calmly went to cropping grass between the tree rows.

"Well, cowboy," Mel said after his laughter slowed and he determined I was basically okay, "you have to get right back up there and ride again. That's the rule. And this time, you just show that horse who's boss."

The spill had shaken my confidence, but I took Mel's word that I had to try again. Mel sweet-talked Dolly into letting him pick up the reins, and he led her back to stand in front of me. As he handed me the reins, Mel advised, "Stand right in front of her and look her in the eye. Make a hard face and tell her you're the boss."

I moved around to face the horse, looking up to her unblinking, brown eyes. I put on my sternest face. "Listen, horse," I growled, "I don't like being dumped that way. Now, I'm the boss, and you just go where I say. If you do that again, I'll punch you on the nose!"

Dolly didn't seem too frightened. All through my threats she continued chewing her mouthful of grass. She probably was distracted by the choking fit that Mel was having behind me.

But Mel assured me that I had given the horse an effective scolding. He grinned and chuckled his approval as he helped me back onto the broad, brown back and handed me the reins.

Dolly, indeed, seemed totally under my control as I walked her back and forth on the open strip alongside the orchard. She reined at my will, and obediently stopped and started at my commands.

"Good job," Mel called.

But horses need to *run*! I knew that from the movies.

Without consulting Mel, I kicked the brown sides with my heels. "Giddup!" I yelled.

Dolly walked faster and then began to barely trot. Drunk with power, I repeated my command and kicks.

Despite my frantic reining and shouts of "Whoa, Dolly! Whoa!" the horse veered toward the nearest apple tree.

Unfortunately, this time I knew what was coming. I grabbed a handful of mane. It took the *second* tree limb to scrape me off.

The scratches and bruises weren't serious. I lived to ride again, but only under Daddy's supervision. I even got so I could make Dolly back up.

Too bad Mel wasn't there to see it. Mamma said Mel had been "a bad influence." I didn't really know why. I guessed that I wasn't the only one who had found Mel's naughty magazines under his mattress in the barn loft.

ORCHARD VISITORS

We had our share of ordinary visitors while I was growing up: relatives, neighbors, out-of-town friends, and couples with whom my folks played pinochle on winter nights. But we had some unusual "drop-ins" too.

When I was very small, during our first few years at the home place, the local Indian band still made annual, summer migrations to the upper Entiat Valley. They spent the summers, I learned later, fishing for the migrating steelhead and salmon, drying and smoking their catch, and gathering their traditional herbs, roots, and berries. Just before their autumn down-valley trek, they killed as many deer as their ponies could carry or drag on pole travois. Their slow passage along the valley road—maybe a dozen swarthy, somber people in buckskins and colored blankets, with a few ponies—was an awesome sight for a small boy.

On their up-valley march, small children and the women with babies rode the ponies, while everyone else walked. On the return trek, however, even the mothers walked, carrying their babies on backboards. The men and boys led the heavily laden ponies.

The homeward-bound Indians camped overnight on the open, down-river part of our property, not yet planted to apple trees. They didn't raise tepees or other shelters, they just slept around their cooking fires under the stars. The ponies were unloaded and hobbled but not tethered, and freely grazed the grass and weeds along our ditch bank.

I don't think the Indians ever asked permission to camp on our property, although Daddy always went out to talk to their leader. Apparently, this had been the band's stopover place through their history, for we later raked up from the orchard soil a beautiful white-and-purple chert spear point, and a well-made grinding pestle of fine-grained basalt.

The Indians stayed only one night each fall, and were up and gone before our breakfast time. One morning, though, I woke early, determined to watch them breaking camp. Imagine my shock when I saw them picking fallen apples from the ground and others from the trees, as their last act before departing.

"Daddy, Daddy!" I called as I raced into the house, "they're stealing our apples!"

Dad was putting wood into the kitchen stove, and Mamma was cutting bacon. Daddy hardly paused at his fire stoking.

"That's all right, Son. They need those apples to keep their kids healthy through the winter."

His reaction to my outburst astounded me—Daddy always got upset about anyone taking other people's things. Mamma got this funny look on her face and hugged me against her. Then my folks hugged one another for one of the few times I ever saw.

I heard that the idea of land ownership was alien to our Indian neighbors, but I'm sure they appreciated my folks' forbearance. During what was, perhaps, their last stopover, two Indian women, in decorated buckskin dresses and with their black hair neatly braided, came to the house and presented Mamma with a pair of beautifully beaded, fringed gloves of the softest buckskin. Mamma oohed and aahed over the gloves, and thanked the women profusely. As far as I know, however, Mamma never wore them, and I never saw those beautiful gloves again. They should have gone to a museum.

*   *   *

Not all the drop-ins to our orchard were human.

One early morning, Mamma, on her way back from the outhouse, rushed into the kitchen breathlessly. "Gerald, Gerald!" she called, "There's a bum in a black coat up in a tree, stealing apples!"

Dad pulled on some overalls and shoes, grabbed his old ten-gauge shotgun, and took off on the run. Dad hated losing good apples to thieves, despite his forbearance with the Indians.

I started to go with Dad, but Mamma held me back. Just as I got to a window, here came Dad, running back to the house about as fast as he'd gone out. In the distance behind him, a black shape crouched between the trees.

Dad's eyes were huge when he burst in. "He dropped out of the tree when I ran up yelling, and he started toward me. I could've shot him with the shotgun, but that probably would have just made him mad."

We watched from the security of the house until the black bear got his fill of apples and waddled away.

"Wish I had a heavy rifle," Dad muttered, peering out at the departing black shape. "We could use some bear meat for winter."

*   *   *

Deer were frequent visitors, especially during heavy winters, when their tastes for tender, budding tree shoots and bark of young trees turned them into destructive pests. They also ate a remarkable array of things around the place—pies and Jell-O left out to cool; soap; the cow's hay; and leather harness. Daddy said they were as bad as goats.

Fences are of little use against determined deer. They can jump an eight-foot fence, and packed or crusted snow along the fences makes their leaps that much easier.

A strong defense against destructive deer is a barking dog. For many of my childhood years we had an excellent watchdog and companion, a black-and-white mix of fox terrier and bulldog named "Prince." For years Prince kept the deer from doing too much orchard damage, although his barking made inroads into Dad's and Mamma's sleep through many a night.

Sometimes, though, watchdogs got beyond control. One winter, the game warden came around and asked for us to account for Prince's where-abouts on a certain night

"We found where a pack of dogs slaughtered two deer," he said.

"They form a pack like their wolf ancestors, run the deer down on the crusty snow, and rip 'em apart," he explained to me. "The dogs go back home come daylight, but once they start that pack activity, they never can be trusted not to repeat it. So if a pet dog is gone during a deer kill, and comes home bloody...." He tilted his head and shrugged.

Daddy was quick to vouch for Prince's presence at home on the night in question. The warden accepted his assurance with a nod.

After the warden left, Daddy explained that if dogs were identified as being part of a killing pack, the warden traced them down where they lived and unceremoniously shot them.

TIPSY DEER

About the only time we welcomed deer at our place was in late winter when they came to dig old apples from under the melting snow. The inevitable wind-fall fruit had lain for months under the insulating snow, receiving just enough heat from the ground to allow fermentation. The deer had an uncanny sense of smell for alcohol fumes. They went after that "packaged apple-jack" with an obvious eagerness and unerring accuracy.

As the deer dug up and ate more and more of the fermented fruit, their antics became a hilarious circus. They would begin to gambol about—both sexes and all ages behaving like fawns. They playfully nudged and jumped at each other, with their slender legs getting less steady and wider apart. Then, as more of the alcohol took affect, one or two of them might put on sudden bursts of speed that ended in stumbles and tumbles. Others would just stand in place, with feet splayed wide, shaking their heads as if to clear the cobwebs. The party would generally continue until several were literally falling-down drunk or already lying in the snow between the tree rows, where they rested before making their stumbling way out of the orchard and up the hill to sleep off their binge.

One winter, when imbibing deer visitors were at their drunkest, Daddy decided to try riding one. He crept up on a big buck that was lying in the snow. While Mamma and I watched from a safe distance, Daddy pounced on its back.

As closely as I was watching, I didn't see that buck gather his legs under him. It happened in a blur. The first jump threw Daddy up completely through a twelve-foot apple tree. His ascent was in slow motion compared to the buck's bouncing departure from the orchard, along with the rest of the herd.

Daddy made a graceful turn in midair above the tree, unfortunately to a face-down position. The awful ripping, cracking sounds of him crashing back down through the tree limbs remain with me to this day.

Blessedly, Daddy landed in soft snow. Mamma and I rushed to help him. His clothes were ripped, and he bled from several places. Broken tree limbs surrounded him on the snow.

"Gerald! That was the *dumbest* thing you *ever* did!" Mamma scolded as she pressed her handkerchief to his bloody nose.

Daddy managed a sheepish grin as he lay there, surveying the tangle of broken branches around him.

He glanced up through the tree.

"Guess I won't have to prune *this* tree soon."

COMPANIONS AND CAREGIVERS

Most children's lives are greatly influenced by playmates, schoolmates and caregivers, and my childhood was no exception. Regrettably, space allows mention of only a few of those influential boys, girls and adults in the Entiat Valley during my time there. A lot of very fine people shared the valley with my family.

The friend with whom I spent the most childhood time was **Bobby Schermerhorn**, whose family lived just a quarter-mile from us, on the next orchard up valley. Bobby was roughly the same age as I but for years I was the taller. Slender like his folks, he had dark-brown wavy hair and a very expressive face. The girls at school, where he was a grade behind me, thought him handsome. But Bobby also was "nervous," as his mother put it, and when we first began playing together he was easily frightened and upset. I'm not proud to say that I and other schoolmates took advantage of him at times. However, he soon grew both physically and socially, and thereafter could hold his own.

Bobby's folks, Rollo and Nora, established their place before we moved onto ours. Their house, yard and outbuildings were "finished," in contrast to ours, which never seemed to be quite done. They had a nice little white-painted, two-story house, a woodshed with a snug bunkhouse attached, a fenced lawn with flowerbeds, and their own small fruit-packing shed with a sawdust-filled ice house and a one-car garage underneath.

The self-priming pump on their well was better than our old pitcher pump, and even their outhouse was better and more attractive. In fact, their outhouse was the nicest I ever saw in the valley. A two-holer like most, it was sturdily built of finished lumber, and was painted white inside and out. It had a finished ceiling under its shingled roof, a tight-fitting door, screen over ventilation openings, and a sturdy wooden floor. In contrast with most other toilets, it was kept "limed" to reduce odors, making it almost a pleasure to use. In fact, when I knew I was going to Bobby's, I sometimes "held it" until I got there rather than going in our more smelly, insect-inhabited outhouse.

Bobby and I spent countless days together. We played carom and checkers in his parlor, and gambled marbles in the loft of the bunkhouse. His house had a fun stairway, where we would race to the top and then purposely bounce from wall to wall as we charged down, until his mother would finally shout, "For heaven sake, put on your coats and play outside. You're driving me crazy!"

Outside, we layered a road bank near his family's garage with spoon-dug roadways for our toy cars and trucks. As we knelt in the roadside ditch, "driving" the toys back and forth along the bank, we had no fear of the real cars passing behind our backs. As long as we remained in the ditch, in plain view, we knew the drivers would take care of us. We made our little roadways in that wall of dirt until a county road worker complained to Bobby's folks that our "excavations" were filling in the drainage ditch.

Later, Bobby and I collaborated on bigger projects, like pooling our meager pocket money to buy lumber and build a leaky rowboat, then spending days learning first-hand what oakum calking rope would and wouldn't do to seal the leaks. Bobby also was a favorite companion for roaming the rocky, pine-dotted hills, with and without other guys.

Bobby and I remained close buddies until I started high school, leaving him in eighth grade. About that time, burgeoning defense industries in the Puget Sound region were hiring, and Rollo, and later the rest of the Schermerhorns, moved to the Tacoma area. I lost track of Bobby after that move.

*   *   *

For a while, I had a playmate living even closer to our home place than Bobby Schermerhorn. His name was **Charlie Gofinch**. Charlie's family didn't stay long, but its link to my family persisted throughout our up-valley days.

In 1931, the year I started first grade, the C. A. Harris and Son Lumber Co. began relocating its mill and other facilities to land near the mouth of the Mad River, within a mile up valley from our school. One of the family men who moved from the former mill site to work at the new construction was Charlie's dad. Mr. Gofinch decided to forego the rental housing the Harris company provided and instead build his own house. The site he chose was on the lower slope of the hillside across the road

Zebra House, built across the valley road from the home place.
Shown are Aunt Achsa and Great Uncle Bright Foxworthy.

from our orchard, almost opposite our house. There, he built a little two-room cabin using salvaged lumber and box-wood shingles from the mill. Part of the lumber was "shiplap" that had been used as concrete forms, and some boards were stained white from the cement. Mr. Gofinch used those form boards as part of the siding for their little home, creating white, horizontal stripes among the other, brown-weathered siding boards. The little outhouse he built also had white-striped sides, vertical in this case. Because paint was a non-essential luxury in those days, those buildings remained striped throughout their existence.

I thought the house would be a perfect place for zebras to live, but I only said that once. Mamma scolded me for making fun of the Gofinch home. Still, I always thought of it as "Zebra House."

Living just across the road, Charlie was handy for me to play with, and we spent a lot of time together for a while. However, he had formerly lived in a mill camp among some tough kids, and Charlie sometimes was too surly and aggressive for my liking. We finally had a falling-out after I accidentally broke one of his few toys, a little cast-iron car. I don't remember ever walking to school with Charlie, probably because an older friend, Lois Johnson, walked me to school during my first few grades, and Lois didn't like Charlie.

Like many other depression-era families, the Gofinchs had no water supply except what they carried to their cabin and stored in a five-gallon milk can. During the irrigation season, they scooped water from the big ditch, named the Spencer ditch, which ran along our place just across the valley road from Gofinch's. In September of 1931, shortly after Charlie and I started school, one of his younger siblings, twenty-month-old Mary Helen, escaped her busy mother's attention, toddled down to the ditch, tumbled in and drowned.

It was my first experience with death. With the despair of a bereaved family. With the sympathetic anguish of mine. With the barrage of scoldings about caution near water.

Not surprisingly, the Gofinch family moved away as soon as they could. Mr. Gofinch offered the cabin to us for whatever Dad could pay. I'm sure that wasn't much, for we didn't have much, but I'm also sure that my folks gave them all they could, even though the Gofinch family did not own the land. We certainly didn't have the money then to buy the land either. In fact, although someone in our family lived there as long as we were in the valley, Dad did not manage to buy the land under the little striped cabin until about 1938.

*   *   *

Lois Johnson was an older playmate, a mentor, and, at times a guardian angel. She was five years older than I, the same age as Uncle Max, and her family lived across the river from Grandma Lillian's place. When I started first grade at Vaughn School, Lois walked me to and from the little one-room schoolhouse, where she was starting sixth grade. We continued to make that walk together until she moved on to high school.

We also walked home together from after-school events, such as practices for school programs. I remember one cold autumn evening, while we walked toward home along the empty roadway in the deepening gloom, that we heard the hair-raising cry of a cougar. We both panicked and, even though the cry must have been from far away, we ran until I fell exhausted with a side ache and gasping for air.

Lois was my first seatmate in the double desks at school, and she promoted my love of learning by helping me through the first confusing weeks. She also intervened at times when she thought I was being picked on by bigger kids.

Our close relationship stemmed partly from the fact that her parents, Tony and Rachel, took care of me in the afternoons when Mamma worked in the fruit-packing sheds during harvest times. "Aunt Rachel" was a kindly woman who had also raised three other children, all older than Lois, so she was tolerant and wise to the way of kids. "Uncle Tony" also was kind, and virtually unflappable.

Tony had carpentry skills, and the home he built, compared to anything I had seen before, was a palace. It was a sturdy, two-story, house, well finished inside and out, with a modern bathroom (tub, sink and flush toilet) and a basement furnace fueled by sawdust from the Harris mill. Tony also built, behind the main house, the first little playhouse I ever saw. Next to it were a neat washhouse, and a fragrant smokehouse where the family cured meat from the hogs they butchered each fall.

Although Lois usually was trustworthy, occasionally, when her cousin Beryl Moe was visiting, Lois might betray me. These cousins sometimes took me to an upstairs bedroom and stripped me down to my underwear.

"Please, no! Please, no!" I would plead.

But, despite my tearful protests, they made me submit to wearing some of Lois's outgrown dresses and party shoes and they groomed me as a girl.

Worsening my humiliation, the girls made fun of my underclothes, which consisted (during spring and fall) of a one-piece vest-and-shorts combination (flap in back, fly in front) with attached garter supporters to hold up my thigh-length, brown cotton stockings. The underwear was called BVDs. In wintertime, I had to exchange the BVDs for full-body long-johns, but I always got to wear long pants over them. Dad said he had hated his own consignment to short pants, or "knickers," and was determined not to make his son wear them.

Despite those traitorous acts involving female attire, I have always felt great warmth for Lois and her family. Lois's older brother Art was particularly kind to me in my later grade-school years by concocting jobs for me to earn spending money, and introducing me to skiing.

*   *   *

Vern Packwood, a class ahead of me, was a schoolmate ever since I started school. He was about two years older than I and, of course, taller. Vern had sandy hair, a quick grin and an amiable disposition. However, he also could be daring, with more verve than common sense.

Vern's family lived on one of the larger nearby ranches, in a house directly across the river from our first school, Vaughn School. Vern was the youngest in his large family and had plenty of playmates. In my early years, I got to play with Vern and his siblings mostly when Lois Johnson wanted to visit the Packwood girls and took me along. I remember a big, high swing the Packwoods had, and Vern's older brother pushing me higher and higher to my first ever frightening "thrill ride." I got to know Vern even better after our Vaughn School years.

*   *   *

Dick Shumway moved to the valley during his seventh-grade year, and entered school a grade ahead of me, in the same grade as Vern Packwood. Dick had a husky build, dark-brown hair, and a quick wit. He and I had a lot in common from the beginning: both of us only children; both in families having rough times; both of us with mothers who were five-foot, plump bundles of sweetness and dads who were less approachable. But I was a little in awe of Dick, too. He had lived in the big city of Wenatchee, where he had actually had a newspaper route and played organized baseball. Also, by being one grade ahead of me, he was roughly two years older. Anyway, we finally got well acquainted and ended up having notable adventures together, some of which are better left untold.

*   *   *

I first heard about the **Morrow kids** in some valley gossip about their mischief. I had no idea then who they were, and could not have guessed how their future in the valley would intersect ours.

The Morrow family came to the valley as refugees from the Midwest Dust Bowl, which added its own special misery to the Great Depression. The family had five kids, all but two of whom were older than I. The Morrows were friends or relatives of the pioneer Cannon family, and for a while the Morrows stayed with the Cannons on their ranch about three miles down valley from our home place.

The Morrows hadn't been in the valley long before we finally lost our apple ranch to foreclosure. By then, the mortgage bank had learned that the ranches they took over needed to be kept in production or else become major liabilities. Through some arrangement, the Morrows became the operators of our old orchard. When the Morrow kids moved into our old house and started at Ardenvoir School, I gradually got to know them, although I admit at first I resented their occupancy of my old home.

I often wondered where all those Morrow kids slept in our old two-bedroom house, still unfinished after the fire we'd had in 1934. Of course, they had the little barn with the loft where our hired men and other male visitors had spread their bedrolls. And the Morrows were the only other family I knew that had kids sleeping in an old car with seats that folded down to make a bed, as I slept in an old Flint sedan behind our tiny cabin, just down the road (see "Our Last Valley Home").

When the younger three Morrow kids, Leslie, Don and Donna, started at Ardenvoir School, they came with something of a reputation, about events while they lived at the Cannon's:

Although the other kids in the valley happily swam in the Entiat River, the Morrow kids decided that they needed their own swimming pool. They chose a small gulley up the hill from the Cannon place, where a major unlined irrigation ditch joined a wooden flume that carried water across the gulley. Needing tools to reshape their "pool," they broke into a nearby road-department storage shed for picks and shovels, which they used to build an earthen dam across the gulley below the flume. Then, for water to fill their pool, they breached the side of the irrigation ditch at one end of the wooden flume.

Not surprisingly, the impromptu swimming pool was not full before major wrath descended on the Morrow kids. Several downstream ranchers raced to the site fearing a ditch break after their irrigation supplies suddenly went dry. They caught the kids red-handed.

Under the wrathful direction of the ranchers, the kids were set to hauling dirt up the hill from their earthen dam and repairing the ditch-bank washout with their "borrowed" tools. Reportedly, the local sheriff deputy also gave the kids and their parents some stern lessons about the inadvisability of breaking into county property and about the sanctity of irrigation systems.

Another anecdote about the Morrow kids came from the boys themselves. One afternoon while at the Cannon's, the kids decided to have a croquet game. As exuberant boys will do, one of the older brothers decided to "kill" a competitor's ball. He took a mighty swing but missed the ball. The head of the croquet mallet came off its handle and struck his ten-year-old brother, Don, squarely in the head. Don dropped like a sack of fertilizer. He seemed not to be breathing, so the others assumed he was dead. They huddled around the body and decided they had to get rid of it or they'd be in serious trouble. So they dragged Don's carcass into a huge lilac bush, planning to come back in the middle of the night and bury him.

Dinner time came before the grownups missed the young boy. The other kids were busy explaining how Don had gotten mad at them and walked away—they didn't know where—when Don staggered in the door, rubbing a lump on his head and asking how he came to be in the lilac bush.

I hung out some with the Morrows, especially Les, who was in my class, and Don, who was one grade behind us. Les was tall, had sandy hair and needed glasses. Don had a sturdy build, dark hair, and a devil-may-care attitude. Les, the more serious and thoughtful of the Morrow kids, turned sixteen before I did, and acquired a 1930 Model A Ford roadster with a rumble seat (but no top). When one of us had money for gas, Les drove his car to school and on occasional dates. I double-dated with Les a few times, but quit that after one miserable night in Wenatchee when his car engine went out of time, and we spent most of a cold night along a roadside trying to get the car running well enough to limp back home.

*   *   *

With a name like Bruce, which often, especially in early years, was used as the diminutive "Brucie," I had to become a bit of a scrapper or else submit to being lower than scum in the cellar. Although my Aunt Achsa assured me that Bruce was a noble name in Scotland, in my world of the 1930s it was seen as effeminate, sissy. If anyone wanted to taunt me in the schoolyard, all they had to do was call, "Oh, Bru-ceee," in a lilting tone, which I soon learned was meant as an insult to my maleness.

For the first couple of years at school, I had to take it. I was too small and frail to do anything else. By third grade, however, I had recovered from a debilitating illness that caused me to miss part of first grade, and was growing a bit. I began to respond by figuring out variations to their names or other ways to insult my tormenters in return. That led to some scraps, which I learned did not kill me. Besides, our teacher Mrs. Parker usually stopped us after a few blows were exchanged.

Two things helped me: One was my quickness—"quicker than a chipmunk," one kid said. The other was the teachings of my Uncle Max. Max, five years older than I, had learned to hold his own against some pretty tough kids in various orchard camps where he and my grandparents had lived. Somewhere along the way, he had learned to hit really hard with either fist. I don't think I ever, during childhood or even later, knew anyone who could hit harder for their weight. (When he was sober, that is; after he started drinking, about high-school age, he was only inclined to fight when he was drunk, meaning slower and unsteady.) Max taught me to plant my feet and put everything I had behind a punch—shoulder, twisting hip, and driving leg. He also advocated: (1) When a fight seems inevitable, get in the first punch, and make it count. (2) Aim for the nose; a hard nose punch will usually take all the fight out of your opponent. (3) Never fight brothers; if you lick one you'll just have to fight the rest of them. (4) Always, *always* keep your wrists straight and your fists tightly clenched to minimize damage to yourself when you make contact.

I'm not proud to say that Max's teachings, put into practice, made me cocky and a bit aggressive. Guys learned that, even if they bested me in a fight, they'd likely end up hurting too.

Enter **Ray Green,** a schoolmate when I was in fifth or sixth grade: One day, in a dispute over playground equipment, we squared off. I failed to heed Max's admonition to make the first punch count. Instead, I feinted a left.

I never got to land my right fist. Ray hit me with a straight right-hand punch that nearly dropped me, and had me stumbling around in circles. Fortunately, he did not follow up, for I was defenseless. Ray had been aiming for my nose, I'm sure. I ducked just enough to take the blow right between the eyes. That one clean, righteous punch turned me black and blue from my cheekbones to my hairline, a sight which I'm sure gave more than one of my former opponents great satisfaction. Remembering it now, I may have to modify my earlier statement that Max hit hardest for his weight of anyone I knew.

So Ray Green taught me three more lessons that Max had omitted: (1) Never underestimate an opponent. (2) Never start a fight unless there's a darn good reason. (3) There is always someone out there who is stronger, tougher, and unwilling to take your guff. Thanks, Ray, wherever you are.

I guess for us smallish males it comes down to the admonitions in the popular song, *The Gambler:* "You have to know when to hold 'em, know when to fold 'em; know when to walk away; know when to run."

GOOD CIDER AMONG GOOD FRIENDS

For a while, the Shumways lived on the Packwood ranch, in one end of a storage building where an apartment had been made. I often walked home from Ardenvoir school with Vern and Dick, after which I took a shortcut through the Packwood orchard and their back pasture, and over a wood-stave pipeline that crossed the Entiat River to the back of Bobby Schermerhorn's yard. From there, I had just a quarter-mile jaunt along the valley road to home.

One late autumn afternoon when I was eleven and they were thirteen, as we three crossed the bridge to his place, Vern asked, "Would you guys like to try some cider?"

This was, of course, a rhetorical question. We were always famished after school, ready to eat or drink almost anything.

Vern led us to a cellar that I hadn't known about, under one end of the storage building where Dick lived. Vern opened the dusty, cobwebbed door and, in the cellar's gloom, I saw two large, wooden barrels atop a sturdy stand. The barrels were on their sides, and one of them had a wooden spigot in the end.

"We make our own vinegar," Vern said, "but right now the cider's pretty good to drink."

I didn't question Vern's remark but, in retrospect, just one of those barrels full would have made an awful lot of vinegar, even for a large family like the Packwoods.

Vern took a small enameled dipper from a hook beside the barrels. My mouth watered as he carefully turned the spigot handle and let the aromatic liquid dribble into the dipper bowl.

"Here," Vern said, handing the dipper to me. "Tell me what you think."

I sniffed the amber liquid. It was cider, sure enough, with a kind of pungent smell. I took one taste, then gulped the rest.

"It's great. Not a bit sour," I assured my friends, and handed the dipper back to Vern.

Dick tried the cider next, then Vern, who took his time drinking his portion. I couldn't wait for seconds.

We stayed there, talking and drinking that delicious cider, long after I should have continued home.

"You're a good friend, Vern," I said at one point, suddenly overcome with brotherly love. "And you, too, Dick." I loved those guys so much that I began to worry about them getting into trouble.

"Won't your folks miss all this cider we've had?" I asked Vern.

Vern shrugged, "They won't know who drank it. My brothers stop in and drink some, too." He offered me the dipper again.

I glanced outside. The sun line was high on the opposite hill. "I gotta go," I announced, shaking my head. "My folks will kill me as it is, for not havin' my chores done by now....Well, just one more sip," I agreed, as Vern continued to offer the dipper.

After that swallow, I rose from the crude bench on which Dick and I sat. "What the hell?" I gasped as I lurched against the doorway.

The others laughed. "I guess the cider's gettin' a little hard," Vern allowed with a twinkle in his eye.

I stood there stupefied, leaning unsteadily against the door frame. My only previous experience with alcohol had been during my recovery from an illness that had left me anemic, and for which the doctor had prescribed liver extract and red wine. I had considered the wine only slightly less nasty than the liver extract, and was totally unprepared for finding alcohol in such a tasty form.

Confused by all this, I had only one overwhelming thought: "Gotta get home."

To the laughter of my schoolmates, I lurched out the cellar door and began trotting unsteadily homeward through the Packwood's orchard. When I got to the pipeline over the river, no question was in my mind about the advisability of crossing in my unsteady state—I simply had to get across without pitching into the water.

I considered sitting and scooting along the big pipe that I usually ran across, but by making concentrated use of the side supporting cables, I edged across okay. On the other side, I skirted Schermerhorn's yard and reached the road—my home stretch.

My Uncle Max had told me that exercise burns off alcohol at a rapid rate, so I ran as best I could that last quarter-mile. Max also had warned me about telltale alcohol breath, so the moment I burst in the kitchen door I stuffed a cookie into my mouth.

Obviously, my folks didn't kill me, although they were plenty vocal in their displeasure about my lateness. My wood box had gone empty, and Dad had to bring in an armload of wood to feed the kitchen fire. That was a sin demanding stern punishment. But I don't even remember what punishment he imposed, I was so relieved that they didn't guess my greater sin of drinking that hard cider. I told my folks that I'd stopped off with Vern and Dick and lost track of time, which was the truth as far as it went. Being teetotalers, my folks may have missed any telltale evidence of my alcohol consumption. Or perhaps I had been "scared sober" or, in fact, had burned off the alcohol through my running.

Or maybe Dad suspected but let it slide; I learned much later that he knew a lot more about my escapades than I would have believed.

And, to this day, I don't know whether good ol' Vern set me up, or whether it was just my own gulping greed that got me tipsy on that delicious cider.

GRADE SCHOOLS

VAUGHN SCHOOL

I started first grade in 1931 in Vaughn School, a classic one-room school about a mile up valley from our home place. I was not yet six years old when Daddy took me for a talk with the lady teacher and a man I didn't know, and they decided I was ready. This suited my eagerness to start school, but I worried about the crowd of other kids I didn't know.

Vaughn School, perched on a knoll above the Entiat River, was built about 1902, the year my Foxworthy grandparents stepped off the steamboat at Old Entiat with their baby Gerald. (My dad and his sister Achsa, however, attended other schools down valley.)

The first thing I learned in school was how to fold a half-sheet of tablet paper to make a paper cup. That skill was essential because the school's only water supply was in a three-gallon ceramic crock with a spigot at the base. Commercial paper cups, if they existed then, would have been an unacceptable extravagance for our poor school district.

To fill the water crock, two of the larger boys got the privilege of taking a bucket down a switch-back trail behind the school to the Entiat River, scooping up a bucketful of river water and carrying it back up the gravelly trail to pour into the crock. Then, the teacher would carefully drip in a few drops of iodine from her first-aid kit and, after an hour or so, we were allowed to get drinks during recesses and lunchtime. The iodine must have been adequate for purification, because none of us got typhus or such. Actually, that iodine treatment probably was progressive for the times; drinking water for some families in the valley came, directly and untreated, from the river or from irrigation ditches fed by the river.

Vaughn School was primitive in other ways, too, but it was sound and functional. The white-painted, wood-frame school building—a single classroom with a small cloakroom on the down-valley end—had a roof of durable cedar shingles. Four sash windows on each side provided cross-ventilation and daytime lighting. The interior walls had wainscoting below the windows and plaster above. The floor was bare, fir wood, preserved with an oil that forever dominated the other schoolroom smells.

Twin outhouses sat in the back, or river side, of the school, about fifty feet away and out of sight of passersby on the adjacent Entiat River Road. Each outhouse was a "two-holer," and the boys' also had a rusty pee-trough cut from a stovepipe. The outhouses seemed no better or worse than I was used to—typically stinky and attracting their share of flies. The flies bothered most during warm days, when the screen-less school windows had to be open for ventilation. In keeping with the times, the fly problem was fought with ribbons of sticky flypaper dangling from the classroom ceiling.

A locally built wood stove heated the school. The stove comprised a stack of two horizontal oil drums, welded together with stub pipes between so the heat and smoke from the lower drum, the firebox, moved up through the higher drum to increase heat radiation. A wire-suspended stovepipe carried the smoke from the upper drum to a chimney at the rear of the building. This type of stove was a favorite for heating any sizeable area in those days, including the local community hall, a mile up valley.

Starting the wood fire each cold morning was one of teacher's duties. Local families donated the firewood. The privilege of carrying in wood chunks from the brown-weathered woodshed at the back end of the school, and stoking the fire, went to older boys. Alas, I never ascended to that cherished role.

The classroom arrangement was, to say the least, compact. Teacher's desk and chair sat in the left-front corner of the classroom, near the doorway to the cloakroom. Other corners of the Spartan classroom held a bookcase for reference books and a small worktable. On the front wall of the classroom was a blackboard, decorated along its top edge with a row of painted-on cursive letters matching the penmanship books. Above the blackboard were window-shade-type map rolls and a wind-up, pendulum clock with Roman numerals. We students occupied double desks—seventeen according to one old inventory—in three rows, as I remember.

The stove took up major space in the center of the classroom, owing not only to its own size, but also because it was enclosed by a U-shaped, galvanized metal shield to prevent accidental burns and to reduce overheating of the closest students. In wintertime, that shield often got hot enough to melt color crayons, if some miscreant was foolish enough to test the teacher's wrath.

The teacher at Vaughn School, during my tenure and for some years previous, was Mrs. Ruth Parker, a mother of two boys whom were not allowed to attend the school where she taught. Women teachers with families were unusual for those times, but I think having children of her own gave Mrs. Parker special patience and understanding. She was one of those teachers whom one would like to seek out later in life, grasp her hand, and say, "Thank you so much."

The school served grades one through eight, although the year I started we had no sixth or seventh graders and only one eighth-grade boy. Still, Mrs. Parker could spend only a brief time with each class on each subject.

In front of her desk was a "recitation bench," resembling a long church pew, where we sat during her class-by-class instructions or our parroting of letter sounds. At first, being called up to the bench was scary, but I soon saw that I was as prepared as most of the others in my grade. Also, this was a chance to show off, which suited me just fine.

Our school day started with the singing of patriotic songs, to music from a pedal-pump "parlor organ" played by Mrs. Parker or one of the older girls. The tiny organ sat just inside the cloakroom, next to the stand that held the water crock. Immediately after the singing, the class-by-class recitations began, each followed by the next assignments for that class.

Most of the time, we worked on assignments at our desks, and soon learned to concentrate on our own work and ignore teacher's instruction of the other grades. If we needed help, we first consulted our desk mate. The whispering about such problems was the only talking allowed at our desks. If we finished our assignments, we were encouraged to work on penmanship, always cursive letters and always starting with rows of circles that looked like tight coil springs, and "push-pulls" of tight, up-and-down strokes. The other subjects being taught were reading, spelling, English, arithmetic, geography, history and civics and, for the eighth-grader, agriculture.

The only subject I really disliked was penmanship, especially when, by third grade, we had to use ink. At that time, we were issued bottles of black ink to keep in the round holes in the top corners of our desks. Getting that ink onto fingers and clothes seemed to be no trouble at all, but getting the ink onto paper in a readable form was a challenge. Our long, wooden pen shafts were unwieldy for small hands, and the sharp, steel points they held insisted on making blobs and digging into the paper. The answer, of course, was dipping just a little ink onto the pen point each time and barely touching the point to the paper. As dexterity training, ink penmanship excelled, but I needed lots of pulpy paper blotters and cloth pen wipes, which came from home. My folks also had to buy expensive "ink paper" from then on. And poor Mamma had ink removal added to her laundry problems.

Another non-favorite subject was geography. My lack of interest in geography, I think, was simply that I could not imagine all those other places and other peoples. I could relate to mountains and rivers and forests,

Students at Vaughn School, 1933. The author is holding base-ball bat. Mrs. Ruth Parker, left rear, taught all eight grades.
Student photo courtesy of Rachel Stanaway Sines.

and also to logging and agriculture. Concepts of big cities, however, and other earth features and industries, were too vague to memorize easily.

Conversely, I was pathetically eager to learn reading and writing. When our "Dick and Jane" type books were handed out, but before we had our first instruction, I laboriously copied to my tablet each letter, in the printed form, and each punctuation mark of the first two pages of my "reader." I might as well have been copying cuneiform, for all I understood, but I was *writing*! When I proudly showed it to Mrs. Parker, she said, "That's very nice, Bruce, but I think you'd better wait until you learn your letters before you start to write."

Still, I was not as impatient as my wife, in her own classroom in Entiat. She came home after her first school day and immediately sought out the comics in the newspaper. Furious, she took the paper to her mother. "Everybody lied to me!" she raged. "You all said when I went to school I'd learn to read. I spent the whole day there and I still can't read a word of this!"

At Vaughn School we got brief recesses mid-morning and mid-afternoon, and a full hour for lunch. The kids who lived nearby hurried home for lunch. The rest of us got our lunch boxes from the cloak room and ate outside in nice weather or at our desks in bad. My lunchbox was black-painted metal with a rounded top that held a Thermos bottle. Even when it meant sacrifices at home, Mamma, bless her heart, always tried to have a nourishing school lunch for me, with hot soup or cocoa in cold weather to go with my peanut-butter or meat sandwich and the inevitable apple. In warm weather, the Thermos might hold milk or even Ovaltine, if we could afford that.

After our hurried lunch, we played until Mrs. Parker rang her hand bell at one o'clock. If the weather was too bad for outside play, Mrs. Parker read to us instead, a treat I always enjoyed.

The games we played were limited by our small schoolyard and by proximity to the river. When we chose up sides for softball, the adjacent graveled road, as well as some lower hillside beyond, was part of our ball field.

In the small schoolyard, we played "pom, pom pullaway," "ante over" (the schoolhouse roof), and jump rope.

We also played on the hillside across the road. In the springtime, we picked wildflowers there, and piled rocks to build forts. The girls brought their dolls and little dishes and played house on the hillside, using stones to outline their "rooms." At low-water times, we were allowed to play down by the river, although never alone. The bigger boys caught "crawdads" (small crayfish) where they dipped the school's water bucket, and they used their catch to chase the squealing girls. We younger kids played in the sand of a tiny "beach" that existed only at low river stage. Our natural play environment was wonderful with its freedom and its space, but no doubt would be deemed too risky nowadays.

Discipline and attendance were taken seriously in those days. If we arrived after the morning bell had rung, we'd better have a good reason or we would be marked tardy—a disgrace—and maybe lose some serious recess time. Never mind if the snow that morning slowed our way to school—we were supposed to allow for that, and run when necessary. Discipline problems mostly involved fighting among the boys, although I remember cases of minor thievery and malicious falsehoods. Mrs. Parker's approach to discipline consisted of keeping the offenders in at recess, clearing out everyone else, and "getting to the bottom of things."

After her inquisition, Mrs. Parker meted out her punishment, usually the loss of recesses or other privileges. I never heard of her resorting to corporal punishment, as did many other teachers of the time, and she rarely contacted the parents about disciplinary matters. By settling the problem at school, she spared some of us from the wrath of fathers who *did* believe in corporal punishment. Miscreants with siblings at school were usually doomed anyway, by a brother or sister who could not wait to tell on the offender at home. If the problem resulted in contact from the parents, that almost always was an apology to the teacher with assurance that little Johnny or Susie would do better—or else!

*   *   *

Among my fondest memories of the Vaughn School years were end-of-school picnics. Two of these which our family attended (1932 and 1933) took place at Pine Flat, a Forest Service campground a few miles above Ardenvoir in the valley of Mad River, the largest tributary of the Entiat River. The grounds presented ample room for happy competitions—foot races, horseshoes for the men, and softball games in which parents and students chose up sides. Identifying unfamiliar grownups with their children, and watching the interactions of the families, became almost as interesting as the games themselves. And, for some of the adults, these picnics were rare times when I saw them looking happy.

The picnic fare was mostly "pot-luck," with food and dessert contributions arranged among the women.

The first year we attended, several of the families also brought hand-crank ice-cream makers, along with supplies and ingredients to make the vanilla-flavored frozen treat. Grandma Lillian furnished one of the ice-cream churns, and Mamma brought some of the liquid mixture. Someone else brought blocks of ice and the rock salt needed to lower the temperature of the melting ice. After adults loaded the ice-cream makers, we boys took turns cranking the rotating freezers until our arms played out and we had to pass the task to others. As the ice cream froze, the cranks turned so hard that only the older boys and adults could finish the task. The rest of us waited, almost drooling, until a small helping of the frozen delight could be spooned into our bowls. Unfortunately, the supply of ice cream barely served the crowd.

For the second picnic, in the spring of 1933, preparations were the same, except that someone decided we needed more ice cream. Cooper's Store agreed to furnish commercial ice cream, and those who could were asked to contribute fifteen cents per family to help defray the costs. Surprisingly, attendance at the second picnic was less than at the previous one, despite the fact that additional kids from new mill families attended our school that year. Mamma thought maybe some families who could not afford the fifteen-cent donation were reluctant to show up because they could not pay their way. Anyway, the result was that a lot of ice cream had to be eaten before it melted, and that picnic was a monumental time when we kids literally had all the ice cream we could eat.

*   *   *

During my Vaughn School days, my folks provided additional education at home. Besides the usual help with my homework, Mamma coached me on reading the Bible, patiently helping me sound out the strange names and the odd Old English phrases. I got to show off my acquired skills at Sunday Bible meetings.

Daddy, in turn, insisted that I learn about current events. He sat me down one evening in November 1932. I was not yet seven.

"Son," he said, "I want you to always remember this day. This is a very important time in our country. We're going to see some big changes from now on, and I want you to pay attention to what's happening."

That day the country learned the results of the 1932 presidential election, after thousands and thousands of American voters—more thousands than ever voted before—swept Herbert Hoover out of office and catapulted Franklin Delano Roosevelt into the presidency he would hold for the next twelve years.

"From now on," Daddy continued, "I want you to try to read the front pages of our newspapers. Anything you don't understand, we can talk about."

Daddy was so serious in this order that he frightened me. So, I dutifully struggled with the front pages of the papers. We still managed to buy the *Wenatchee Daily World*, and the Sunday *Seattle Star*.

Many of the longer words I sounded out seemed vaguely familiar but their meanings remained unclear. In the end, my folks had to explain so many words to me, and then discuss the contexts, that my reading chore was gradually allowed to slide. Still, my vocabulary improved and, as my reading skills progressed, so did my understanding. Dad's basic admonition stuck, for I did think more about things beyond our valley and I have tried to pay attention to the goings on in our government ever since.

ARDENVOIR SCHOOL

Vaughn School might have seen me through the eighth grade had not the largest employer in the valley, C. A. Harris & Son Lumber Co., decided to relocate. During 1931-32, the company relocated its mill to a site about a half-mile up valley from Vaughn School, from a more remote mill camp ("Old Camp," on Muddy Creek) which had its own school.

Relocation of the Harris mill resulted in a sizeable new community. The labor force from Old Camp, with its school-age children, moved in to workers' housing built nearby, and a new general store (Cooper's Store) was built halfway between the mill and our school. The mill owner named the community "Ardenvoir" after his first-born, Arden Harris.

Obviously, Ardenvoir needed a larger school and more teachers. But this was during the heart of the Great Depression, and local funds for another school seemed out of the question. Fortunately, the federal government's New Deal program, designed to spur the nation's recovery from the depression, included grants for school construction under a Public Works Administration. Through diligence of the local school board, funds for a

Ardenvoir School, my "learning center" for grades four through eight. Lower end of galvanized-pipe fire escape is left of entrance. Courtesy of Rachel Stanaway Sines.

new school were thus obtained through the PWA, which carried the bonus benefit of requiring employment of local workers for the construction. The new Ardenvoir School was built in 1933-34, complete enough to house students during most of the 1934-35 school year.

My dad helped to build a stone retaining wall in front of the new school. His WPA job not only brought in much-needed money but also made our family eligible to receive free surplus commodities, which included bags of grapefruit, flour, and lentils.

The benefits also included materials and a local class for making cotton mattresses, which Mamma seized upon to create a sturdy mattress for my folks' bed. I was one of the boys pressed into service to beat the mattress batting into shape with lengths of broomsticks during assembly by the neighborhood ladies. We child laborers were forced to beat on those blessed mattresses until our arms threatened to unhinge. I quickly learned the wisdom of being in school instead, and of doing my home chores without complaint, lest I be forced back into that weeks-long mattress-making sweat shop.

Even though we students moved into the new school while the outside walls were still unpainted and the upper level unfinished, the place seemed like a palace. Two brand-new classrooms gleamed with bright walls, varnished floors and woodwork, huge windows—and marvelous electric lights! We sat in single desks, smooth and sturdy. We had drinking fountains fed by the school's own well. Below the classrooms was a full, concrete basement, half of it a playroom with natural light from window wells. The other half of the basement contained a room for an oil-fired furnace, and restrooms so modern they could have been in a city hotel. The whole building smelled of paint and fresh concrete.

Ardenvoir School was nearly a mile farther up valley than Vaughn School, but being in the newer, nicer school more than made up for my extra travel. Also, I soon had a bike which I could ride to school in all but the snowiest weather.

As I recall, dear Mrs. Parker finished out the 1934-35 school year in the new school, teaching grades one through three in the south classroom. A second teacher was hired for the rest of us in the north classroom. Other teachers appeared after Mrs. Parker retired, and yet another came after an upstairs classroom was finished to house grades seven and eight. In the meantime, enrollment swelled as other small nearby schools consolidated with the new Ardenvoir School District, designated No. 119.

The new school's spacious grounds, although never landscaped beyond the initial leveling and smoothing of the dirt, gave us ample playgrounds for softball and touch football. In bad weather, we played dodge ball and relay games in the basement, or jacks, "hangman" and tic-tac-toe in various out-of-the way corners above. Jump-rope and fiercely competitive marble games began outside as soon as the ground became firm enough in spring-time. I had a "lucky" amber-colored agate shooter, and I am proud to say that I usually won more marbles than I lost.

An unusual aspect of the Ardenvoir School was its second-story fire escape—a large tubular, galvanized-steel slide starting at a sash window in the school's upper, and largest, classroom. That big metal pipe on the north side of the building was a bit of an eyesore, but it allowed evacuation of the upstairs classroom in less time than was required to march the younger students out from the first-floor rooms.

We boys were especially fond of the fire-escape slide, a favorite place to meet after school and take turns crawling up inside and sliding down. The long slide had a good gradient that gave us a nice ride, especially after we learned to bring waxed paper to sit on. This left a good wax residue on the slide even after the paper wore out. However, the pipe had a rather sharp flattening at the bottom and, the faster the ride, the greater the jarring jolt at the end. The wax also made the pipe harder to climb, but we learned to force our tennis shoes against the metal on either side of the slide-way as we climbed up inside.

When girls came down the slide, we boys below might get an exciting treat. Especially if the girls got frightened of the speed and tried to slow themselves with their feet, we were likely to get a glimpse of panties under their flaring skirts and petticoats—very thrilling indeed!

The year after completing grade six in the north classroom of the first floor, we moved up, for grades seven and eight, into the large second-story classroom. The rise was symbolic as well as literal. We now were in The Big Room at the Top!—the room where the big pipe started, where we couldn't wait for the next fire drill. The room where English was now called "Language" and Arithmetic was "Math." The room from which there was no return, for our next move would be to high school!

During my two years on the top floor, our teacher was Kenneth Long, a very capable teacher but a stickler for discipline—probably a good thing for our crowd. He kept a wooden paddle at his desk and used it on us, girls as well as boys, when we strayed. About the worst sin in his eyes was talking back. Yet, he was especially kind to some kids, like me, whose families were on unusually hard times and living rough.

THE FORBIDDEN SUBJECT

Even for that time, when sex was a forbidden subject that nice people simply did not mention, I probably was one of the least informed kids in the valley. It was not for lack of curiosity—I had plenty of that. Lack of opportunity was the reason. For years, I was totally uninformed about the process of human procreation. As for female anatomy, in the absence of sisters or other female relatives inclined to enlighten me, my early, meager knowledge consisted of fleeting glimpses of Mamma, and what I saw—nay, studied—in the mail-order catalogs in the outhouse.

The big, thick Sears and Roebuck or Montgomery Ward catalogs were not there so much for reading material as they were as a source of toilet paper, store-bought rolls being an almost sinful extravagance. Among the hundreds of catalog pages, offering everything from automobiles and wagons to mousetraps and candles, were ads for women's clothing, including illustrations of women wearing "unmentionables" including corsets.

Although nothing in those illustrations (drawings or, later, black-and-white photos) showed anything bare except legs, arms and shoulders, the ads were snickered at as borderline indecent. I'm sure Mamma would have used those pages first to be rid of them, except that they often were among the few "slick" pages of the catalogs. The slick pages always survived the

*Corset advertisement of the kind that titillated adoles-
cent boys reading mail-order catalogs.*

longest, for, no matter how one crumpled those pages into a ball, smoothed them out and crumpled them again, they were never very satisfactory for their intended purpose—well, their secondary purpose. Therefore, the underwear pages commonly persisted to titillate young boys until the catalogs were finally used up.

I've heard that some kids tried to see more by tilting the pages to look up the corset skirts, but I don't think I was ever that naïve about the limitations of two-dimensional pictures.

Women and older girls took young boys to the outhouse, of course, as part of their care-giving, and sometimes "went" too, on the usual "two-holer" bench. This never resulted in enlightenment for me, however. All females wore skirts and petticoats in those days, and those ample garments obscured everything of interest.

Those coed outhouse visits, of course, became taboo as we boys got older. During the first week of my attendance at Vaughn School, the teacher made it painfully clear to me that a boy does not go into the girls' outhouse, even when the boy is invited. That whole outhouse episode was a disaster: Not only was my scolding much harsher than that received by my "hostess," but the object of her interest had been clearly exposed, whereas the object of my curiosity remained hidden the whole time by skirt and petticoat.

Most of my early information (and misinformation) was from other guys, notably boys who lived in crowded proximity to their sisters, and from my uncle Max. Because Max was five years older than I, he seemed to be a more reliable source of such information than he really was. Other sources of information were the crude drawings among the men's toilet graffiti. I was always willing to visit a strange men's "can," no matter how smelly, just for the chance to broaden my education. Still other sources were the pulp magazines acquired by some of our hired hands and stashed in the barn loft. I was a snooper and an early, precocious reader. I devoured those magazine accounts, wherein things were more hinted-at than explicit. I sensed some of the excitement of the sexy passages even though I didn't really understand all they implied.

Some of the most reliable information and advice I received on the subject came from our favorite hired man, Archie Bond. Archie was a wholesome Christian young man who understood better than my folks did my need to know. He gave me sound, clinically correct answers to my questions, at least those he thought were appropriate for my age.

*   *   *

My earliest actual observations of grown-up female anatomy, beyond the fleeting glimpses of Mamma, came, of all places, in Mamma's kitchen.

During our early years at the home place, my folks hired a few local girls to help with household chores and to ride herd on me whenever Mamma had an outside job.

Marie, whom my folks hired one summer, was a girl just beyond high-school age, living with neighbors. She was fairly pretty, with curly blonde hair and a figure at least as nice as my Aunt Achsa's. One fine day in early fall, when I was about eight, Mamma assigned Marie the duty of canning a big batch of green beans.

The bean-filled jars had to cook atop our kitchen wood stove in our big, oblong copper boiler for at least an hour, which meant that a stove's fire had to burn for considerably longer to heat the water to boiling while Marie filled the jars. My part in the operation was to bring in wood and keep the fire roaring in the firebox.

As I recall, Marie didn't get the jars into the boiler, onto the wooden slats that separated the layers, until after noon, when the sun already was hot on the kitchen side of the house. Our tiny kitchen, even with its two windows and the door open, became stiflingly hot as I kept stoking the fire box.

Both Marie, working next to the stove, and I, on the floor beside the wood box, sweated profusely. Marie's blonde hair became a soggy mat, and her simple cotton dress was soon soaked at the neck, waist, and underarms. She constantly wiped her brow and eyes with a kitchen towel so she could see. She looked about to burst with anger.

About the time her dress became soaked to her hips, Marie muttered something and abruptly walked out the door. I expected her to just keep going out the driveway. Instead, she stopped at the clothesline, peeled her dress off over her head, and draped it over the clothesline. With a resolute look on her face, she strode back into the kitchen wearing only her shoes, white panties and brassiere. "Don't tell your mom," she ordered sternly.

Tell Mom? Was she kidding? Even at that young age, these new visions enthralled me. Telling was the very last thing on my mind. I shook my head. "I'll go get you a dry towel."

Marie used the towel to mop the rivulets of sweat as she continued to work by the blistering stove. As her underwear got wetter and wetter, she began to show through—first, intriguing shadows, then details that had my young eyes bugging. I don't know whether Marie realized what an education I was getting. She didn't try to hide anything from my staring eyes, but neither did she seem to be showing herself. I think she was just too miserable from the hellish heat to care.

"Let the fire die," Marie said finally, and shortly afterward she had all the jars out of the boiler, cooling on Mamma's counter with dishtowels over the jars to slow their cooling.

"You stay right here till I get back!" she ordered, and went out the door again. I watched her underwear-clad body trot to the clothesline, where she snagged her dress, then past the outhouse. Her dress, and the towel I had given her, flapped in her wake as she ran on toward the river and disappeared over the bank.

Marie came back up over the riverbank a few minutes later, in her dress and fluffing her curly hair. She stopped again at the clothesline, where she hung her underwear and the towel.

When she reached the house again, I was outside to avoid the kitchen heat. "You won't tell your folks, will you?" she asked.

I did not, in fact, ever tell my folks. But that didn't matter to Marie's future with us. When Mamma and Daddy got home, Marie, fully dressed by then, met them with the proclamation that she didn't mind the other work, but she would do no more canning in this heat. Mamma bristled and replied that the canning was one of the main reasons she had hired her. Marie was adamant, and that was her last day with us.

Mamma seemed relieved at Marie's departure. I think Mamma considered her just a little too pretty. And we could tell from her breath that Marie smoked, which Mamma considered a likely sign of a loose woman.

*   *   *

Something happened at Ardenvoir School in my sixth grade, involving one of the older girls, that prompted our woman teacher (name escapes me) to announce to our class, "If you are curious about the opposite sex, you should get your answers from your parents, not try to get them from your fellow students."

This, of course, was sound advice—theoretically. However, I think our whole class was stunned that the teacher had even mentioned the dirty word, "SEX." And, for most of us, the chance of raising that subject with our folks was slimmer than a spider's thread. At that age, the world was clearly divided—kids versus grownups. Also, in those times parents were not encouraged to get too close to their kids. Sociologists were preaching that parents, especially fathers, should not demonstrate closeness, lest the child leave home unprepared for the harsh world beyond. No kid I knew felt comfortable in talking openly about many subjects with their folks, especially of things that went counter to the strict codes about modesty and privacy.

Therefore, the afternoon of our teacher's bizarre suggestion, I went home without the slightest intention of following that teacher's advice. But when Mom asked, "What went on at school today?" I suddenly blurted out the whole episode.

Mom's eyes went wide. Her face flushed and stayed that way. "Okay," she said finally, "what do you want to know?"

I immediately felt as embarrassed as Mom looked. Not having intended to raise the issue, I had no questions prepared. I think I muttered a bit before I stammered the first thing that came to mind: "Wh-what's ass?"

Mom looked a bit relieved. She solemnly patted a plump buttock. "What else?"

"Uh, uh…how do people *do it*?"

Mom, still blushing, thought a bit. "Well…about the same way your rabbits do it," she answered finally, referring to the rabbits I raised for their meat and hides.

"Okay," I blurted on my way to the door. "Gotta get my wood in."

Outside, I shook my head. I simply could not envision a man jittering himself against his woman's backside for a few seconds, thumping a foot rapidly and letting out a massive groan, then falling over backward stiff as a plank, the way my buck rabbit did with his females.

COMINGS AND GOINGS

During my early childhood, horseback travel was still common, and even a horse-drawn wagon or sleigh was not an unusual sight on the valley road. But most transport, by far, was by motor vehicles. Even the logs coming from the woods to the Harris mill were, by then, transported by trucks—big snub-nosed Mack trucks with solid-rubber tires and chain-driven rear wheels. We were well into the Age of the Automobile.

We owned many vehicles during the up-valley years, but three kinds were prominent in my memories: Fords, a 1928 Pontiac two-door sedan, and big old cars that Dad bought cheaply and either repaired and sold, swapped, or modified into a type of orchard tractor called "puddle jumper."

My dad came of age with the Model T Ford. He loved those Fords. And he understood them. Neighbors came (often on cold mornings) to ask Dad's help to get their balky "tin lizzies" running, or for advice on repairs. This was not surprising, considering that Dad, in his late teens, had built a Ford "racing bug" boasting seven speeds ahead and three reverse.

And there was a legendary shade-tree repair Dad made to his Model T touring car, named Jim, on a drive back from Spokane. In the middle of nowhere, Jim developed a knock that Dad recognized as a bad connecting-rod bearing. Dad knew the engine might be ruined if he pushed on to the

Dad mimicking film actor Harold Lloyd while working on Jim, our Model T Ford.

next town, but he managed to coax Jim to a farm near Waterville. In the yard of that farm, Dad took out his ever-present tool kit and got down on the dirt under the car. He removed the oil pan from the bottom of the engine, handling it carefully to save the oil, and unbolted the bearing cap from the damaged piston rod. Lacking facilities for proper repairs, Dad begged a strip of bacon rind from the farmer, cut it to fit around the crankshaft inside the bearing, and bolted on the bearing cap as tightly as he could. After reinstalling the oil pan, Dad was able to pamper the tough old Model T to a place where he got proper repairs. I forget other details, if I ever knew them, but the story helps explain Dad's reputation and also his respect for the rugged Model Ts. We had at least one "T" in the family, though not necessarily in complete, running condition, from before I was born until after Dad died.

As I recall, two starting problems seemed to dominate with the "Ts." One problem was the coils, four blocky things in wooden boxes, each about twice the size of a pound of butter. They had external contacts which were subject to corrosion, and a vibrating leaf spring that had to be adjusted so that it would "buzz" just right. The coils fitted into a dash-mounted metal box which, for obvious reasons, gave easy access for service.

The other starting problem was simply getting the correct setting for the spark lever and the throttle lever, both of which were mounted under the steering wheel. If they were set correctly, the spark plugs would fire at the right time, and the gas mixture would ignite properly in the cylinders when the hand crank at the front of the car was spun. These settings seemed to be a little different for each Ford, and changed with weather extremes and the condition of the engine. If the spark lever was set incorrectly, the engine was apt to backfire and break the cranker's arm, as a crank did once to Dad. If the gas throttle was set too rich, the engine could run away with itself before the cranker got back to slow it down, and might break a piston or something just as serious. No wonder electric "self starters" were so welcome when they came out.

The Model Ts had magneto ignition, which meant that the faster the engine was cranked, the stronger the electrical "juice." Therefore, being brawny enough to really spin that crank was a big advantage. Of course, if a "T" engine was well tuned, and the controls were set just right and the weather was warm, even a small person could go to the front of the car, give a sharp lift to the crank, and the engine was likely to start.

The problem of cranking a balky engine got worse in cold weather, when the crankcase oil became thick enough to retard the cranking effort. Dad could be lax about certain things, but on one thing he was scrupulous: During cold weather he always drained the oil from the vehicles and stored it so that it could be heated (on the kitchen stove) before being poured back into whatever rig was driven that day.

An emergency substitute for draining and heating the crankcase oil was to build a small fire underneath the oil pan to heat and thin the oil. This also was a good way to set fire to accumulated engine grease, resulting in a lively scramble by all nearby to snuff the flames with water or dirt or snow—whatever was handy—before the entire car caught fire.

This happened to a neighbor, Rollo Schermerhorn, one cold morning when Dad was called to get Rollo's Buick started and I tagged along. Rollo, a nice man and ordinarily sensible, tended to lose judgment in a crisis. That morning, when his engine blazed up from the warming fire underneath, Rollo grabbed a grey lap robe from inside the car and threw it over the top of his engine. The blanket settled in place just in time to deflect the handful of dirt that Dad was throwing at the fire.

"Rollo! What the friggin' hell are you doing?" Dad shouted as charred, acrid-smelling spots grew in the blanket and then blazed through. By the time Rollo finally snatched the flaming cloth away, Dad had found a bucket and was scooping up dirt and showering it on the engine compartment at blurring speed. That finally killed the fire before gasoline ignited, even though the blanket had done a fine job of concentrating the flames around the engine. Most of the engine's wiring was ruined, and also the lower radiator hose, but not much else. That was one of the few times I heard profanity from my dad.

Disgusted as he was with Rollo's mental lapse, Dad helped fix the Buick. That's what neighbors did in those days.

Another thing Dad was strict about was the care of wheels and tires. Many vehicle wheels of the day had wooden spokes, which shrank and loosened in our dry summer heat. Dad taught me to bring buckets of water from the irrigation ditch, splash it over the wheels, inside and out several times, and then drape wet gunny sacks over the wheels and wet them down again. That kept the spokes damp and tight even in the hottest, driest weather and also protected the tires from sun damage.

When I grew heavy enough to push down the handle of our tire pump, I also became responsible for checking tire pressures and adding air when needed. I was not always good about remembering this task, but all it took was a stern "Son, do I see a low tire in the driveway?" to get me back to duty.

Our family's ownership of motor vehicles began in 1917, when Grandpa Bruce registered a 1912 Model T, one-ton truck, license number 1748. Dad was sixteen, and undoubtedly was as ecstatic as any normal boy that age at having a motor vehicle to use instead of horses.

But the first vehicle of my memory was that black Model T touring car named Jim. Dad had used Jim to court his girlfriends, and had somewhat of a reputation as a wild and crazy guy behind the wheel. Jim also was the car in which Dad transported Mamma and me to the Entiat Valley from her parent's home in Spokane, where I was born.

In 1929, shortly before the Wall Street crash, my folks traded Jim in for a green '28 Pontiac two-door sedan. I reportedly howled my head off when we left the familiar Model T behind at the dealership. The Pontiac was the last "newer" car my folks ever bought, and we drove that old green car, in which I learned to drive, up to the beginning of my high-school years. When the years of weather and gravel damage finally rendered the Pontiac's appearance intolerable to Mamma, she sandpapered and repainted the entire car to a lighter green. She worked outside in the shade of our apple trees, using only a three-inch paintbrush to apply the enamel.

Other Model Ts figured prominently in the family's activities. For example, in 1925 my aunt Achsa, as a reward for her excellent grades and as a reliable way to and from her high school, received a shiny black Model-T coupe. Having her own car gave her personal freedom almost unheard of for young ladies of her day—to say nothing of her choice of companions. With her own fresh beauty and that splendid little coupe, she must have been the envy of the county. But in that time of hedonistic "flappers," Achsa remained a sweet, conservative young woman, and one of my favorite relatives.

Later, a stripped-down Model T truck played a key role in reshaping the landscape at our last home in the valley (see *"Clean Fill Wanted"*).

Most of the cars in our family developed sloppy steering and loose front ends because of the rough roads. Between trips of the county road grader, the graveled valley road soon developed ruts, gravel ridges and a special kind of roughness called "washboards." None of our early cars had shock absorbers, and the washboard stretches caused teeth-rattling vibrations and made driving in a straight line difficult. The only ways to combat the washboards were to either drive very, very slowly—an idea that never caught on in our family—or speed up so that the tires floated from one ridge to the next. The worst stretch of washboard roadway I remember was a half-mile or so up valley from Cooper's Store. However, speeds upward of 45 mph smoothed the road there acceptably well.

Front-wheel shimmy was a common ailment among used autos of that time. A few years of travel on those rough roads hammered and loosened the simple steering-systems and front-wheel bushings of cars as well as trucks. All the drivers in our family knew how to respond to the shimmy: You slowed, jerked the steering wheel from side to side to break the rhythm of the shudder, and when the vibration stopped you gradually resumed speed. And the driver vowed, aloud or silently, to rebuild that darn front end—just as soon as time and money allowed.

Dust, of course, was an unavoidable byproduct of driving on the gravel and dirt roads during the dry seasons. Driving etiquette required slowing to reduce the dust when passing someone walking or working along these roads. Houses built during the era of abundant vehicles and unpaved roads tended to be set back from the main valley road to avoid the dust, whereas after paving the home construction moved closer to the road. Some driveways were sprinkled with used motor oil to reduce the dust, a practice that we now know could be harmful to underlying ground water.

Snow and slick roads were unavoidable problems in the winters, and mastering the skills needed to get around under those conditions was the greatest challenge of learning to drive in those days. County road crews did the best they could at clearing the snow, and a heavy snowfall brought out volunteer efforts of anyone with equipment that could move snow. For example, bulldozers from the Harris mill often were pressed into service. School grounds and school routes were given high priority for clearing, just as they are today. I don't remember equipment or effort directed toward a general sanding of the roads, although volunteers might haul some dirt and throw it around school driveways and steep hills.

Tire chains had been around forever but, even if we happened to have a set that fit whatever vehicle we were using, Dad used them only as a last resort. I think it was some kind of male defiance of the elements, as well as a natural reluctance to lie in the snow and wrestle with the beastly chains of those days.

Families were on their own for clearing their driveways. Most of us simply "bucked the snow" on our way out to the main road, racing the cars forward until stopped by the loose snow, and then backing up for a straight run and charging into the snow again. Shoveling might be required where the snowplows left snow piled at the road's edge, but otherwise the access to most homes and ranches was by two ruts in the snow until the spring melt. As the sun melted the surface snow and the nighttime temperatures refroze it, those ruts often became glare ice that made the driveways all but impassable.

MAMMA'S CAR WOES

Mother cherished the independence of being able to drive, which many women of the times couldn't do. Dad respected this and encouraged her to drive the family cars. Mom drove well enough—she, not Dad, taught me to drive—but first she had to start the car. That was her nemesis.

Admittedly, part of her problems lay with the cars. Dad did all our tune-ups and repairs, and scarcity of money and his time meant that most of the maintenance came only after a vehicle quit running. Each car had its own quirks that had to be dealt with at starting time. But Mom understood only the rudiments of motor vehicles, and certainly lacked Dad's knack of dealing with the cars' peculiarities.

Usually in a hurry, Mom became her own worst enemy when she slid behind the wheel. If one pump of the accelerator did not cause the engine to catch life immediately after she stepped on the starter button, Mom added a couple more pumps. It was always touch-and-go whether the engine started before she flooded it.

The only successful response to a flooded engine in those days was to simply wait until the excess gasoline dissipated from the tops of the cylinders—twenty minutes or so to be safe.   I'm sure that Mom understood this, but she seemed psychologically incapable of enduring the wait. *Her* response was to fidget and mutter for about five minutes, then stand on the starter button again, pump the accelerator pedal some more, and scold the car while she let the starter grind away. Car batteries of the day did not have abundant cranking power, and I clearly remember sitting beside Mom in our '28 Pontiac, praying silently for the miracle of engine life before she drained the battery to death. If the car was already flooded, my prayer was seldom answered.

One particular episode involving Mom's car-starting problems occurred before I started school but after we had the Pontiac and were living in the home place. The unfinished attic of that house, above the lath-and-plaster ceilings, was our main dry-storage area. A few miscellaneous boards lay across the 2 X 4 ceiling joists to support stored items, but most of the attic "floor" consisted of exposed ceiling laths, with oozed-up white plaster, between the joists. The only way to get to some of the stored boxes was by balancing your way across the on-edge 2 X 4s.

That's how Mamma got in trouble that day—tight-roping across the attic. I sat playing in my room, listening to her movements above, when suddenly there came a ripping sound and a plump, white leg protruded through the middle of the ceiling. The leg was accompanied by a high-pitched wail and a rain of plaster. I watched in fascination as a slipper came off the foot and fluttered down like a wounded bat.

Mamma let out a massive groan and tried to pull her leg out, but the bent-down laths had trapped her like a Chinese finger grip, digging into her thigh and drawing blood. She tried again and they dug deeper. Blood trickled down her leg.

"Brucie!" she wailed. "Go get Daddy! Quick!"

I ran out to the orchard as fast as I could and found Daddy. As we ran back together, I breathlessly tried to explain what had happened. "Is she hurt?" he asked.

"Yes! She's *bleeding*!

That sent Daddy sprinting ahead of me.

But Daddy's mood had changed by the time I got back to the house. He was laughing while he set up a short ladder to free Mamma. Even to me, this seemed strange—Daddy down below laughing while Mamma was up there bawling her head off.

Mamma was mad as a stirred-up wasp when Daddy finally helped her down from the attic. I sensed trouble and made for the space under our big oak table, one of my sanctuaries.

Mamma lit into Daddy even as she wrapped up her bloody leg. If he cared about her he wouldn't have laughed while she was trapped—that sort of thing. Then voices rose to what probably was the biggest fight I ever saw them have. I think all grievances were aired that day. One that Dad threw out was her insistence on spending precious money on her Bible tracts. That *really* blew the lid off.

The upshot was that Mamma, bawling all the while, quickly packed a valise, pulled me out from under the table, and announced that we were "going to stay with Grandma."

Mamma towed me out to the Pontiac, put our stuff in, and slid into the driver's seat. The car failed to start on her first try. She tried again. And again. Finally the starter growled down to a stop. Mamma, bawling again, pounded her fists on the big wooden steering wheel.

Finally, after another futile attempt to start the car after the battery had rested, Mamma gave up. She went back into the house, leaving me in the car. Long minutes later, Mamma came out crying again and took me and the valise back in the house. She didn't explain about the change in plans, but I learned later that she had asked Daddy to start the car for her, and he refused.

Not much talking happened the rest of that day, but Mamma did fix supper, and we stayed the night—and from then on.

TRAINS AND AIRPLANES

While cars and trucks captured my boyish interest, two other forms of mechanical travel fascinated me more—steam trains and airplanes. Airplanes were by far the most exciting, but I saw few of them in my early years. The rare sound of a plane over the Entiat Valley was an occasion to call everyone out to scan the sky. But trains were as near as the mouth of the valley, at the Entiat depot.

The Great Northern Railroad had extended its tracks northward from Wenatchee through Entiat and beyond, reaching Oroville, almost to Canada, in 1914. Thus, ice-refrigerated boxcars became available at Entiat for shipping the valley's fruit to markets in the East. The railroad also provided passenger service north and south and, by connection at Wenatchee, to the rest of the country. The coming of the railroad soon ended the era of the Columbia River steamboats, such as the one that had brought my Foxworthy grandparents to Old Entiat in 1902.

In my youngest years, I preferred to watch trains at the Entiat depot from a safe distance while hanging onto one of my parents. The shiny-black, smoke-belching, steam-chuffing monster locomotives excited me to the edge of fright, especially when an idling engine suddenly released a sideward blast of steam. But I loved the chugging sounds and, especially, the steam whistles.

About the time I started school, my Bedient grandparents rented a small house in Entiat, where I frequently stayed overnight. They and my Uncle Max, with whom I slept, were so used to the train sounds that they didn't seem to hear them. I, however, seldom missed those sounds.

In the fall of the year, the railroad ran a southbound night freight, which stopped at every siding to hook onto refrigerated boxcars that had been loaded during the day with boxes of packed fruit. The train arrived at Entiat with a long warning whistle, which instantly woke me. That melancholy wail in the night always sent a shiver through me as I pulled the covers around my ears. I lay hardly breathing, listening for the next sounds—the switching and backing and bumping which seemed to take forever as freight cars were hooked on. And then the three short whistle blasts that signaled the train's departure.

By the time the night freight left Entiat, the string of cars had become long and heavy. The locomotive began chugging slowly southward toward Wenatchee—chuff…chuff…chuff… chuff. Then, more often than not, came a brief, sudden speeding of the chugs—chu-chu-chu-chu-chu—until the former slow rhythm resumed. Only later did I realize those rapid chugs meant the drive wheels of the locomotive had lost traction in starting the massive train, and ended only when the engineer backed the throttle off a bit. Then, as the train picked up speed, came the clacking of the steel wheels on the rail joints and, finally, one last far-away whistle as the train neared the next crossing down the tracks. Those fascinating train sounds remain indelibly imprinted from my boyhood.

And the train smells: the black coal smoke from the engine stack, and the oily, white steam that leaked and spurted from the locomotive's sides. In our wood-rich region, only the blacksmith and the railroad used coal as fuel. Even the tiny Entiat depot—where the Stationmaster served as janitor, ticket-seller, handler of freight and mail, and operator of the clacking telegraph—smelled of coal he burned in the pot-bellied heating stove.

Despite the easy access to the train, our family seldom used it for travel. Trips by auto were more convenient and cheaper, with gasoline costing less than twenty cents a gallon in those days. Only in late 1943, when I rode the train from Wenatchee to Spokane on my way to join the Navy, did I begin experiencing major train travels.

* * *

Airplanes became a near-obsession for me. Nothing, to my boyish mind, approached the excitement and intrigue of those soaring, roaring mechanical birds. The fact that my Uncle Max also loved airplanes no doubt fueled my interest.

An event that also fanned the fire was the emergency landing of trans-Pacific aviators Clyde Pangborn and Hugh Herndon, at the small airstrip serving Wenatchee, after accomplishing the first-ever non-stop flight from Japan. That globally acclaimed flight of the *Miss Veedol* occurred in 1931, shortly after I started first grade. It spurred local interest in aviation as nothing had before and, as Daddy said, "put Wenatchee on the map." My family didn't visit the landing site, but for years afterward I used to pop into the Wenatchee City Museum just to stare at the plane's bent metal propeller, on display there.

During my grade-school years, I devoured everything I could find about airplanes and pilots. I scanned newspapers and listened to radio news about aviation-record attempts that were common in those days. I followed the results of air races the way some modern kids follow auto races. Oh, how I longed to be up there piloting one of those speeding, graceful birds.

My favorite after-school radio program was "The Air Adventures of Jimmy Allen," a fifteen-minute show about a teen-age pilot who had earned his own airplane. Jimmy's exciting adventures were shared by his older mentor, Speed Robertson, who, of course, also owned a plane. Sometimes during those broadcasts I would don my aviator helmet—my preferred cold-weather headgear—pull a kitchen chair close to our radio, and "fly" along with my heroes with a wood-lathe "joystick" between my knees. When the radio signal sometimes faded, I thrust my ear against the speaker, seeking to not miss a single word.

In addition to newspaper stories about aviation, I avidly read pulp-fiction magazines about flying. Two favorite monthlies were *The Lone Eagle* and *G-8 and His Battle Aces*, both about imaginary World War I exploits. The Lone Eagle was an incredibly skillful American fighter pilot, flying a Spad biplane, who preferred to fly combat and rescue missions alone—against impossible odds, of course. G-8 was part indomitable fighter pilot and part secret agent. His squadron, combat aces all, fought in the skies and on the ground to foil nefarious, science-fictionish plots by the "dirty Krauts."

I got most of these magazines from my Uncle Max, who in turn scrounged them from orchard hands where Grandpa Bedient worked. We almost never had the fifteen to twenty-five cents to buy them new. Mamma disapproved of these stories about war and violence, but she stopped short of forbidding them.

During my middle grade-school years, I avidly built model airplanes, as did my Uncle Max and many of my schoolmates. At first, I got the model kits as gifts; only later in my model-making years did I earn enough money to buy my own. Most of the available model kits were for World War I warplanes—the kinds that I read about in the pulp magazines. I loved those war-bird models, but they did not please my pacifist mother. She preferred that I have models of non-combat planes, and always tried to select those for me.

The model kits supplied the aircraft plans, sheets and sticks of balsa wood, rice paper for "fabric" covering, and necessary hardware such as wheels, propeller, and the rubber-band "motor." No snap-together plastic in those days—in fact, very little plastic. We cut the parts from the balsa with a razor blade, pinned the cut-out parts down on top of the plan sheet, and glued the pieces together with airplane cement. I invariably over-applied the glue. For years, I picked dried cement from my fingertips and carried the acrid smell of airplane glue on my clothes.

Nearly all my plane models were designed to fly, and fly them I did. At least, I tried. Almost before the wetted rice-paper fabric had completely shrunk-dried onto the balsa frame, I was test-gliding the model across my bedroom toward my bed. If the model had a reasonable glide path to the bed, I tried sailing it outside, over the lawn. If the model passed the test-glides, I gingerly finger-wound the propeller to twist up the rubber-band motor for powered flight.

That first launch of a new model into the sky—a model on which I'd spent many concentrated hours—always was a nail-biter, a mixture of exhilaration and apprehension. A smooth, steady flight and soft landing marked a total success. Anything less was a disappointment, although I learned that some flight irregularities could be corrected. In one or two maiden flights, major damage occurred, such as collisions with apple trees that punctured the paper covering or broke a wing spar. Usually I could repair the damage so it didn't look too bad. After I repaired the crash victims, or decided that luck was running out on the good flyers, I hung the models from my bedroom ceiling on threads. I arranged them in various attitudes of flight. There, I could stare up at night and imagine they were real planes in a "dog-fight over no-man's land" and that I was piloting one of the "good-guy," Allied warplanes.

One summer when my Uncle Max and his folks lived in workers' housing at Wagnersburg Orchards south of Entiat, Max and I each selected our most beat-up flying model and took the planes to the top of a cliff above the orchard. With each plane in turn, we wound the propeller, lit a match to the front part of the plane, and launched the model off the cliff top to watch it "go down in flames," as planes did in the flying-aces novels.

As we watched breathlessly, the paper skins of the models burned in brief "poufs," after which the skeletons dropped like rocks, and any remaining flames were blown out during the fall. Disappointing as they were for us, those quick burn-outs may have prevented a major grass fire on the hillside below the cliff.

I also flew store-bought gliders and toy planes, mostly after I was old enough to earn my own money for them. My favorite flyer was a rubber-band-powered plane from pre-war Japan, a soldered-wire frame with flying surfaces covered by silk fabric. The soldered-wire construction made them very durable in the inevitable crashes. I spent uncountable hours standing on the road edge above our home place, patiently winding the propellers to twist up the rubber bands, then launching the planes toward our driveway and running down to retrieve them.

*   *   *

My first airplane ride was in a silver-colored, open-cockpit Waco biplane, flying out of the local airport, Fancher Field. I don't remember the year, but I was in my early grade-school years. Dad took my Uncle Max and me to the field where airplane rides were being sold. At first, the pilot wouldn't let me ride because I was under his arbitrary age limit. But good old Dad, knowing how desperately I longed to fly, argued that Max, five years older and much bigger, could sit with me and keep me in line. The pilot, looking every bit the part in his leather jacket, helmet and goggles, finally agreed. Then, while I fairly danced from one foot to the other, Dad began dickering about the price. Dad argued the fare down from ten dollars, the regular price for two, to eight dollars, with the reasoning that the pilot was still making extra money for the flight because the two of us would be occupying the single front-cockpit seat. I could scarcely wait while Dad handed over the money. I have no idea how he could spare that much cash, but I'm sure it represented considerable sacrifice.

Max and I, both with our airplane helmets strapped tight, were helped into the single seat of the front cockpit. Instantly, my thrill began to wane. When the pilot snugged down the seatbelt over both of us, it forced me so low into the seat that I couldn't see over the padded cockpit rim. The pilot lectured Max about making sure I remained secure. Max nodded vigorously.

The pilot disappeared from view. I strained against the lap belt to raise myself. Max reached a hand to my helmet top and pushed me down. The plane's starter whirred. The big radial engine coughed a cloud of blue exhaust flavored with hot oil. It clattered to life and smoothed to a steady roar. The roar increased and the plane began a bumpy roll down the airstrip. I put both hands on the cockpit edge and pulled myself up against the restraint of the seatbelt. I could almost see out—almost! Max pushed me down.

The bumpiness stopped and I felt a little thrill as we zoomed upward. Max shouted something. I think he said, "We're flying!" but the engine and the wind roar covered his words. Several times I strained upward in attempts to see out; the only times I came close were when Max was so enthralled with looking out that he failed to push me down. I may have glimpsed some hilltops when the pilot banked the plane.

Finally, I felt the plane straighten and descend. The engine noise cut down, and a jolt came as the wheels hit. The plane's tail settled and thumped. For a while, the plane taxied. The engine roared briefly while the plane swung around, and then it died with a little cough. The quiet assaulted our ears.

Max let out a jubilant hoot. The pilot appeared and released our lap belt. We stood up on the seat and the pilot hoisted me to the ground. I politely thanked the pilot as he helped Max out. Then I ran over and thanked Daddy, who stood grinning nearby. On the walk back to our car, parked at the edge of the airfield, Max jabbered non-stop about the great view from the plane.

I had gotten my long-dreamed-of airplane ride—and about the only things I'd seen were the sky above and the inside of the cockpit. Still, experiencing the sounds and smells, the feel of leaving the earth, and the knowledge that I actually *flew* in a real airplane, were sweet indeed.

Only several years later, at about age eleven, did I finally see from the air the terrain Max and I had flown over in that open biplane. This flight, also from Fancher Field, was in a red, high-wing monoplane with an enclosed cabin. I sat in the right-front seat beside the pilot, a dour, balding man who obviously didn't like young boys. But this time the view was superb, and I also got to watch every move the pilot made, from starting the engine before the flight to landing and taxiing back to the flight line.

For this flight, too, Dad drove me to the airport and handed over my fare. But this time, I was earning a little money and had saved up half the fare. Money was still tight, but my dear folks, knowing my consuming passion to fly again, somehow came up with the other half. That second flight was my last childhood airplane ride. I didn't fly again until my Navy service.

My folks never experienced flight, even after commercial flights became commonplace.

RISKY TIMES

During my growing-up years, folks encountered considerably more and greater risks than most of us face today. According to Census Bureau data, for an American born in 1900 (my folk's generation), average life expectancy was only 50.2 years for white males and 51.1 years for white females. By 1930 (my generation), those life expectancies had improved to 59.1 years and 62.7 years respectively. For our Indian neighbors, life expectancy was even shorter.

The major killing diseases of the time were heart diseases, influenza and pneumonia, cancer, and tuberculosis. And childbirth was riskier than it is today; women spoke of "going to death's door" to bear a child.

Serious accidents were mainly workplace accidents—on farms and in factories and logging operations. I don't know how many fingers and hands were lost to saws and other equipment in the local Harris mill and box factory, or how many crippling accidents occurred while falling timber. But those risks were accepted as part of life, as part of having a job. If any workplace-safety guidelines existed then, I never heard of them, or of any lawsuits about workplace accidents.

Although deaths from automobile accidents were rising nationwide, surprisingly few deaths or serious injuries resulted from the many car crashes along our twisty valley road. One reason, I am sure, was the sturdiness of those old cars. Some of their fenders could have doubled as boiler steel. Another reason was that the roughness of the roadway, especially before it was black-topped, and the frequency of sharp curves, held down the speeds. I believe that a couple of car occupants did drown in the Entiat River, unable to get out after their cars went off the road into the water. Seat belts were not a factor in car crashes, because those restraints did not exist.

During the worst of the depression, many Americans succumbed to direct effects of poverty—starvation, exposure, and lack of medical help. Big-city dwellers suffered most. A member of my extended family told of desperate depression times in South Philadelphia, when hard choices had to be made between buying food or winter fuel. He was part of a youth gang that robbed coal trains, he said. A few of the fastest and nimblest boys scrambled onto the trains that slowed to enter the rail yards and threw coal from the open coal cars as fast as they could. Others of the gang ran along the tracks, collecting the coal in sacks and buckets before scattering in all directions and meeting later to divvy up the stolen coal. Few of the boys were ever caught, he said.

We in the Entiat Valley were better off, even in the worst of times, than poor big-city dwellers. Living in a forested valley, we had access to wood for fuel. Also, our family and neighbors grew fruit and vegetables, caught fish and hunted wild game, and had cellars to store home-canned food to get us through the winters.

For kids like me, the risks, other than sickness and disease, included insufficient respect for the stern environment in which we lived—and our own damn foolishness.

Considering what my folks had gone through with my early illnesses, it is a wonder that Mamma ever let me out of her sight. But after I progressed in school, and especially after I learned to swim, my folks allowed me to roam the nearby hills and fields as long as they knew my general plans and territory. As an only child I was often alone, but seldom lonely because I was an imaginative and eager explorer and observer of Nature. The rock outcroppings, the trees I climbed like a squirrel, and the hills all held an irresistible appeal. In fact, I never did get to all the high places and canyons I wanted to explore.

Water—namely, the Entiat River and the larger irrigation ditches leading from it—was the biggest hazard for kids. Several youngsters drowned while we lived in the valley, including the toddler from the neighbor Gofinch family who drowned in the very ditch that watered our orchard. Yet, with the ditches so prevalent, there was virtually no way to keep kids from coming in contact with water. All the parents could do was drum the dangers into us and watch us closely until we became swimmers. Even then, the water risks remained ever-present.

My own close call with water came on the way home from a picnic in the upper Entiat Valley. Our family group, including Grandma Bedient's brother, Earl Zesiger, had stopped along a beautiful stretch of smooth, deep, river water. I had recently learned to swim in the river, was already wearing my swimming trunks, and was eager to show off my new skill.

"Watch me, Uncle Earl," I called, and dove into the smooth stream.

In an instant, I learned that smooth water doesn't always mean slow water. Although I swam vigorously, having no trouble staying afloat, I was being swept downstream faster than a man can walk. The realization hit my adrenalin button, but my frantic swimming tired me rapidly.

Uncle Earl, however, did not panic. Before the others could move, he dashed downstream. He found a log extending into the river, and edged out onto it. Timing my arrival perfectly, he bent down and plucked me out of the current. I almost dumped us both into the water with my frantic clutching at him, but he got me back to shore.

I've often played the "what if" game with that incident: What if Uncle Earl had not acted instantly, or what if he had missed me with that one-time grab? What if that log hadn't been just so, protruding into the river just far enough, at just the right place? Would I have had the presence to swim back to the shore and grab a rock or bush, or would I have known enough to try to float and rest? Would further immersion in the icy water have quickly sapped my strength? At the time, I treated the incident as just another childhood adventure. Contemplating it as an adult, however, never fails to make my neck skin crawl.

*   *   *

Another early "close one," though perhaps not as risky as my reckless swim, occurred before I started school. It involved my unauthorized use of Daddy's 10-guage shotgun.

That old, double-barreled shotgun was the only firearm I can remember Daddy owning. For deer hunting, he always had to borrow a rifle from someone else in the family—someone he could trust, because he usually did his hunting out of season and at night. As I remember, he used the shotgun only to hunt grouse and kill birds that were intent on eating our ripe fruit. With as many crows and magpies as we had pecking at the apples, the bird-shooting probably was a waste of time and shotgun shells, but I guess it made Dad feel a little better. It certainly fascinated me.

One fall morning when I was about five, several squawking magpies in a large pine tree across the road attracted my attention as I played in our yard. Just then, my folks announced that they needed to go to the store and I had to take care of myself for a little while.

Ahah! My chance to try out the shotgun and get rid of some bad birds.

Being a snoop, I of course knew just where the shotgun shells were "hidden," so I was able to quickly load the gun for action. Carrying the heavy gun in both arms, I ran across the road and onto the hillside, and took cover behind a large sage bush. From there, I sneaked up on the bird's tree. Small as I was, I could barely raise the long-barreled weapon, much less aim it steadily, but I pointed it up in the general direction of the magpies. I slipped my fingers into the trigger guard and pulled.

The roar deafened me! The recoil knocked me down so hard that impressions of my back and head showed in the hillside dirt. Nobody had told me the two barrels fired separately, so I'd just pulled both triggers.

Barely conscious and with ears ringing, I staggered to my feet and looked around for dead birds. No birds were down, but a few fresh branches lay at the base of the pine tree.

Shaking from the scare, I picked up the shotgun from where it had dropped and ran back to the house. I found something to wipe dust off the gun, and put everything back carefully.

Although for days I lived in fear of being found out and skinned alive, nothing was ever said. I guess Daddy must have used the shotgun again without noticing that the barrels hadn't been cleaned. I couldn't conceal a massive black-and-blue bruise on my shoulder, but I claimed it was caused by a fall from a tree. Thus, I survived another risky "adventure," this time gaining respect for firearms.

*   *   *

The valley's pine-spotted hillsides are underlain by granitic rocks and generally thin soils. Some of the rock outcroppings where I roamed were massive and steep, which made for great play opportunities.

By the time I was old enough to explore the hills and rocks, I had a dog named Prince, a fearless mix of fox terrier and bull dog. Prince accompanied me almost everywhere, although he was apt to get distracted and range off by himself at times. During one of those hillside roamings with Prince, I wandered farther than usual seeking wildflowers for Mamma. Rounding a knoll, we came upon a magnificent granite rock face that just begged to be climbed. I quickly found some shade for my handful of flowers and went back to the base of the cliff, automatically looking it over for hand and foot holds. Without further thought, I began to climb. Prince watched me quizzically, with his head cocked, and whined.

"It's okay, boy," I assured him. He sat watching me as I happily inched upward, grasping cracks with fingertips and jamming the toes of my tennis shoes against protrusions of the rock.

Soon, the shrill whistle of a groundhog sounded, and Prince charged off to one of his favorite pastimes, hunting rodents.

My climb progressed well until I neared the top. Suddenly, my fingers found no more handholds above. I reached to the right. Nothing I could grasp. I carefully changed hands on the last grip I had. Only smooth rock to the left, too. Adrenalin shot through me, with panic as a chaser. I frantically felt again, as far up as I could reach. Nothing!

I was stuck! I hadn't planned for climbing back down. I had been confident in making it up over the top.

I clung there and began to cry, with my cheek pressed against the rough granite, trying to plaster myself against the rock. My muscles tired. I began to shake. My mind raced. I wondered about injuries from my inevitable fall. How hard was the ground below? Should I push off backward to clear the base of the cliff?

Suddenly, two sharp barks sounded below. They somehow brought me reason. *Calm down*, Prince's barks seemed to say. *You had hand- and footholds to get up there, you can surely find them to get back down.*

Deep breaths helped. I focused on remembering. Where was my last foothold? Prince whined his concern, keeping me in reality. I tentatively reached a foot down, feeling for the last toehold.

"Help me, God," I prayed.

My sneaker toe caught. I added weight. It held. The new position eased cramped muscles. Confidence returned. My trembling stopped.

That was the turning point of my peril. With the return of confidence came new strength and reason. Breathlessly feeling for successive grips on the rock, I managed to work my way back down off the cliff.

At the bottom, I dropped to my knees and hugged my happy dog, rolling my eyes heavenward and silently thanking God, too.

Who knows whether I'd have returned to calm and reason while frozen on that cliff without the timely return of Prince and his blessed barking? I would like to think so, but I'll never know. I easily could have fallen and been badly hurt—too injured to get home on my own. But even then faithful Prince probably would have saved me, by going for help.

Recalling that scary time always reminds me: Panic subverts reason, and can turn us into our own worst enemy in a crisis.

Mamma loved the wildflowers, and gave me a hug. "What took you so long?" she asked.

I think my answering hug was extra tight. "Oh, Prince went off huntin' groundhogs, and I climbed a rock."

*   *   *

Forest fires, then as now, were serious dangers, especially for herders and loggers in the woods and families in forest homes. In those days, nearly all forest fires were started by lightning, rather than by other causes such as careless campers. But because the forests were more extensive then and less accessible, dangers from large fires could be great indeed.

Lacking the observations from today's artificial satellites, or even abundant aircraft, we depended on human fire lookouts to detect the forest fires. Throughout the dry seasons, these solitary sentinels lived in and kept watch from tiny lookout towers on high peaks in the West. When a forest fire started, the lookouts would report the compass direction and estimated distance of the smoke plume to the authorized federal agency, the U.S. Forest Service. During my boyhood, before the availability of small, reliable short-wave radios, the fire spotters reported over primitive telephone lines strung all the way to those remote lookout towers—hundreds of miles of single, grey iron wires strung through porcelain insulators along forest roads and trails. Upon receiving the fire reports over the old, crank-style telephones, the Forest Service quickly plotted the location of the fire on maps and mobilized teams of fire fighters.

No smoke-jumpers existed then to drop in by parachute or helicopter to snuff out small fires before they expanded, nor any planes dropping fire retardant. Fire fighting then consisted of the dangerous and back-breaking work of climbing through the steep terrain, setting backfires and clearing firebreaks with picks, shovels, axes and handsaws.

The firefighters in those days were mostly locals—loggers and mill workers, ranchers and their orchard workers, and men from the nearby towns. They worked under the direction of the Forest Service, which furnished equipment and supplies for the "volunteers."

Not all the men pressed into service as firefighters went willingly. Local men were expected to do their firefighting duties but, if larger crews were

133

needed, local authorities didn't hesitate to declare a community emergency and conscript into service any able-bodied man who came into the valley.

I remember one story about a salesman, dressed in suit and tie, who had the bad luck to drive into the valley during one of these emergencies. The sheriff promptly ordered him to park his shiny car and join the fire crew. Over his violent protests, he was issued boots and coveralls and taken to the fire line. However, he reportedly was totally inept, blistered his soft hands severely on the tool handles, and became such a burden that he had to be evacuated.

During one bad fire season, three young men from South Bend, Indiana—two cousins of Dad's and a friend of theirs—were visiting our home place, sleeping in our barn loft and eating with us at the house. Lifelong city boys, they were fascinated with the West but were total greenhorns. For example, Dad convinced them that a slab of bacon came from the flat side of a cow's neck. They willingly tried every kind of work on the ranch, but were not very successful—falling off ladders during thinning, damaging trees, and letting our cow get loose on the roadway. Dad adamantly refused to let them try chopping wood.

When the call for firefighters went out that year, our city boys couldn't wait to sign up despite Dad's advice against it. They cheerfully trudged off to Forest Service headquarters, and we didn't see or hear from them for six days. "I hope I don't have to write letters to their folks," my worried father said.

Then one evening an outbound truck stopped at our driveway and our three guests hopped off. Unshaven, dirty and disheveled, they limped down to the house. Their red-rimmed eyes sparkled with excitement, and they couldn't wait to tell us of their adventure:

"The first day we hiked fifteen miles with a pack train of mules to get to the fire line," they said. "After that we worked twelve-hour days using pick-axes to clear brush and cross-cut saws to fall trees, making firebreaks."

They told of exhaustion so deep that any level spot of dirt felt like a featherbed, of bad drinking water and worse food, and of nearly getting trapped by a wildfire. Despite blistered hands and feet, scratched and bruised bodies, they showed a pride that we hadn't seen in them before, especially when they pulled out the government vouchers for their pay—a dollar each per day.

Mamma handed out soap and towels, sent our guests to the river, and told them to change clothes before dinner. But after they had bathed and climbed up to their sleeping quarters in the barn loft, we didn't see them again until morning.

Our former greenhorns thereafter confidently took on any chore around the place, including wood-chopping. And a few weeks later, when they went back to Indiana, riding the Great Northern boxcars, they still maintained that their fire duty was the highlight of their trip.

*   *   *

I never got to serve on a fire crew. The nearest I came to fire duty was going to the local Forest Service headquarters with Mamma and Aunt Achsa while they helped pack food for firefighters. By the time I was old enough for the fire crews, the Civilian Conservation Corps (CCC) had established a camp in the upper Entiat Valley, and those strong young men, when they weren't building trails, bridges, campgrounds and other forest facilities, became the first line of defense against fires.

My dad, however, got involved several times, with his truck.

When remote fires broke out, one of the biggest problems was to get men, supplies, and equipment to the fire sites. The Forest Service had trucks and pack animals of its own, but those seldom were enough, so locals again had to pitch in. Private packers and their animals were pressed into service. Logging trucks were not suitable for transport, so local trucks such as Dad's were sought out. The trucks hauled pack animals, men, and equipment as far as the roads extended toward the fires. There, pack trains were assembled and loaded, and men and animals trekked on to their destinations. Later, the private trucks again served to bring men and animals out. Dad never hesitated to answer the call with his truck, not only out of community spirit but also because the truckers received modest payment, which we could always use.

One day, while Dad was driving his empty truck back toward home along a narrow hillside road after delivering firefighter's supplies, he came across a spotted baby deer, curled up in a ball in the middle of the dirt road. The road was barely wide enough for his truck wheels, he said, and the hillside precipitous on either side. There was no "around" to drive to miss the fawn. Dad looked for the mother, but couldn't spot her. He gunned his engine and honked his horn. If anything, he said, the fawn just coiled tighter. Typical of the species, the mother deer had left her fawn with "instructions" to wait right there for her return, and the fawn was obeying this imperative.

Dad wasn't about to run over the cute little fawn, but he had to get through to pick up another load and return that way. He had to clear the road. Setting his truck brakes, he got out, walked to the curled-up fawn, and prodded it with his toe. It refused to move. Dad squatted down, talked to the baby deer and tried to push it, but it remained still except for trembling. If there had been any kind of space alongside the road, Dad said, he could have just picked up the fawn in its curled position and moved it aside.

Dad climbed back in his truck and waited, hoping that the mother would return and take her fawn. Time passed without the appearance of the doe. Finally, Dad just had to get going.

He decided that, if the fawn had stayed curled up all this time, maybe he could load it in the truck and drive it to a widening where he could set it back down. But the truck bed was enclosed in side racks and a tailgate, so the easiest place to transport the fawn was beside him on the truck seat. He got out, opened the passenger door, and walked back to the fawn.

He didn't have much trouble getting his arms under the fawn, Dad said. He picked it up carefully. As he hoped, the little animal stayed in its curled-up position, trembling with terror. With the baby deer in his arms, Dad edged slowly along the side of his truck, mindful of the precipitous slope behind him. He elbowed the door open and laid the fawn neatly on the truck seat. Dad lightly latched the passenger door, went around the front of the truck and slid carefully into the driver's position. He stepped on the starter button.

Chaos erupted before he got the truck in gear. The fawn uncurled like a broken spring. It kicked and stomped and tried to get out through the windshield, then Dad's window, then the other window. It blatted and kicked some more.

It might have kicked him to death, Dad said, if the partly latched door on the passenger side hadn't given way, allowing the terrified fawn to leap out, down the steep slope below the road.

To his credit, Dad finished hauling another load of supplies in to the fire crew. He came home that night limping, with a black eye and torn overalls that were bloody where a little hoof had punctured his right thigh. The cute little fawn also had left slobbers all over the truck's windshield and dashboard, and had made Swiss cheese of the leather seat, puncturing both the bottom cushion and the seatback.

Dad never did patch the seatback, but one of his old cars yielded a seat cushion that almost fit the truck. That cushion was grey instead of brown, and upholstered with cloth instead of leather. It made the décor of Dad's truck cab rather bizarre.

As I watched Dad force the new seat cushion into place, I ventured, "Daddy, I don't think deer like you very well."

Dad snorted. "Deer would be just fine with me, if I had the good sense to leave 'em be. Puttin' that fawn in the truck wasn't the smartest thing I ever did.

"And by the way, you don't need to tell your friends about it," he added.

AILMENTS AND TREATMENTS

When someone fell to illness or accident, family members or neighbors rushed in to help the afflicted and pick up some of the burdens. Few in our valley were so isolated or lacking in friends that they were truly alone in such an emergency. Seriously ill or injured employees of the C. A. Harris and Son lumber company also might receive help from the company.

However, few social "safety nets" existed for the indigent. One of those few was the County Hospital in Wenatchee, which did not turn away those who couldn't pay. Dad had to go there once when we were really broke and he developed pleurisy. But if you could pay or barter anything for your medical care, society expected that you do so. Inevitably, some people, especially very young and the old, died simply because the family had no money to pay for medical help. Sizeable medical expenses were a serious burden to most people, who might require years to pay them off. If medical insurance existed in those days, it was surely too expensive for the average family.

Reaching medical care was another problem. Even for us, who always lived beside the valley road, major medical help was twenty-nine miles away by car. Families more remote might have to ride a horse or walk to the road, then try to get auto transport from there to the nearest medical facility.

One woman, bitten by a rattlesnake while working in her garden, had to walk a mile to the highway and then catch a ride to town. She nearly died. However, she had increased her risk immeasurably by pumping water and taking a bath before she went for help.

Families did not seek medical help for every little illness or accident. If they were lucky, the County Nurse, who periodically visited the schools, might have time to see the patient; otherwise, the families treated themselves as best they could. Most parents knew the rudiments of first-aid, and grandparents seemed especially adept at diagnosis and treatment, including setting simple fractures and stitching up gashes with sewing thread (no anesthetic, of course).

The simple, direct first-aid of the time is exemplified by my experience with a large wood sliver that penetrated full-depth under my right middle fingernail. A friend and I went to Entiat to the drugstore and showed the problem to Walt Gerson, the druggist. He took out his pocket knife and got a bottle of rubbing alcohol from his shelves. He opened the bottle and dipped the knife blade into the clear liquid, swishing it around. Then he asked to see my finger again.

"Hang on," Mr. Gerson said calmly. Holding my finger firmly, he jammed his knife point under the full length of my nail. He deftly used the back of the blade to wedge out the big sliver in one smooth move. While I was catching my breath, he grabbed the alcohol bottle, stuck it over my finger, and let the stinging alcohol seep under my bleeding fingernail. It was over in seconds and, after that one stabbing moment, it immediately relieved the deep, throbbing ache the sliver had caused. When we tried to pay him, Mr. Gerson would not even let us buy the bottle of alcohol.

"Taking any payment would be against the law," he explained, "for practicing medicine without a license. That was just first-aid." Needless to say, I couldn't thank him enough. And the finger healed without a problem.

Parents often deliberately exposed kids to common childhood diseases to give them future immunity. A notable exception was smallpox, which was still around, but was being eradicated through widespread vaccination. For the less dangerous childhood diseases, "Get it over with while they're healthy," was a common attitude. Kids were sometimes infected by taking them to play, or even sleep, with the sick kids. I don't think that ever happened to me. Much as I might have liked being put to bed with some of my schoolmates, I'm sure Mamma wouldn't have agreed with my preferences.

I seemed able to get infected on my own with whatever was going around. I had whooping cough, measles, chicken pox (three different strains) and mumps. Whooping cough was the earliest and scariest; I still remember my panic from the extended, exhausting coughing that blocked my ability to get my breath. The most embarrassing was mumps, because I got it during high school. Before I developed the symptoms, I infected my high-school sweetheart, Cleo Buckley. She came off sicker than I and she claims, furthermore, that I laughed at her facial swelling, something she never let me forget.

Home treatments often seemed as bad as the ailments they were supposed to help. Poultices, usually something very hot wrapped in cloth such as a dish towel and held against the affected part of the body, were big in my family. Mom applied them for "drawing out" things—deep slivers, boils, infection from wounds, even muscle soreness. I never knew all of Mom's concoctions, but one poultice contained hot oatmeal. Other hot poultice fillings, used by neighbors or my wife's family, were salt pork, and milk-soaked bread. For chest congestion many favored the mustard plaster, a paste of mustard powder and flour between two layers of cloth or newspaper, "plastered" against the chest skin overnight. The skin heating generated by the mustard was supposed to loosen the congestion so it could be expelled. Although I never had a mustard plaster, that traditional treatment must have helped, for it was even used in hospitals. A similar home treatment, which I only heard about, was a poultice of hot sauerkraut, used to treat a schoolmate's facial acne. His acne did improve, whether the sauerkraut treatment worked or he just grew out of his pimply phase. During that treatment, he had a perpetually red face from the near scalding by the hot poultice.

A variation of Mom's poultices was her "cold pack" for sore throats. A thin cloth, such as a strip of flannel, was wetted in cold water, wrung out and wrapped around the neck. This layer was covered by an outside wrap—a dishtowel or diaper—and fastened with a safety pin or two. The cold pack was applied at bedtime and removed in the morning. The initial cold did seem to soothe the soreness, and also reduced the urge to cough. Then, during sleep, after our body warmed the wet cloth, the moist heat remained against the throat. After a night or two of this, the sore throat was gone. Of course, one might argue that the sore throat would have disappeared in the same time without her cold packs, but the wraps may have helped, and at least were soothing and reassuring.

Gargling was a sore-throat treatment, as it is today. Warm salt water was a favorite, then as now. Other gargle liquids were less pleasant. These included Sloan's Liniment ("Good for Man or Beast") and my Dad's favorite—turpentine. My family subjected me to both these liquids, along with a little sugar, as cough suppressants. They surely were an incentive to stop coughing, just to avoid another dose of the horrible stuff.

If a bad sore throat persisted, Dad had a last-resort treatment. He would roll a sheet of paper into a small tube, load one end with a quarter-teaspoon of "Flowers of Sulfur" powder, and put that end of the tube into the patient's mouth, holding down the tongue. He put the other end to his lips. When the patient said "Ahh," Dad puffed the yellow powder into the other's throat, coating the affected areas and inducing gagging and coughing. "Now don't you throw up!" he'd order immediately.

When some of my schoolmates got tonsillitis, they got their tonsils snipped out, got to stay in the hospital overnight and have all the ice cream they wanted. I got to gag and choke on nasty tasting, eye-watering yellow powder blown down my throat. However, I still have my tonsils, which nowadays are considered beneficial.

Turpentine and liniment were fed to kids for other ailments too, including pin worms—which probably came from unsafe drinking water. In my wife's family, treatment for worms was peach-leaf tea, which she assures me was vile enough to drive out any kind of demon.

Constipation and, indeed, any complaint involving abdominal cramps in kids were treated with terrible-tasting, slimy castor oil. My folks took a foul-tasting brown pill instead, called "NR-Nature's Remedy," for their "irregularity."

Bleeding wounds were mostly treated by allowing the blood to flow until the wound had "cleaned itself," then binding it with clean rags, such as strips of worn-out sheets. Because the family seldom had adhesive tape, or money for such a luxury, the binding cloth usually was torn into two strips at the end, and the strips tied together to secure the wrapping. Wounds that today would be stitched were just pulled together and bound up; the big concern was stopping the bleeding. Whopping big scars resulted from some of those wounds.

Dad always liked to douse a cut with turpentine, his universal medicine. It was cheap and always on hand for dissolving pitch from saws and axes, and for other general cleaning. Alcohol-based liniment also was a favorite antiseptic. Fighting infections was no joke; several people in the valley died of "blood poisoning" and one from an abscessed tooth.

Teachers liberally applied Tincture of Mercurochrome as an antiseptic for small wounds and scrapes. It stung like fire and dyed the skin red, but the red was a badge of honor after the stinging stopped. Tincture of Iodine was another popular antiseptic for minor wounds. Mercurochrome and its widely used successor, Tincture of Merthiolate, later dropped from favor because of their risks of giving kids too much mercury.

Salves and ointments were popular, both for their purported healing properties and to keep bandages from sticking to wounds. Clover Leaf Salve was a favorite, as were carbolic acid ointments, sold farm to farm by salesmen for Watkins or Raleigh products. The best thing we ever had for chapped and cracked skin was Bag Balm, kept handy for the care of cows' udders. Mentholatum and Vicks Vaporub were available even then for relief of nasal and bronchial congestion.

Some of these medications and treatments clearly helped as intended. Whether or not all our home remedies were medically beneficial, they made everyone—kids as well as parents—feel that we were doing all we could.

*　　*　　*

Dental care was far different than it is today. For one thing, I don't remember brushing my teeth until I was in Vaughn School and the County Nurse handed out toothbrushes and coached us on how to use them. After that, mother, too, became a regular brusher at home. Our dentifrice was a half-and-half mixture of dry salt and soda; we couldn't afford the tooth-pastes like Ipana and Pepsodent that were being widely advertised by radio and magazines.

For kids, a visit to the dentist could be, quite literally, torture. Dentists were coming around to the realization that decayed "baby teeth" had to be preserved for the sake of healthy permanent ones, so they were advocating the treatment of kids' dental carries. For some reason, however, the available anesthetics such as Novocain were considered unsuitable for children. Therefore, when we kids got our teeth drilled and filled, we had to just sit there as still as we could—gripping the arms of the dentist's chair until our small hands ached—and suffer not only the pain of the drill assaulting the raw tooth nerve, but also the stabbing heat as the low-speed drill burned our dentine to an unforgettable stench.

Our family dentist then was a Dr. Hutchinson, a kindly man whom, I'm sure, suffered almost as much giving this "cold-turkey" treatment to kids as we did. For me, the post-treatment benefits, in addition to elimination of toothaches, usually included some treat such as a movie.

I have no idea how long my folks had to make payments for my dental bills, or where the money came from. I'm sure they let their own teeth go untreated in order to pay for mine.

Considering the childhood pain we endured in the dentist chair, it is a wonder that everyone of that era didn't loath going to a dentist. Of course, many did fear the dentists, to the extent that bad teeth were endured until they could not be salvaged. Many people of the time ended up toothless or with false teeth at early ages.

*   *   *

Bedbugs, though not exactly an ailment, certainly were an affliction for many families in the valley. Bedbugs are dark, wingless, nocturnal blood-sucking bugs (*Cimex lectularius*) about the size and shape of an apple seed, which infested many homes, especially bedrooms. They are very flat, and spend their days in the cracks of furniture, woodwork, mattresses, and the seams of clothing. They can even live under wallpaper. At night they emerge and become little vampires, seeking out the warm bodies of people and other mammals to bite and suck their blood.

Bedbugs didn't seem to be especially dangerous to people, besides the itchy welts they left, and some families in the valley remained infested with them for years. The little critters spread from home to home mainly through exchanges of furniture, bedding, and clothing. Kids' sleep-overs were another route. I remember how Mamma immediately checked every seam of every garment I brought home after those. Of course, I was not allowed to stay long at any home known to have bedbugs. As I remember, we were lucky enough to avoid the little critters altogether.

Having bedbugs did not indicate filth or sloth on the part of the afflicted family, although some neighbors seemed to act as if they did. At the first sign of a bedbug, most women of a family would clean the entire house to the point of disintegration, wash and (or) sun-dry every piece of bedding and clothing, and check and pest-spray (with pump-style "Flit guns") the undersides of furniture. Fortunately, bedbugs do not like either the sun's heat or winter's chill, so exposing infested objects to hot sun or subfreezing temperatures killed enclosed bedbugs. Even those heroic efforts, however, usually could not kill all the bedbugs and their eggs. In fact, I never heard of an infestation of the little critters being eliminated by any means other than sealing the house with a fumigation "bomb" inside, and letting the penetrating fumigant kill the bedbugs and their eggs overnight. Of course, fumigation cost money that some folks simply did not have to spare.

Signs of bedbugs include blood spots on the bedding, where the blood-engorged bug has been inadvertently mashed by a "donor;" pinhead-size spots of the bugs' excrement, black and indelible on bedding as India ink; and a distinctive smell which Mamma described as musty and "mediciny." Her sensitive nose could detect the bedbug smell in an infested house the minute the door opened.

*   *   *

The earliest injury I remember receiving was an accidental burn from boiling teakettle water, one morning when I was three or four. Daddy wanted hot water for shaving but the kitchen stove had no fire. So Daddy put the teakettle on top of the heating stove, a fancy black-and-nickel stove with a rounded top. I was still in my heavy flannel, footed sleepers, playing on the floor in the warmth of the stove. I remember noticing that, as the water heated, the teakettle began to rock on the round stovetop. I thought this was strange, and probably would have brought it to my folks' attention if they had been in the room.

The inevitable happened. The teakettle walked its way off the rounded stovetop. When it fell, the top came off and the hot water splashed my way, soaking my flannel sleepers all down the left side. My screams brought my folks running, but before they could strip my sleepers off, I had third-degree burns on my left thigh and upper arm.

Mom and Dad did all they could, applying cool water to the burns and pumping a cold bath to soak me in. Then Dad raced to the nearest neighbor who had a phone and called a doctor. The doctor recommended a prescription which he called in to the Entiat drugstore, and Dad sped the nineteen miles to the drugstore and back.

The medicine turned out to be yellow creamy liquid called picric acid. At first it only increased the raging pain, and I cried and writhed in agony for what seemed like forever. Then, a strange thing happened. My stern, distant father, with tears in his eyes, came over to my couch of pain and told me how sorry he was. He sat down beside me and began lightly blowing on my burns. That gave me some relief, and I managed to calm down a bit. Daddy stayed there for what seemed like hours, blowing and blowing, until I was exhausted enough to sleep. That was the most tender care I ever knew from Dad.

The intense pain lasted for several hours and then, amazingly, just stopped. I guess I then slept around the clock and, when I awoke, I was able to tolerate dressings on the burns. They took weeks to heal, and left large, pebbly scars that still remain. The Navy liked them as an aid to possible body identification.

My next major ailment, a true brush with death, came in my first school year, when I had just turned six. One evening after school, abdominal pains came on just as I started my evening chore of carrying in fire wood. I complained that it hurt too much, and kept whining as I carried in smaller and smaller armloads. I guess Mamma thought I was faking, and she finally motivated me with a swift swat on my behind. I did finish filling the wood box, although I was doubled over with pain, and asked to skip supper and just go to bed. My folks then knew I wasn't fooling, and Mamma put me to bed with a hot-water bottle. The next morning I had a fever and worse abdominal pain, so my folks wrapped me in a blanket, loaded me into our 1928 Pontiac sedan, and drove the twenty-nine miles to the old Deaconess Hospital in Wenatchee. There, a surgeon wanted to take my appendix out, but Mamma disagreed with his diagnosis and wouldn't let him operate. That's about the time I lost touch.

I awoke days later in a strange bed in a strange room, too weak and hurting to be frightened, but dying of thirst. I called out until a strange woman showed up. She was kind and reassuring, saying that Mamma wasn't there right now, although she would be later. For my thirst, she gave me sauerkraut juice, which she said was better for me than water. I was not overly fond of the stuff, but it did quench my thirst a bit. That effort and the continuing pain exhausted me, and I fell back to sleep.

The next time I woke, I had to pee. The same woman helped me out of bed, onto a chamber pot, then back to bed. She fed me more sauerkraut juice, and I went back to sleep.

I went in and out of consciousness some more, and suddenly I woke having to poop—really, really bad. The same motherly woman helped me back onto the chamber pot and then stood by expectantly. When I told her I couldn't go with her standing there, she laughed and said I must be feeling better. That was the first time I realized that I really did feel better, although I was tremblingly weak.

After my BM, I felt so much better that I apparently slept around the clock again. When I woke, my folks and Grandma Edna were there, smiling down at me. Mamma fed me some warm potato soup—potato cubes cooked soft in rich milk. That soup was about the best thing I'd ever tasted.

The room where I passed that crisis was in a private clinic of an alternative-medicine practitioner, which Mamma had insisted on after her disappointment at the hospital. That clinic "doctor" diagnosed my problem as an impacted bowel, and had prescribed prayers and sauerkraut juice. The grownups all rejoiced at my deliverance, and my family took me home for a recuperation that included abundant potato soup. I later learned that I had been at that clinic, teetering near death, for nearly a week.

I was out of school for about two weeks, but my teacher, Mrs. Parker, and some kindly schoolmates supplied me with schoolwork that I had missed, and Mamma and I worked on my catching up and keeping up while I gradually got stronger. Weak as I still was, I was delighted to be able to go to school again and to remain in my same grade. My enthusiasm was dampened, however, when I learned that I would now be sharing a desk with Shirley Green, who was always asking for lesson help, and who's chronically runny nose kept her sniffling beside me through the rest of that school year.

For a couple of years after that illness, Mamma worried over me like a mother bear with a sick cub. It was no wonder, though; even I was shocked the first time I looked in a mirror after coming home from the clinic.

My face looked like a resurrected death head with dark crescents painted under the eyes. My folks pampered my appetite with special food that I'm sure we couldn't afford, and bought me a nifty metal lunch box with a thermos bottle for hot soup at school. I was so small and skinny that one of my schoolmates nicknamed me "Bird's Egg." I found that name much preferable to "Brucie," and I laughed along with the others when that tag was used.

The real cause of that illness came to light later in my childhood when the symptoms recurred and my folks took me to another doctor, this time a pediatrician. The doctor immediately had me bend over and did an anal finger probe. He announced that I'd had a colon abscess, which had just burst on its own, so I would be fine now. He also said that he'd felt a much larger scar from a former abscess. My folks then told him all about my earlier illness, and the doctor just shook his head. I remember him gripping my shoulder and looking me in the eye. "You're lucky to be alive, young man," he said earnestly. "You could easily have developed peritonitis and died."

I left that doctor's office remembering some of Mamma's words after my earlier, near-fatal illness—that God had spared me to use my life to "make a difference."

If I ever was sent a sign about my mission in life, I missed the message. But perhaps hearing those things from people I trusted made me take my life more seriously than I might have otherwise.

FUN TIMES

Despite the hardships and the things we couldn't afford, our up-valley days held many fun times, too. These were mostly simple pleasures, which included swimming, fishing, camping and picnicking, skating, holiday celebrations, and visits to the big city of Wenatchee.

Valley kids were encouraged to learn swimming at an early age because of the obvious drowning hazards presented by the river and large irrigation ditches. I don't remember exactly who taught me to swim or where, but I sharpened my aquatic skills in the cold water of the Entiat River, and later in Lake Chelan at Manson, where my Aunt Dorothy and Uncle Dick Bedient kept me for days on end so I could be with cousins Virgil and Jean. During summer vacations when I stayed with them, my cousins and I swam unsupervised in the lake at least once a day, usually until our skins got pruney.

The Entiat River ran full and swift during its springtime flood stage, then declined and slowed until its lowest flow in fall or winter. I vividly remember my impatience, checking the river day by day as the weather turned hot, yearning for the level to drop enough that we kids would be allowed to start swimming.

Water temperature had no bearing on the start of swimming for us kids. The river, draining snowfields and the Entiat Glacier less than thirty miles upstream from us, always remained numbing-cold until the low-water stage in autumn when it warmed slightly, especially in its lower reaches.

A favorite summertime escape from the heat was a swimming hole about a quarter-mile downriver from Grandma Lillian's house. This was no more than a large eddy of quieter water below a huge boulder of granitic rock at a bend in the swift river, but it was big enough to hold a couple of kids at a time..

I don't remember just when my folks started letting me go to that swimming hole. The only restriction I remember was that I mustn't swim alone. There, other boys and I played in the water until we shivered so hard we could no longer swim, and then flattened ourselves on the big, granite rocks like the local blue-belly lizards, to warm and brown in the sun. In that cold, moving water, strong swimming was a necessary skill, and I remember my pride when, by thrashing my feet and stroking as fast as I could, I first managed to swim across the current to the opposite side of the river.

Another favorite swimming place on the river was the deep pool behind the Harris millpond dam, which blocked the river just below the company's stout wooden bridge from the valley road across to the mill yard. The bridge and dam sat just upstream from Cooper's general store and beer parlor, so we swimmers had only a short barefoot walk to use the store's restroom or, if we had money, to buy a snack or soda.

At about the age when I started Ardenvoir School, I was allowed to ride my bike to the millpond and join other kids who invariably were there swimming on any summer afternoon. I learned to dive, about twelve feet down to the water, from the rail of that old bridge. The millpond, with its expanse of relatively quiet water, got a few degrees warmer, in its top layer, than the free-flowing river. It was a fun place to swim, and it drew lots of kids from the mill camp and the nearby valley homes, as well as a few adults after working hours.

The mill-pond swimming crowd also allowed curious boys like me to check out female schoolmates who had been maturing during the school year, even though the girls' swim suits were very modest by today's standards.

Neither of those swimming places exists today. Both were washed out by a flood of historic proportions in 1948. The mill resumed operations after that flood, but the dam was not rebuilt because advances in log-handling machinery made a mill pond unnecessary. And at the swimming hole near Grandma's, the flood took out the big rock that had created the large eddy, leaving only a small backwater at the same bend in the river.

I heard that, even before the 1948 flood, the Harris company had posted "No Swimming" signs at the mill pond, over concerns about legal liabilities from swimmer injuries. Thank heavens such concerns didn't arise during my up-valley days.

*　　*　　*

Fishing was a favorite pastime for our family, and all my male relatives frequently took part. Mamma also fished occasionally, usually in the company of one of my aunts.

During my boyhood, the Entiat River produced abundant fish, mostly Rainbow but also Dolly Varden, Eastern Brook trout and (seasonally) Cutthroat and migrating salmon. Scaly whitefish also lived in the bottoms of the deepest holes, especially near the mouth of the river. Anything we caught, we ate. Fried fish was a summertime staple on our plates.

Our favorite mode of fishing was wading downstream with a fishing rod, zigzagging across the river from one rock-defended eddy to the next, playing our lures across the eddies well in front of us, and also working the swift riffles as we moved. I began wading to fish when I finally got heavy enough to maintain an upright position while scrambling over the loose cobbles of the stream bottom in the quieter parts of the river. Before that, I sometimes got to go with Daddy to fish from the river bank at a safe streamside fishing hole. During my high-school years and even before, I often waded into the river at the upper end of the home place and caught a limit of trout (then twenty-one fish) by the time I reached the lower end of the property.

Like all our activities, our fishing had to be done in the most economical ways possible.

Our fishing attire was generally old clothes, worn rubber-soled shoes, and maybe an old hat or cap. Our extra gear consisted of a spare hook or two, a length of leader, and a tube of lead-shot sinkers. I fished for years with a battered steel-tube rod, a basic reel, and a canvas-bag creel. Daddy had a genuine split-bamboo rod, acquired during earlier, prosperous times. Not for years could he afford to replace that fishing rod and hand the old one down to me.

While wading, we landed most of our catch by reeling in line, dangling the fish and swinging them in to clasp against our chests. If they were too big for that, we had to keep them hooked while we worked our way on the unstable footing through the river current to the nearest river bank or bar, where we could drag the flopping creatures out of their element. A good sense of balance, and the ability to keep a tight line throughout the scrambling rush to shore, were essential for success.

In the springtime, when the river was too high and swift to wade, we fished along the banks, clambering through the brush and rocks from one streamside fishing hole to the next. Dad, who had fished the river since before his first pair of long pants, knew intimately each reach of river from below our place to the headwaters, and knew which fishing holes would be accessible and productive at any particular river stage. He not only loved to fish at every opportunity but, more importantly in those days, he knew how to put fish on the table.

We were not so much sport fishermen as meat fishermen, although we generally obeyed the size and catch limits. I saw Dad try fly fishing a few times, but mostly we fished with wet flies and natural bait. The preferred kinds of natural bait were: (1) caddisfly larvae, locally called periwinkles or "pennywinkles;" (2) the pupae, or "eggs" of red ants; and (3) grasshoppers. As a last resort, we might use pieces of angle worm on the wet-fly hooks, or even the eyes of fish from our creel.

One of my summertime jobs was to gather the bait, especially the cadd-isfly larvae and grasshoppers. The larvae, encased in little tubes of chitin ornamented with coarse sand particles or fir needles, attached themselves to rocks in shallow, quiet backwaters of the river. Harvesting them needed patient searching and knowing where to look. The grasshoppers only required carefully moving through the vegetable garden and pouncing on the hoppers when they landed. Ample angleworms were in the soil beneath Mamma's compost pile, where she dumped vegetable waste and peelings from the kitchen.

Gathering ant eggs was more complicated. First, one had to find a red-ant nest, marked by a characteristic gentle cone of sandy soil. Observing ants going in and out of the summit opening confirmed that the nest was alive. Dad would take a stick and carefully stir the soil of the sandy cone, taking care to avoid collapsing the central opening. Then he would immediately lay down an open, pocket-size Prince Albert tobacco can or Watkins spice tin beside the ant-hill opening, and wait. The ants, responding to the disturbance of their nest, would immediately try to save their next generation, the pupae. Ant workers poured from the nest opening, each carrying an "egg," each intent on putting it in a safe place. Behold, here was a handy enclosure—the tin can. If the ant hill was stirred properly, the ants would stock the tin can with hundreds of their pupae in a few minutes. And two of the "eggs" on a small hook were almost guaranteed to attract a hungry trout.

*　　*　　*

Much of our best fishing came during camping expeditions in the upper Entiat Valley, where we stayed at U. S. Forest Service campgrounds in the Wenatchee National Forest. In those days, the campgrounds were basic streamside clearings in the forest, reached by dusty, narrow, extensions of the unpaved valley road. The campsites provided simple, rock-lined fire pits, split-log camp tables, and smelly pit toilets as the only "facilities." We scrounged deadfall firewood and dipped water from the river, believing the myth that rushing water in a primitive area would, by definition, be safe to drink. We were lucky not to contract some water-borne disease.

We nearly always camped with one or more sets of my aunts and uncles. Each family brought grub boxes and a few blackened pots and frying pans, and cooked over an open fire. While the men fished, the women gathered wood and prepared the meals over the smoky fires—an arrangement that didn't seem to me unfair at the time. We counted on fried fish to be the staple meat, but always brought a slab of bacon, just in case. The meat topped off meals of bread, canned beans, and potatoes—plenty of fried potatoes. A fire-blackened coffee pot usually perched on one of the fire-pit rocks. The women washed our dishes in the river, scooping up sand in an old rag to scrub the pots and pans.

Nobody in the family owned a tent. The weather almost always cooperated during those July and August camping trips, and we all slept under the stars, on the smoothest ground we could pick. A piece of tarp went down first and, if you were lucky, an old quilt over that. On top went a couple of blankets, which seemed excessive at bedtime but woefully inadequate in the shivering cold of dawn. And, no matter how good the "bed" might feel at first, all too soon matching one's protrusions with hollows in the ground, and visa versa, became impossible. So campground sleep was fitful, especially for the adults, who might jokingly compare their aches and stiffness over morning coffee.

Dad solved sleeping problems for himself and Mom by driving his truck to the campgrounds carrying their mattress along with our other gear. The mattress and blankets would be covered tightly by a tarp to keep out the ever-present dust, and, when bedtime arrived, my folks had only to climb up on the truck bed, turn back the tarp, and crawl into their made-up bed.

This arrangement evoked either derisive laughter or envy from those who saw it, and was a typical example of Dad's inventiveness.

To my knowledge, no one in the family owned a sleeping bag until the bags became available as cheap war surplus after World War II.

On most of our family camping trips I was the only kid in the party. Rarely did I have the company of another youngster, such as my Uncle Max or one of the neighbor boys. However, I was used to being by myself, and I credit my free hours on those camping excursions with many cherished observations of the natural world. I learned to distinguish trees and other plants not found in lower parts of the valley, as well as birds we didn't have at home. Our camp invariably attracted amusing chipmunks and ground squirrels, and nighttime raids by deer. But my most cherished and enduring memories are of the basic natural wonders of the place—the clear air, perfumed by the evergreen trees and streamside willows; the brilliant sunlight reflected from near-vertical granite valley walls, carved here and there by steep canyons carrying lacy, rushing streams. And over all, the panoply of Milky Way stars, sprinkled thickly on the inky blackness of the night sky, seen between the patiently swaying tops of magnificent evergreen giants. Add to those inspiring images the intermittent whispering of breezes through the treetops, the hypnotizing flames and crackling of the campfire and, incessantly in the background, the voice of the river.

The Entiat River at low stage, viewed from a favorite campground.

The sounds of the Entiat River, varying with the seasons, were virtually constant in my life until, at the end of my seventeenth year, I left the valley for enlistment in the Navy. At flood stage the river's roar, loud enough to drown out streamside conversation, is punctuated by the clack and thump of rocks that bounce along the bottom in the swift current. At low water, the millions of ripples, gurgles and tinkles multiply and magnify into a kind of undulating sigh that never ends. I still find that quiet voice of the river unsurpassed for soothing and recharging the soul.

At intermediate levels of flow, the river's voices range from the near-silence of slow-moving reaches to the constant roar of white-water cataracts. Many of its best fishing reaches were always loud, but not so loud as to prevent a dad from instructing his young son: "Now if you stay low, and don't let your shadow hit the water, you can catch two or three nice trout in that hole right there. Use a short line, and be patient. Keep casting out toward the middle, minding the bushes behind you, and let your hook drift toward that swirling foam. I'll be fishing just downstream. You stay right here till I come back for you."

*   *   *

During my up-valley years, winters usually were cold enough to freeze thick ice on the Entiat River, especially in relatively still reaches such as the Harris millpond. Winter flows were the lowest of the year, and the ice growing outward from the river banks muted the voice of the river to a tinkling whisper in open channels between the ice.

Despite dire threats and warnings from the grownups, we kids regularly tested the thickness of the ice on our way to and from school, by walking out on it until it began to crack under our weight. With this constant testing we were sure that we knew, better than the adults, when and where the ice was fit for skating and other play. I remember only one report of a person breaking through the ice and getting trapped underneath, and he was a mill worker. I think he survived.

Daddy, who had been an amateur hockey player on the Ardenvoir town team, tried to teach me ice skating at an early age. His first attempt came during the winter of 1932-33, when I turned seven and was still rebuilding strength after a debilitating illness. My first skating was not on the river ice, but at a temporary outdoor rink at the Harris mill, which was flooded by a fire hose and allowed to freeze naturally. At that rink, Daddy patiently strapped on for me some ill-fitting, nickel-plated, hand-me-down skates which clamped to my winter boots by use of a skate key. Then he sent me forth to "have fun" while he laced on his hockey skates.

The first tries left me bawling in utter despair. My winter boots, bought large so they would last two years, simply were too loose to support my weak ankles or give me any control over the skates. As a result, I spent most of my "lesson" on my knees or backside, while Dad glided and twisted around the other skaters, practicing stick work with his hockey puck. Totally defeated, I finally asked Daddy to take off my skates so I could go to the car and wait for him under a blanket.

On the way home, Daddy raised my spirits by saying he'd figured out a way to help me skate. The next time we went to Entiat, he took me to Worby's Hardware where he bought a piece of firm, dark-grey felt, about a half-inch thick. Back at the house, Dad cut the felt into strips that fit into my boots, around my heels.

"There," Daddy said with a grin as he tied the second boot. "That'll take up some slack and support your ankles, and we can get you back on the ice."

I was skeptical, because the felt pushed my toes hard against the ends of my boots, but I was pleased that he was trying. Mamma, too, was beaming. Looking back, I'm even more grateful for his caring. And I still wonder where he found the money to buy that felt.

The felt in the backs did make my boots fit tighter and stiffened my ankles for skating. Still, I essentially learned to skate on the inside edges of my boots and skate blades, with my legs spraddled and ankles bent awkwardly. Nevertheless, I embraced skating with a persistent vigor that only youngsters can muster. Besides, most of the other kids were skating with caved-in ankles too.

*　　*　　*

When roller skating was introduced at the Ardenvoir Community Hall a few years later, I easily made the transition to the clamp-and-strap roller skates. Roller skating at the community hall worked about the way it does in rinks today: separate timed periods of skating for men, ladies, and couples, and "All Skate" periods. Then as now, floor monitors—older boys skating backward with whistles in their mouths—were needed to keep order, especially during the wild "Men Only" periods. At one Saturday afternoon session, the manager waved me off the floor during a typical "Men Only" period, in which older boys were speeding around the rink, swerving among slower skaters, racing their buddies.

"It's pretty dangerous out there, young fella. I think you'd be better off skating just during 'All Skate,' and maybe with the ladies."

With the ladies?! No greater insult existed.

Mortified almost to tears, I dropped to a bench and stared at the floor. If I hadn't already invested fifteen whole cents in this session, I'd have pulled off my skates and gone home.

People are always treating me like a baby, I fumed silently, *just because I'm small for my age.*

The manager must have read my despair. He skated over and sat beside me. Putting an arm around my shoulders, he said, "Sorry kid. I know you need to be out there for 'Men Only.' Just watch yourself and stay toward the center of the floor."

Given back my young-manhood, I spurted off the bench and back onto the floor. Following the manager's wise advice, I stayed toward the middle of the floor, inside the ring of pounding racers, and I don't remember ever being in a serious collision in that rink.

*　　*　　*

The skating sessions were in the second of two community halls in the middle valley. Both halls occupied roughly the same site, about 0.8 mile up valley from the Harris mill and a hundred yards or so northward from Ardenvoir School. The first hall burned down during one of my summer vacations from that school, probably in 1936. The replacement building was built by volunteers a few months later. I can't recall all the details, but I have strong memories, mostly pleasant, of events in both community halls.

Both halls were centers for community social and service events in the valley, especially events requiring sizeable space. These included meetings of social and service groups, school programs, political rallies, and Saturday-night dances.

Ah, the dances. I remember them well, especially those in the old hall, when I was little and impressed by every aspect: the big space, everyone in dress-up clothes, and all those cheerful, mostly unfamiliar adults, clustered in conversation groups or gyrating around the floor to the music of the band. I always looked forward to the special treat of one snack and one drink, "all we can afford." Depending on the time of year, the drink was either punch or cocoa. The snack was either a cookie or one half-sandwich on home-baked white bread. We probably got in to the dances free when Daddy was part of the band, but the refreshments were strictly cash-and-carry.

Valley folks of all ages came to the dances, from babes in arms to grandparents and all ages in between. We kids were allowed a certain amount of charging around before the band tuned up, but then were apt to get a sharp grab by a parent and a stern, low-toned admonition if the horseplay didn't end "right now."

My folks always came early, because Daddy often played drums in the band. He had only a basic drum set, but what set it apart was a painting of a Hawaiian scene on the big bass drumhead and a light inside that flashed on and off. To me and my friends that drum was nifty. The rest of the band usually consisted of a piano and a fiddle. The fiddler I remember was Charlie Mathews, who worked in the woods or the Harris mill, and who had two daughters in my school. A couple of different ladies played the piano, though I confess I don't remember who they were. I used to nag my Aunt Achsa to play the hall's old, battered upright piano, but she always alibied that she didn't play well enough.

Sometimes a banjo player showed up, too. Dad had a banjo, but he, like his sister, didn't play well enough for dances. Dad greatly admired that instrument, but never had much time to practice, and as the years of hard work went on, his hands got too stiff to finger the strings.

The little band played old standard music including peppy tunes like "Buffalo Gal," "She'll Be Comin' 'Round the Mountain," "Five-Foot Two," and "If You Knew Suzie," as well as more romantic songs like "Moonlight and Roses," and "In the Good Old Summer Time." The musicians played from memory and by ear—not a sheet of music to be seen. The band always wound down the evening with "Let Me Call You Sweetheart," followed immediately by "Goodnight Ladies," which officially closed the dance.

We boys would never, *ever* dance with a girl our own age for fear of being teased to death by other kids. However, young boys might work up the courage to ask a nice older girl to "dance," which mostly meant walking her around the outside of the floor in time with the music. And little girls, seemingly always eager to dance, sometimes got some man like their dad or uncle to dance them around.

The old Community Hall was an impressively large building by my early standards, although I doubt that the rectangular floor was more than sixty feet long. Plain, continuous wooden benches lined the walls on both sides of the oiled-wood floor.

Wood shingles covered the old hall's windowless sides as well as its roof. As I recall, pairs of windows high on each end provided ventilation and meager daylight. The entry door, with its tiny, roofed porch, was at the front end, toward the valley road. At the back end, a lean-to building added spaces for the stage, a tiny kitchen, and stove-wood storage. A door at the rear of the wood-storage area provided exit for emergencies, such as quick trips to the outhouses in back. I think the little kitchen had emergency egress only by way of two sash windows.

The old hall had electrical service for as long as I can remember, and lighting could be controlled somewhat by a few "zone" switches. Heat was another matter. The room could get stiflingly hot in summer and was hard to heat in the winters—but of course we were used to such temperature extremes. The heating stove sat in the back of the hall to the left of the stage. The wood-fired stove, typical of local construction, consisted of two stacked, rust-colored oil drums vented to a black stove pipe that led to the hall's chimney. One of the men would be in charge of the big stove throughout the evening, controlling the heat by varying the stove's wood load and adjusting its dampers.

As the evening went on and the younger kids tired, parents started bedding them down along the benches. The preferred locations for sleeping kids depended on the season. In the winter, the kids who faded first were laid on coats placed nearest to the stove. Those put down later got bench space farther from the heat. In warm weather, kids could be bedded on the benches toward the front door, where the lights were dimmer and the music less loud. (The hall had no amplification, of course.) Mothers stayed close to their babies, who might waken and need to be taken to the kitchen (strictly women's territory) for changing or breast-feeding.

After I reached a certain age, when I got tired at a dance or other function I was allowed to go out to our car in the parking lot to sleep. In those times, kids alone in cars were just as safe as in their own beds. As for sleeping during a dance, though, the activities in the parking lot sometimes were too interesting for that. The parking lot was where the drinking happened, and the fighting, and the secret wooing. Some dance nights, while I lay on the back seat listening, and sometimes peeking out a car window, were quite educational, although Mamma wouldn't have approved of some of the things I learned. I always stayed still as a frozen mouse and tried to be invisible while I listened intently, and I only worried when a fight got close to our car. Among other things, I learned that women, fighting drunk, could cuss just as bad as men, and that it wasn't always their own wives whom some men visited in the parking lot. I never discussed those parking-lot happenings with my folks, knowing that if I had they would have made me stay in the hall and miss all that action.

At least one fight seemed to erupt outside every Saturday-night dance. The fights I heard or saw always seemed to happen after drinking. According to one saying in the valley, Saturday entertainment for a single man was:

draw his pay, go to the dance, get drunk, get in a fight, and speed up and down the road until he wrecked his car. My Uncle Max, unfortunately, sometimes fit that pattern.

The activities outside the Saturday-night dances didn't change much when the hall was rebuilt after the fire. The new hall, however, was much nicer and perhaps a little larger. It was of a hemi-cylindrical ("Quonset hut") shape, supported by overlapped, bent-beam arches, nailed together on-site by local volunteer workers. As with the former hall, the outside was shingled, but this time also painted grey. Also like the former hall, the new one had windows high on the ends (two sash windows each) which could be opened for ventilation. As with the burned-down hall, a lean-to addition on the back provided an emergency exit and extra space for the stage and kitchen, as well as two restrooms.

Inside, the new hall was much nicer. The lean-to extension held not only a more modern kitchen to the right of the stage, but two flush toilets on the left side. A large space heater (oil-fired, I think) replaced the old wood stove. This floor was hardwood, durable enough for roller skating and basketball, which was one of the phys-ed activities for the adjacent Arden-voir School. And the floor was a delight for the Saturday-night dances.

Use of the hall for both roller skating and dancing, however, created a conflict. The dancers loved a slick floor, just the opposite of a floor that gripped roller-skate wheels. Before the dances, a material called "spangles," probably some kind of soap flake, was sprinkled on the floor. After the dances, no matter how well the floor was swept, it remained too slick for skaters without some sort of counteragent. At least one of the compounds tried was baking soda, which eventually counteracted the spangles and helped the skates grip the floor, but also caused a haze of throat-searing soda dust throughout the skating sessions. Who knows how much soda dust we racing, panting kids drew into our lungs during those sessions.

*   *   *

Fun times included holidays—some holidays more fun than others.

Christmas, a time of joy for kids in the better-off families, a time of anxiety and envy for the poorer kids, became a stressful time for me. For our first two or three years in the home place, we had traditional, decorated trees that dazzled me as a toddler, with gifts that appeared magically underneath. Daddy would go out and cut a perfect young fir tree, and set it up in our living room. Mamma would decorate it with painted-glass baubles and little clip-on candle holders. With the holders secure on the tree branches, my folks inserted little candles, similar to those used on birthday cakes. At the appropriate time on Christmas Eve, with the rest of the family and guests waiting in the kitchen, Daddy carefully lit all the little candles from a larger taper. Then, he extinguished other living-room lights, and the rest of us came in to ooh and ahh over the beautiful sight. This "lighting of the tree" was a risky practice—dozens of little fires on a combustible tree—so the grownups blew the candles out after a short interval. Also, I'm sure they had pans of water handy in case of a flare-up.

After those first few years of traditional Christmas celebration, Mother and her side of the family rejected Christmas. Among other things, they came to believe that: (1) The holiday had evolved into crass commercialism, leading families who could not afford gifts to buy them just to maintain a hollow tradition. (2) The aggrandizement of Santa Claus constituted worship of a spirit other than God. (3) Adornment of Christmas trees equated to pagan (Druid) rituals.

All this left me walking a social tight-rope through the Christmas season. I dared not disavow the existence of Santa Claus, much as I was tempted. At school, where Christmas programs were a big thing, I had to decide what I could join in and what I needed to sidestep in order to conform to Mamma's religious beliefs. As Christmas seasons came and went, I got better at this, and most schoolmates didn't realize I operated by a different set of rules. I do confess that, when backed into an unavoidable corner, I sometimes caved in and violated principles taught at home. If I helped with the school Christmas tree, or sang a "pagan" carol, it created a certain amount of secret guilt that further tarnished Christmas for me.

Mamma's anti-Christmas stance, with which other relatives complied, meant that I got no Christmas presents. But then, half of my extended family didn't, either. However, all the family celebrated birthdays, when those of us who did not celebrate Christmas got our "big" gifts. But I was lucky in a way. Because my birthday (December 30th) fell within the holiday season, I always had gifts to talk about like other kids when school resumed after the Christmas break,

St. Valentine's Day was another touchy holiday. Mother did not really approve of it because it originated as a celebration of two 3rd Century Roman martyrs (both named St. Valentine). However, I was allowed to exchange valentine cards. Some families could afford kits of pre-printed cards that only had to be cut out and addressed. Most kids, like me, made valentine cards from scratch, using the nicest paper we had, such as carefully saved gift wrap. Someone in the family, perhaps Grandma Lillian, had a thick book of wall-paper samples, and I used sheets selected from that book to make valentines and other things. I made valentines for just the girls in my class and for other special girls and women, including women teachers. Giving valentines to other males was unthinkable. Mrs. Parker, my first teacher, gave valentines to all her students, and included a few little candy hearts bearing printed mottos, such as "Be Mine," and "Kiss Me."

Easter was more fun. I could participate in school Easter activities, except for any acknowledgement of the Easter Bunny myth (Mother insisted on truth). I especially enjoyed the school Easter egg hunts, which used boiled eggs we children decorated at home and brought to school. After recovering the last egg, we hungry kids gobbled up much of our booty. I learned to bring salt and pepper from home, and with these seasoning I came to enjoy eating the hard-boiled eggs.

For my family, Easter resembled our Thanksgivings—part religious and part family gathering and feast. During the worst of the depression, the meat for the family dinners might include roast venison (legal or illegal) plus fried chicken supplied by one or both of my grandmas. The dessert always included pies, not only pumpkin, mince or apple pies, but also

Mother's incredible butterscotch-cream pies, for which I've never found an equal.

A springtime celebration which kids of my day looked forward to, but I hear little about nowadays, was May Day. We in the valley did not dance around May poles, decorating them in the process, as did grade-school children at Entiat, but we did hang May baskets. The baskets were paper pouches, with secure handles, that we pasted together using the nicest paper we had. We filled the baskets with seasonal flowers, mainly fragrant lilacs and showy "snow balls," and often added a few pieces of homemade candy. The morning of May 1st, we stealthily hung the baskets on neighbors' door knobs and knocked on the doors before running to hide nearby. From our hiding places, we enjoyed watching the pleased reaction of whoever answered the door and discovered our simple gift. Sometimes they would call out, "Thank you, wherever you are." Some neighbors played a game with us, waiting to answer the door in expectation of a repeat knock, when they could swing the door open and catch us before we hid again. However it played out, the day was fun for us kids—fun to please the neighbors, and fun when we got caught.

Mamma made a great divinity candy for my May baskets, and someone else made delicious peanut-butter fudge. I think the fudge maker probably was "Aunt Rachel" Johnson, Lois' mother, because I sometimes went with Lois to hang the baskets. I remember the fleeting guilt when that fudge became irresistible and I secretly slipped a piece from a May basket on its way to a door knob.

Independence Day (July 4th) was a big holiday for us, because we almost always extended it through Dad's birthday, July 5th. This two-day celebration usually involved a family picnic, sometimes with hot dogs and homemade ice cream—major treats at that time. It often included an overnight camping and fishing trip up valley in the national forest. One year, when I was maybe four, Dad started our holiday early by driving us north to Penticton, British Columbia, where we stayed with some former valley neighbors who had emigrated, and we joined in celebrating Canada's Dominion Day (now Canada Day) on July 1. An enduring memory for me came when a Canadian Mounted Policeman, in full dress regalia, rode his horse up beside me, leaned down and told me to grab onto his arm, and swung me up behind his saddle for a brief ride around a fairground.

At Fourth of July, I envied kids who had money for fireworks. I've always loved them—the louder, the showier, the better. Mamma, however, said they were too dangerous, and Grandma Lillian snorted and said they were "good money gone up in smoke." Dad was noncommittal, but I think he really liked fireworks, too. I lusted after fireworks even after I tried to make them myself (see "Income, Any Income") and finally earned enough money to buy my fill of firecrackers (see "Our Last Valley Home").

Halloween was not the mild-mannered "trick-or-treat," kid's-costume holiday of today. No one expected treats—just tricks. Some of these were rather benign practical jokes. Others were out-and-out vandalism, usually perpetrated by older teens or young adults, sometimes as grudge revenge.

Some of the tricks were truly spectacular, like taking a farm wagon apart, hoisting the pieces onto the roof of a building, and reassembling the rig up there to appear magically in dawn's light. This obviously required a well-planned, night-long effort by a talented team of mischief-makers, the kind we boys admired and envied. I've heard that a wagon thus appeared on the roof of our Community Hall, but I did not see it for myself.

Another major prank, probably advertised more often than actually performed, was outhouse tipping. The ideal situation, from the prankster's perspective, was to wait until someone came to use the outhouse before retiring for the night, and then quickly run up and tip the little building so the door was on the ground with the person still inside. I think I heard about this prank every Halloween, but don't know anyone who actually became a victim. A variation on this theme was to not topple the outhouse, but merely slide it back about four feet to expose the pit. I did hear of a victim of this prank, but it was one of the saboteurs, who lost his bearings in the darkness and fell into the pit himself. Reportedly, his fellow pranksters would not let him back into their car until he walked to the Entiat River and waded around for a while.

My own pranks, in company with my closest buddies, seem relatively benign. My favorite was to stretch white string across the road at windshield height and enjoy the startled reactions of drivers when they drove through the string. The best place we found for this prank was near Vaughn School, where two utility poles happened to be directly opposite on either side of the road. The infrequent traffic usually gave us time to retie the string after each car went through. In the unlit road, drivers didn't see the string until just before it hit their windshields. Their reactions ranged from a slight swerve and momentary slowing to a larger swerve while hitting the brakes. If we got lucky, a car would skid to a full stop, a car door would pop open, and someone would yell obscenities out into the blackness, while we in our hiding places giggled in delight.

*   *   *

The most exciting times for up-valley kids included trips to the big city of Wenatchee (1930 population 11,627). Even when my parents admonished, "Now, don't ask for anything," just being in the city enthralled me. In my early years, the city was altogether too much to take in. The streets and sidewalks seemed so orderly, the bustle of all those cars and strange people so busy, and the rows of shops seemed endless. The multistory buildings and the expanse of grassy park in front of the courthouse seemed so grand. Wenatchee is where I had my first elevator ride, and where I first saw a black man, a shoe-shine "boy" in a white-tiled barbershop where Daddy often took me to the men's room.

I got to roam the city by myself at an age that now would be considered dangerously young. In those days, my parents' biggest concerns for me were crossing streets and missing meeting times.

I was always eager to watch a movie, especially the westerns, and, when my folks had money for my ticket, they used the movies to keep me occupied while they shopped. Ten cents got me into any of the four downtown movie theaters—the Liberty, the Mission, and the Vitaphone theaters on Mission Street, and the Rialto on Wenatchee Avenue. An extra nickel would buy a treat that made me feel like about the richest kid in town. The theater lobbies then sold only popcorn and a few kinds of candy. I usually passed on the popcorn, because we had plenty at home, and I soon learned that I could get a much better deal on candy if I bought it someplace else. Often my five-cent treat was pickles—two fat, succulent dills from the pickle barrel at the Public Market on Wenatchee Avenue, dark green and soft inside from the prolonged curing. I carried them into the theater in a white deli box with a wire handle, and tried to make them last through the entire double-feature show.

The movie ticket windows had two clocks, one showing current time and the other showing when the movie would be repeating. That's how we kids, lacking watches of course, knew when we should leave the show to meet our folks. Often, I met my parents at the shady park in front of the courthouse. If I arrived at the park early, I could climb all over a brass Civil War cannon kept polished by kids' pants, or watch old men push painted blocks of wood around a huge, concrete checkerboard. If Dad was feeling flush, we might meet at Meadowmoor Dairy store on Orondo Street and split a fifteen-cent milkshake, which filled a milkshake glass twice and gave all three of us a cooling treat.

When I was old enough to earn money, I took pride in being able to finance my own activities in Wenatchee. In addition to movie tickets (continuing to lie about my age until I was thirteen), I could afford the dill-pickle treats and an occasional milkshake of my own or, for a short walk down Mission Street from the theaters, a visit to "Peppy Service."

Peppy's was a small place, on a drab side street a few steps east of Mission. The proprietors served beer and wine at a side counter, but the place was famous for its five-cent hamburgers, served at the front counter. The small meat patties, perhaps "stretched" with cereal, sizzled on a grill behind the counter, producing mouth-watering smells that overpowered the stench of beer. The patties were served on small, plain buns. The only condiment I remember was a mustard—a secret mixture with a drool-inducing cheesy flavor—that I've always sought since but never found. Peppy's must have been one of the most prosperous enterprises in Wenatchee, even during the hardest times. Everything about the place was geared toward fast, labor-saving service, long before the MacDonald chain. On many visits, we found few stools available. Standing to eat one's hamburger was okay but, under the liquor laws of the time, the drinkers had to remain on their stools, no matter how crowded the food area became.

I adored Peppy's, and tried to guide my family there as often as possible. One time I got Grandma Edna to walk there with me for lunch, and she foolishly agreed to pay for all the hamburgers I could eat. My conscience stopped me after I'd finished eight, costing her the considerable sum of forty cents (about an hour's orchard wage at the time), but I could have eaten a couple more.

Another favorite establishment was the Kress variety store, which carried by far the best toy assortment in Wenatchee at reasonable prices. There, I shopped for model-airplane kits and for my all-time favorite toys—Japanese rubber-band-powered airplanes with soldered-wire frames and silk coverings that survived a remarkable number of crashes.

We usually ended our Wenatchee trips with a visit to the Public Market in the heart of downtown, where my folks stocked up on the basics, which were much cheaper than at Cooper's Store or even the Entiat stores. Shopping was a serious matter, for every penny truly mattered. Dad loved to dicker with the produce manager over the price of aging produce. He often bought browning bananas for next to nothing. I clearly remember the drives home, with Mamma sorting the bananas, handing out the ripest to eat immediately. After we got home, we would have a supper of banana fritters, which Dad loved, and that meal might be repeated the next morning. One of our many small pleasures earned cheaply.

PEDDLING APPLES

"The Fouchs are going to California to sell their apples this year," Daddy said one evening at supper. "Earl leased space in a warehouse in Bakersfield, and he'll have his whole crop shipped down there. They'll peddle their apples around the city next winter."

"Oh, my," Mamma said. "Are they moving there for good?"

"No, Earl says they'll close up their house when they leave, but come back as soon as they sell their crop."

That was the summer of 1933, during the heart of the Great Depression. Most of the country was just getting by at best, and many Americans suffered in severe poverty. Fruit ranked low on the list of family necessities, and even as our apples grew and ripened on the trees, markets for them were expected to be at rock bottom. To worsen matters locally, the largest single employer in the valley, the Harris mill, ran on short hours. Much of its production was lumber for apple boxes and, because apple sales were down, so was the need for the wooden shipping boxes. The whole valley was in tough times. Money seemed almost nonexistent, with few honest ways to get any. Some general optimism for the future had resulted from the 1932 presidential election, but most orchardists were desperate to just hang on, to get through one more year by any means possible.

My folks continued to discuss our neighbors' move while we finished eating. I think the conversation went something like this:

"Fouch is on the right track," Daddy allowed. "By selling his apples direct and doing the warehousing himself, he'll save a bunch on expenses and commissions. Of course, he'll still need to have 'em packed and inspected to get 'em into California, and pay the shipping costs, but...."

"What makes him think the folks in California have any more money than they do other places? And why wouldn't they just buy California apples?" Mamma asked.

Daddy chuckled. "Knowin' Earl, I'm sure he's done plenty of checking before he makes a move like this. He's convinced there's a market."

I knew about the importance of a market for apples, and for the need to avoid expenses. I also knew the general location of California, having received a jigsaw puzzle of the forty-eight states for my previous birthday. But I was a bit confused about what Daddy meant by "peddle." I envisioned Mr. and Mrs. Fouch on bicycles, with their bike baskets heaped with shiny red apples, riding around city streets. "Will the Fouchs take their apples to all the houses, like the Watkins man comes here?" I asked.

Daddy started to laugh and then stopped. "I don't think that's what he meant, but maybe that's not a bad idea. I think Mr. Fouch hopes to sell his apples mostly to stores and restaurants."

"Will he sell apples to Tom Mix and the other movie stars?"

This time both my parents laughed. "No, dear," Mamma said, "the movie stars live in Hollywood. That's another California city quite a way from Bakersfield. I doubt that Mr. Fouch will take his apples that far."

With my questions answered, and being seven years old, I promptly forgot about the matter. It came up again while Daddy and I were visiting Grandma Lillian and he told her about Mr. Fouch's plans.

"Y' know, Mom, maybe the secret to getting people to spend some of the little they have on apples *is* to make it real easy, like Fouch is going to do. Take the apples right to them—like the Watkins and Raleigh salesmen come right to our homes.

"If only my truck was in better shape," Daddy went on, "I think I'd try it this year, with whatever apples don't sell right off. If I hauled the fruit myself, and didn't take it out of state, I could sell it loose in the box and save even more on expenses than Fouch will."

"What's wrong with your truck?" Grandma asked, referring to the first truck I remember, an old Chevrolet truck with dull black paint—a 1926 model, I think.

"The motor's knockin' and it won't stay in second gear. I've been able to baby it along on the short hauls, but it just wouldn't make a long trip. I'm afraid it's about used up."

Grandma thought a bit. Finally she said, "Well, you're going to need a truck sooner or later. Why don't you look around for one when you get time? If you need to, you can use some of my money."

Thinking back, I can imagine how reluctant Dad would have been to touch any of Grandma's money, what little she might have had. I'm sure he already felt guilty about her losing the major sum of $124.26 in one of the many bank failures of 1931-32. Dad had induced her to put her money in the bank where he worked, the Commercial Bank & Trust in Wenatchee, which locked its doors the morning of February 2, 1932. (I was the first person in our immediate family to trust a bank account again—and that wasn't until World War II.)

Whether or not he used any of Grandma's money, Daddy did start scouting for a better truck. He drove as far as neighboring Okanogan, Grant, and Kittitas Counties, and I accompanied him on several trips. Even with prices at nineteen cents a gallon or a little less, he surely burned more gasoline than we really could afford.

Alas, all that scouting failed to turn up a suitable, affordable truck. In the Grant County village of Quincy, however, behind a run-down commercial garage, he discovered a large, dark-blue delivery van that had suffered body damage in a roll-over accident. Daddy decided the van was worth another look, so he and I set out one sunny morning in our Pontiac sedan on the sixty-mile drive to Quincy.

On the way, Daddy explained that, if the van engine was in good shape, and if he could buy the van for the right price, he might be able to make it over into a truck. The very idea amazed me, but I didn't question him.

At the garage, Daddy and the garage owner began an amiable negotiation. Soon bored, I ask permission to look at a damaged biplane parked behind the garage, and amused myself at the old airplane until Daddy called that we were leaving. He seemed pleased and said, "I think we need an ice-cream cone before we drive home."

Over our ice cream, Daddy told me he had decided to buy the wrecked van and had put money down to hold it. He said the van was drivable and that he had gotten it "for about the price of the tires."

The next morning, the three of us set out again for Quincy. Once there, Daddy checked the van once more, and he and the garage owner got it ready for the road. Daddy finished paying, and seemed pleased with the engine sounds. Then, he shook hands with the garage owner, climbed in the battered van, and drove off toward home. Mamma and I followed in the Pontiac. As I recall, the drive home was uneventful, although Mamma worried all the way about the van's expired license plates.

At home, Daddy parked the van in the shade of an apple tree and checked it over again, this time crawling underneath. He emerged whistling tunelessly, a sure sign he was pleased.

The van stayed there for several weeks. Whenever he could find time from his busy orchard chores, Daddy attacked the bus body with a hacksaw, finally cutting it off completely just behind the front seat and front doors. Then he unbolted the rear part of the van body from the frame beneath and, using levers and ropes, he tumbled it onto the ground beside our driveway.

I don't remember the fate of either the old truck or the cut-off van body. I do remember, however, my folks having one of their "discussions" about "more junk in the back yard."

The parts remaining made a strange sight—a naked steel rear frame between large wheels, a hollow cab with all the usual controls and fixtures, and a normal front end. If I had known the word "grotesque," I might have used that. Daddy, however, seemed very pleased. He draped a tarp over the open back of the cab and started doing things with the rear springs, no doubt to strengthen them.

Soon after, Daddy brought home a bundle of nice, new tongue-and-groove boards. With careful sawing and fitting, he formed them into a wall of horizontal boards that closed the rear of the cab, building in a sliding rear window using glass pirated from one of his old cars awaiting repair. Later, Daddy acquired enough beams and boards to build a truck bed. He treated the wooden bed with linseed oil and painted the wood of the truck cab with some left-over white paint. The result looked strange—a normal dark-blue truck cab when seen from the front, with a sharply contrasting flat, white, wooden back to the cab. The odor of linseed-oil paint thinner forever dominated the smells inside the cab.

On that smallish, home-fashioned truck, with all the boxes of loose apples it would carry, along with our suitcase, food box and lap robes, we set out on our first peddling trip. We left soon after Mamma's packing job ended, in late fall. Our pets stayed with relatives.

In the truck, I sat between my parents most of the time, learning to keep my knees out of the way of the gearshift lever during start-ups and shift-downs. Sometimes I was allowed to crouch on the floor on Mamma's side next to the truck's heater. While we drove, Mamma often drilled me on school work, mainly reading, spelling, and arithmetic.

We zigzagged across eastern Washington, driving long hours and calling at grocery stores, restaurants, and other businesses along the way. We ate from the food box and at restaurants, especially at those that bought apples. We dropped in on every shirttail relative on either side of the family that lived along the way; despite the impositions, we were always treated graciously. Between towns, Daddy sometimes stopped at prosperous-looking farms to offer the apples, and once we stayed overnight with a kindly family we met that way. Only one night do I remember sleeping in the truck cab, wearing layers of clothes, huddled together under the lap robes.

A few times we stayed in cheap hotels, where the people and the night noises were fascinating and sometimes scary. At one, our sleep was disturbed by a lot of hall traffic and what sounded to me like scuffling and giggling in the next room. I asked Mamma about it the next morning.

"The women next door were entertaining men during the night," she said, "and they aren't nice women." I thought she meant that they weren't nice because they kept other people awake.

If the hotel rooms were cold, we three slept together in the bed. If our room had a working steam radiator, I preferred sleeping on the floor near the heat with a lap robe over me, especially if the room had a rug.

Those hotels, bleak as they were, had amenities we lacked at home—a sink in the room with running water, usually hot as well as cold, and a bathroom with toilet and tub on each floor. Mamma did a lot of fussing about cleanliness, and made me wash my hands a lot.

My least favorite hotels were those where breakfasts were included with the lodging. Although I welcomed the cereal, toast or pancakes, my folks always made me eat eggs as well. Because they both liked theirs sunny-side up, they expected me to eat eggs that way too. I could tolerate the partly soft egg whites, but hated the runny yoke. I would stall and whine, and nibble at the hardest parts, and eat everything but the "sunny" part. My folks laid on the whole guilt load—wasting good food, the starving Armenians, my need for the nourishment—everything. Finally Daddy would mutter, in no uncertain words, "Eat that egg—now!" and I would tearfully mop up the yellow mess with scraps of toast and gag it down.

Daddy was good at bargaining, and he willingly bartered the apples instead of selling for cash. He exchanged some of the fruit for gasoline and oil, meals and lodgings, and groceries for our food box. I remember vividly a Chinese restaurant in Ellensburg, where Daddy sold several boxes of apples for cash and our dinner. All the workers spoke Chinese. It was my first exposure to a foreign language, and I could scarcely believe these smallish, different-looking people could understand each other in that rapid, sing-song talk.

In the larger towns, my folks would often drop me at a library while they canvassed the businesses. That way I stayed warm and safe, amusing myself with new and wonderful books, until they returned for me. I felt as though I started more books without finishing them than any kid in history.

Other times in the cities, for a ten-cent admission plus five cents for a lunch of popcorn, they would put me in a movie theater while they sold apples. There I stayed through the continuous showings—two feature films, "newsreels" of current events, previews of "coming attractions," and cartoons—until they came for me. At one Spokane theater, I sat through a Shirley Temple movie three times, long enough to memorize most of the dialogue.

Whatever maintenance or repairs the truck needed, Daddy took care of on the way. Most of it, I'm sure, was done when we stayed with friends. I don't remember any particular delays because of repairs.

When all the apples were finally sold or traded away, we gratefully headed back to the snowy home place. The house took more than a day to warm up with fires roaring in both wood stoves. I had a bunch of school-work to catch up, but I was the envy of my schoolmates for my "adventure," and I passed my grades easily. I certainly had gotten enough practice with reading during the trip.

Daddy said we didn't bring home much money, but enough to get through the winter.

Among the fruits of Daddy's bartering were two large gunny sacks of wheat. My folks gave one sack to my Bedient grandparents and kept the other. I had wondered what use the wheat would be, but learned its value a few days after we got home when Mamma served up steamed wheat kernels as hot cereal. It was soft yet chewy, and had a nice nutty flavor. Served hot with either butter or milk and sugar, it was delicious, and I much preferred it to oatmeal. Daddy, however, did not seem thrilled with eating wheat, and soon Mamma stopped serving it. One reason, I am sure, was the work needed to prepare the wheat for human consumption: After the supper dishes were done, Mamma would pour some dry wheat onto her countertop and sort out imperfect grains, chaff, and grit. After rinsing the sorted wheat vigorously in a covered pan, she measured small amounts into our two Thermos bottles. Lastly, she filled the Thermos bottles with boiling water, corked the Thermoses and set them aside. By the next morning, the wheat had cooked and swelled to fill the Thermos bottles. Despite my frequent pleas for more of the delicious wheat, almost all of it was ground up to feed Grandma Lillian's chickens.

The results of our 1933 peddling trip encouraged Daddy to repeat the effort the following winter, during which we revisited each business or farm that had taken apples the first time, according to Mamma's careful records. That second year we ranged as far as northern Idaho. At St. Maries, Idaho, we stayed with some "friends of friends" who treated us so nicely that I was sorry to leave. They let me look through their microscope at bugs, fish scales and other fascinating things.

As I recall, that second year of peddling apples from the truck went faster and we brought home more cash. We probably would have gone again in 1935, had not other events intervened.

FIRE AT THE FOXWORTHY'S

On a sunny, early-summer morning of 1934, while playing on the front lawn of the home place, I noticed steam rising from the house shingles. I wondered about that briefly, because the roof didn't seem damp. However, at eight years of age, I shrugged it off as being just another phenomenon that kids don't understand.

Not two minutes later, Mamma burst from the house. "GERALD! GERALD!" she cried, "THE ATTIC'S ON FIRE!"

I ran to the front end of the house. Grey smoke streamed from the attic access hatch in the gable wall.

Daddy raced in from the orchard.

"Get buckets from the barn!" Mamma ordered. I dashed to comply. When I returned with two buckets, Dad was hurriedly priming the pump. Mamma, carrying the kitchen bucket, was climbing an orchard ladder to the attic hatchway. She recoiled from a gust of smoke that billowed out, then threw her water into the smoky opening.

"Come down and pump!" Dad shouted, "I'll carry the water up!"

Mamma came down the ladder. I stood by, frightened and wanting to help but not knowing what to do. She rushed to the pump and began working the handle as fast as she could. "Bruce, keep the buckets under the spout," she ordered.

I jumped in, making sure most of the water that Mamma pumped frantically from the little pitcher pump got into a bucket. Daddy raced up the twelve-foot ladder with each full bucket of water, throwing it as hard as he could into the smoke now pouring from the attic hatchway, then practically ran down the ladder to grab the next bucket.

The author and feline friend beside our house prior to our attic fire in 1934.
Water from the hand pump proved to be inadequate for fighting the fire.

182

I glanced up at the black smoke, now pouring from under the roof shingles as well as the hatchway. Mamma, gasping for breath, was slowing her pumping.

"Help me pump!" Mamma ordered.

I added my hands to the pump handle until each bucket was filled, then I made sure another bucket was under the spout as Daddy grabbed the full one and dashed back up the ladder.

But we were clearly losing to the fire. The smoke poured out more densely. Daddy now pulled himself up the ladder with each water bucket. Mamma was about played out at the pump. We had no telephone to call for help, no pressurized water, nowhere to turn.

Luckily, Aunt Achsa, then living in the little Gofinch house across the road, happened to go outside. She saw the smoke and realized that the only major help was at the Harris mill, about a mile up valley. She jumped in her car and roared up the road toward the mill. On the way she met men from nearby homes, drawn by the smoke.

"FIRE AT THE FOXWORTHY'S!" she shouted to each one, barely slowing down. The men began running.

At the mill, Achsa burst into the office. "The Foxworthy house is on fire! Roll out the fire truck!" she demanded.

The Harris fire truck was strictly for protection of the mill buildings and nearby worker housing. At first, Achsa told me, the office staff just stared, as if amazed at her audacity. But my blessed, feisty aunt ranted and cajoled until they gave in and ordered the fire truck out.

Before the fire truck arrived at our house, the Albin brothers ran in from the nearest house, and Rollo Schermerhorn drove in from the next ranch up valley. The Albins formed a bucket brigade, with one brother standing on the ladder. He chucked buckets-full of water into the black smoke billowing from the attic hatchway as fast as his brother could bring them the two strides from the pump and hand them up. Daddy worked the handle of the pitcher pump so hard that water spurted up through the priming hole on top. Mamma took me inside to help grab our belongings and carry them out to the front lawn. Daddy and the Albin boys continued, but the water thrown in through the attic hatch was doing little more than soaking the kitchen ceiling.

"Whoosh!" Flames broke through the back part of the roof. Nobody had to tell me our house was doomed.

Men began arriving from the mill, including my Uncle Frank. He dashed inside the house and helped to remove bedding and furniture. He was there when Rollo Schermerhorn arrived.

Rollo was a nice man, but inclined to lose perspective in emergencies. He shouted, "Save the doors!" and headed for the two French doors at the front of our living room. Before anyone could stop him, Rollo ripped the wood-frame doors off their hinges and tossed them onto our lawn. Uncle Frank was moving our big oak table at the time, and could only watch in amazement.

That oak table was the last piece of furniture in the living-room. When Rollo saw that go out he yelled, "Save the linoleum!" He grabbed one edge of our linoleum rug and started to roll it up. Unfortunately, our heating stove still held down one end of the linoleum. But Rollo could not be stopped, even though Uncle Frank shouted, "Rollo—the *stove!*"

"Oh, yeah!" Rollo responded. But he kept rolling up the linoleum, ripping it off along the edge of the stove base. He then dashed out the splintered doorway and threw the roll of torn linoleum onto the lawn, where it promptly unrolled.

Bounding back into the living room before Frank could stop him, Rollo grabbed the stovepipe at the back of the heating stove and knocked it aside. A cloud of black soot billowed out, covering the living room. Wild-eyed, soot-blackened Rollo was about to pick up the stove when Frank knocked his arms aside.

"Don't touch another thing, you muscle-bound fathead!" Frank shouted. "Get outside and take a breath!"

The fire truck arrived from the mill about the time the main contents of the house were outside. Flames now roared and crackled from the back part of the roof. Black smoke was filling the valley.

The fire crew unreeled their hose and swung into action. All the men seemed to yell at once. The leaping, roaring flames seemed unstoppable. No one had time for me. I watched transfixed in a wide-awake nightmare.

By concentrating their water hose on the fiercest part of the fire, the mill crew finally beat the flames down and saved most of the house. Only the roof was a total loss, although all the plaster of the ceilings and much of the walls was soaked and darkened. Smoky steam still wafted up from the attic remains. As the fire crew prepared to return to the mill, water still dripped down onto the floors, and part of the ceiling plaster had fallen into my old bedroom. A stench like scorched cardboard was overpowering.

Then Daddy was thanking all the folks who had come to help, and Mamma was crying on Aunt Achsa's shoulder. I joined those two in a three-way hug, devastated that the only real home I'd ever known was now a soggy ruin. I didn't realize that, without Aunt Achsa's quick thinking and desperate tenacity, that day would have ended much worse for us.

"We're insured," I heard Dad saying. "We'll rebuild." My relief was immense.

As soon as I could, I asked Dad, "Where will we live now?"

"Son," he answered with a comforting hand on my shoulder, "we'll live in the woodshed while we rebuild our house. It'll be just like camping out," he added with a smoke-streaked grin.

I don't remember where we stayed that first night, but by next morning the three of us, and maybe Aunt Achsa, were restacking wood in the wood-shed to form walls on three sides of the open shed. The south side, the highest under the sloping roof, we left open.

As soon as the dirt floor of the woodshed was cleared, Daddy raked the dirt smooth and we tamped it down underfoot. Then Daddy brought the piece of our old living-room linoleum from the lawn, and unrolled it onto the dirt.

"I'll have to thank Rollo," Dad said wryly, "for tearing this to just the right size. It wouldn't have fit in here otherwise."

By midday, when neighbor ladies started showing up with sandwiches and casseroles, we had moved the kitchen stove to our new "home" and had wooden apple boxes stacked beside the stove to hold utensils, salvaged foodstuff and personal items. Our clothes hung on hangers from a rope strung between the woodshed rafters.

We also had brought our little weathered-oak ice box, which served double-duty as our washstand. One of the most precious gifts that day was a block of ice that Nora Schermerhorn brought from their ice house. After that ice was gone, the only way we could extend food life was to open the icebox to the cool night air, close the box at dawn, and hope the food inside would not spoil during the day.

We still had our little dirt cellar, too. Although it was at the back of the house where the fire had raged the hottest, its earth-covered roof had protected it. The vegetable garden beside it had survived as well.

My folk's white-enameled metal bedstead barely fit into the woodshed, crammed next to my cot. My cot was conveniently at the end of the wood-shed nearest the outhouse, but I had to crawl into and out of bed over the pillow end. Nights were cool, and I enjoyed snuggling under the blankets and listening to the loud voice of the nearby river as I sank into sleep.

In a day or two, a portly insurance man came, driving a big, shiny car, wearing a suit and tie and carrying a briefcase. He and my folks huddled around our big oak table under the apple trees on our lawn. I hung around close by, trying unsuccessfully to hear the talk while the insurance man wrote on some papers. Finally, everyone stood up. Daddy and the insurance man shook hands. Mamma had tears in her eyes and a smile on her face when the insurance man handed over a bank check.

Fortunately, the weather stayed dry until we could move furniture and other things back into the part of the house that still had a roof. Then my folks started the depressing job of tearing off parts of the house that could not be salvaged, including, eventually, the entire roof and much of the plaster ceilings. Daddy hauled the waste material to the edge of our property near the river bank, where we always disposed of trash, in the manner of those times.

Using the fire-insurance money to hire rebuilding was not even a consideration. Daddy knew he could do things cheaper. He calculated what materials he needed and went shopping for them—or swapping, such as roofing materials for truck-hauling services.

The biggest need was for lumber. If the Harris mill had specialized in dimension lumber instead of materials for apple boxes, I'm sure Daddy would have bought lumber from the local mill no matter the price, out of gratitude for the mill crew putting out our fire. But he had to look farther afield. He finally determined that, to get the best lumber price, we needed to go to western Washington, where those mills, too, were hammered by the depression. Accordingly, we packed some bags, hung tarps around our woodshed "home," and the three of us drove out in the truck Daddy had refashioned from a van.

Arriving safely in north Seattle, we stayed with former residents from our valley, the McKeever family, while Daddy went around dickering with nearby sawmills. In two days, he had purchased a full load of lumber, actually exceeding his truck's permitted weight, for $213. I remember the amount because such a big thing was made of it—a princely sum indeed, but oh, so much lumber!

Daddy celebrated the coup by inviting our host family out for a movie and supper. We rode an electric trolley car into downtown Seattle, where we went to a theater so grand that it could have been a palace, and saw a black-and-white thriller, "The Invisible Man." Afterward, Daddy treated everyone to supper at a nearby restaurant. I had a huge bowl of vegetable-beef soup—all I could eat—for a nickel.

With the lumber acquired, the next challenge became getting it home. Hauling it over Stevens Pass on U.S. Highway 2 proved to be slow and uncertain. The poor, overloaded truck labored up the steeper hills in compound-low, or "creeper" gear. Even so, it overheated, and the grind up to Stevens Pass was interrupted by stops to let the engine cool and to refill the radiator from roadside streams. Dad apparently knew exactly how much his truck could tolerate, and had loaded it to the limit. As I remember, after we topped the mountain crest, the rest of the haul was uneventful.

Once we arrived home, my folks, aided sometimes by neighbors and my uncles, went to work rebuilding. Even I, young as I was, got to learn some of the labor-saving tricks of moving boards around.

In the process of rebuilding, they widened the house by moving the back wall, thereby creating a larger master bedroom, a back porch, and space in between for a bathroom. The bathroom, however, never got finished, and served as storage space as long as we lived there. They topped the building off with fire-resistant roofing instead of wooden shingles.

Daddy erected new interior walls with sheetrock, then called "plasterboard," and replaced the unsalvageable ceilings with an insulating paneling called "Firtex." Some remaining plaster walls were badly water-stained and, although Mamma repainted them repeatedly with kalsomine (similar to white-wash), the stains kept showing through. Lacking the better paints of today, she finally gave up, and the stains remained as a shadowy reminder of the fire.

During the rebuilding, Daddy replaced all the electrical wiring, which had been concentrated in the attic and therefore was ruined. As I recall, before the fire the only electrical fixtures we had were light-bulb sockets hanging from the ceilings and turned on and off by pull chains with dangling strings. The only way Mamma could use her cherished electric iron was with a plug-in adaptor in a ceiling light socket, and an extension cord to her ironing board. The rewiring, I believe, provided the house's first wall outlets.

As soon as a neighbor rebuilt the upper part of the brick chimney between our kitchen and living room, we moved our kitchen stove from the woodshed back into the kitchen, onto Mamma's brand-new linoleum floor. From then on, we ate in the house. We continued to sleep in the woodshed through most of the summer, however, while my folks refurbished the bedrooms. Gradually, room by room, the house became livable again.

To me, it was just one big adventure, but it must have been terrible for my folks—Daddy especially. In addition to doing most of the rebuilding to save every nickel he could, he also had to work our orchard and that of his mother. Nobody spoke about his beloved drums, which had been stored in the attic.

While we still lived in the woodshed, I asked Mamma what had caused the fire. She seemed uncomfortable when she answered that the insurance claim said the fire started from "spontaneous combustion of oily rags in the attic." Only decades later did I learn from Aunt Achsa that, the evening before the fire, Dad had been in the attic burning out a wasp nest with his blowtorch. For my compulsively truthful mother, that deception, which probably assured our insurance payment, must have been painful indeed.

A BICYCLE!

Thanks to my folks' frugality and hard work, they had cash left over from the fire-insurance money we received in the summer of 1934. I have no idea how much that surplus amounted to, but it made a wad of bills in the fruit jar that Daddy buried in the back yard. (Banks were not to be trusted after the many recent bank failures.)

I can only imagine that Daddy used some of the insurance money to make a mortgage payment or two. And I remember that Mamma got a used washing machine. But the only other special purchase I remember was for me—the most expensive gift my parents were ever able to give me—a brand-new bicycle.

One morning that summer, my folks left me with Aunt Achsa and drove the truck to Wenatchee for shopping. I didn't know, of course, but Daddy had been scouting for just the right bicycle for my diminutive size. He found the perfect one at the Sears and Roebuck store. Dubbed the "Elgin Falcon," it was a red, balloon-tired, streamlined beauty with a chromed electric headlight and a motorcycle-style "tank" to hold the battery. It was full size, but its design allowed a very low position for the seat. It sold for the grand sum of $34.95, equivalent to several hundred present-day dollars.

When ready for the drive home, Daddy wheeled the new bike out to the truck and laid it on the middle of the open flat bed behind boxes of groceries. The bike rode well on the truck bed, according to Mamma, until they were doing about fifty on the open highway. Then, without warning, the bike rolled around the underneath pedal and flew off the truck, bouncing this way and that on the asphalt roadway before coming to rest far back from where Dad managed to stop the truck.

My Aunt Achsa was in on the surprise plan, of course, and when she heard the truck pull into our place, she sent me running home. When I dashed up, my folks were standing somberly beside the truck. Daddy was holding a shiny red bicycle!

"Wow! A bike!"

Advertisement for my bicycle, the Elgin Falcon.

Daddy's sober look stopped me in my tracks. Mamma burst into tears.

"I'm sorry, Son," Daddy said. "It fell off the truck."

Only then did I see that one side of the bike seat was scraped down to the padding, one handlebar corner looked as if it had been attacked with a rasp, and the shiny headlamp was skinned and dented. My heart sank.

"Will it run?" I asked finally.

"Oh yes," Daddy answered quickly. "It runs fine—and I can fix a lot of the damage."

"That's great. A bicycle! Thanks a lot! When can I start riding?"

Mamma smiled with brimming eyes. Daddy grinned.

"You can start learning right away," he said, "as soon as I get the seat set down to your size, and fix a couple of other things."

"Can I help?" I asked. Daddy nodded, and together we rolled the bike closer to the barn and his tool box. On the way, I ran my hands over the smooth, red enamel of the streamlined cross bar.

Together, Daddy and I unclamped the damaged headlight from the handlebar so he could tap out the dents. He straightened a bent pedal and fixed some dents in the fenders so they were less noticeable.

Daddy set the seat as low as it would go, but when I mounted it, my feet still could not work the pedals.

"Well, that's why we bought this kind of bike," Daddy said calmly. "Hop off and get my hacksaw."

When I returned with the saw, Daddy pulled the seat and its post out of the vertical tubing that supported it. He laid the bike onto the ground and unceremoniously hack-sawed off about three inches of the tubing. After jamming the seat post back down into the tubing and twisting the seat into position, he raised the bike. "There, try that."

Daddy held the bike. I stepped onto a pedal and swung up onto the seat.

"Oh, yeah!" By shifting on the seat, I could reach the pedals in their lowest positions. My folks beamed.

The headlamp repair wasn't very satisfactory, and I soon removed the lamp. Also, because I no longer needed the battery tank underneath the crossbar, I took that off as well. I ended up with quite a nifty, stripped-down, streamlined bike, albeit with skinned handlebars and seat. We never tried to raise the seat, even when my legs grew. The "low-rider" seat added to the streamlined effect.

I'm sure the damage already done to it helped my parents tolerate the rough treatment the poor bike received while I learned to ride it. At eight and a half, I had never ridden a scooter or anything else, except ice skates, that required balancing. The concept of turning the front wheel to balance my new steed was totally foreign to me, although I do remember being deluged with that advice. And I had to learn mostly alone. Daddy was too busy to help much, and Mamma had never learned to ride a bike. Training wheels would have helped, but even if they existed then they would have been an unacceptable extravagance.

The only attributes I brought to the challenge were tenacity and toughness. I learned to ride by wheeling the bike to the upper part of our sloping driveway, stepping on a pedal to swing my small frame aboard, and letting the bike coast downhill until it fell over onto the driveway or into the softer dirt of the adjacent orchard. After each fall, I dusted myself off and wheeled the bike back up the driveway for another try. I measured my learning progress by the distance I got before the inevitable crash.

For days I coasted down that driveway, crashing every single time, receiving countless minor scrapes and bruises. I remember bawling from frustration more than from pain, and hiding my injuries so Mamma wouldn't make me quit. One lesson I soon learned was that purposely flopping the bike was much preferable to letting it crash into a tree with me aboard. Another thing I learned was that, when the bike started over, I could jump off and let it crash without me, thereby reducing bodily wear and tear.

I probably was an unusually slow learner, but finally I got the hang of turning the handlebars to maintain balance. Even so, another few days passed before I could maintain that tenuous balance while pushing on a pedal to operate the coaster brake. More frustration, more private tears. Eventually, as with every young bike rider, coordination happened. I could actually ride as far as I liked and then stop the bike in the upright position. Oh, glorious day!

Once I learned to ride it, I virtually lived my daylight hours on that bicycle. I visited every nearby friend who had a bike, and proudly rode it to school, where, in my eyes at least, it almost equaled the fancy bikes owned by more affluent kids. If no other bike riders were available, I rode for hours by myself, up and down the valley road in front of our place.

Soon, I was allowed to ride my bike farther afield, as long as I had at least one companion. Bobby Schermerhorn usually was it, after he too got a bike and learned to ride it. Our normal range was upriver to Ardenvoir School and downriver to the swimming hole below Grandma Lillian's. During summers, whoever got his morning chores done first would just show up at the other's house. If the preferred companion was busy that day, we took no offense, we just biked on to another friend's, with our ever-present swim suit draped on our handlebars. We all had to be at our respective homes in time for evening chores and supper, but we were welcome for lunch at whomever's home was nearest to our midday location.

The thousands of hours spent pedaling that heavy, single-gear bike certainly helped my bodily development, but occasional spills took their toll in skin and blood. Still, I never broke a bone that way, as some of my contemporaries did.

RIDING THE FLUME

We were the Terrific Trio, indomitable as Captain Marvel, daring as Tom Mix, loyal as the Three Musketeers. We were starting fifth grade.

Bobby, Vern and I, on our well-used bikes or roaming the pine-spotted hills with dogs and Bobby's BB gun, had wonderful adventures. Some were death-defying in truth; many more risked virtual death from our folks, had anyone ever "told."

We usually got along fairly well, partly, no doubt, because few other guys our age were nearby to play with. If we tended to pick on one, it was Bobby. Lanky Bob maybe was growing too fast for his coordination. And he was "nervous," as his mom put it, meaning skittish as a chipmunk and likely to get shaky on the face of a rock cliff or while walking the water-slicked, wooden pipeline that crossed the river near his house.

Vern was cocky and fearless. He often thought up the riskiest adventures and shamed Bobby and me into following, sometimes while Bob was scared to tears. Bobby got little sympathy from me, I confess. I was small and had been sickly, and was too concerned about proving myself to worry much about others.

In those days, most of the irrigation water for the valley's orchards flowed through ditches dug into the hill slopes and, where necessary, through pipelines and flumes. The flumes were wooden troughs built in places that lacked soil for a ditch. One ditch-and-flume system ran along the rocky hill about twelve feet above the main road near the home place. Each year after harvest, men from the ranches joined in cleaning and repairing their ditch systems. This particular fall, they decided to rebuild the flume around a rock point above our place.

We boys spent after-school hours there, fascinated by the art of building timber trusses from the foundation of irregular rocks to create a level flume up above. We watched from the road below, perched on the worn saddles of our balloon-tire bikes, between impromptu races to work off our energy. We chewed snitches of coal-tasting tar used for sealing joints between flume boards, practiced spitting, and debated fine points of the carpentry above. Sometimes we met with our Radio Flyer wagons to divvy up the treasure of board scraps for toy boats and wood-stove kindling.

It was a Saturday evening when the truss-building crew finished at the point. The workers' trucks weren't out of sight before the Terrific Trio stashed bikes and raced up the hillside for a close inspection before dark.

The new flume base was a course of level boards, butt-joined at slight angles, curving left around the rocky point. The boards were of rough-cut fir, maybe fourteen inches wide, fresh and bright from the mill. Where the ditch ended, the end board extended smoothly from the bottom of the unlined ditch, inviting us like Dorothy's yellow brick road.

The base boards were nailed solidly to the trusses underneath, bouncing little when we jumped on them. There were no side boards yet. Vern and I grinned. Our eyes agreed: A perfect track for our bikes! Vern let out a joyous "Yeah!"

Bobby looked at the drop to jagged granite on the downhill side. "It-it's high, isn't it?" he said. Vern hooted in derision.

We agreed to meet there next day after church. It would be our only chance to ride the flume. On Monday, we had heard, another crew was coming to add side boards and cross braces, which would turn this treasure into just another flume.

Sunday came sunny and cool, with a breeze carrying the smells of autumn leaves and overripe apples. By noon we had dragged our bikes up the hill into a brush-screened section of the ditch, upstream from the rock point. The unlined ditch had a two-foot-high bank and a bottom of coarse sand which resisted as we pushed our bikes toward the point.

At the upstream end of the flume boards, we planned the ride. We would build up speed in the ditch and then coast the hundred or so feet around the point, pedaling only if our speed dropped too low. I argued for starting from this curved section of the ditch, despite the blind approach, because the straight ditch on the other side was visible from my house. If Dad saw us, he could guess what we were doing, and I wanted at least one ride before he grounded me.

I went first. After salutes and handshakes, I took my bike about a hundred feet up the ditch, settled myself and dug out, pumping the pedals full-force.

Trouble dogged me from the start. The loose sand held me back and the grassy sides of the narrow ditch caught at my pedals. When I coasted past my open-mouthed buddies out onto the flume boards, I knew my speed was borderline.

The smoothness of the boards gave me hope. But half way to the other end a gust of wind slowed me like an anchor.

I ducked forward to cut wind resistance. My front wheel wandered— nearly to the edge. My bike wobbled again. Now I had no choice. With my heart beating wildly, I began to pedal—ever so carefully, ever so steadily. I dared not look down past the board.

I was across! With my front wheel firmly in the ditch sand, I leaned on my handlebars and gasped my relief. What a rush! Shaking down to my toes, I heard Bobby shout, "Yea! You made it!"

"Y-yeah!" I managed.

After pulling my bike out of the way, I walked shakily back across the boards, daring now to look down at the rocks. The thrill of risking everything and surviving had me laughing like a fool when I reached my friends.

I controlled myself enough to describe my problems, advising the others to start farther up the ditch for more speed. And I warned about the gust of wind.

"Don't over-steer if it hits you," I advised, seeing my front tire again, two inches from disaster, "but it can slow you some."

Vern went next. With a longer run in the ditch and his greater wiry strength, he was going plenty fast when he coasted onto the board. His course was smooth and steady around the point, and he yelled promptly that he'd made it. But on his walk back to us his laughter was uncertain.

"I was fine till I looked over the edge. Then I damn near pissed my pants!"

That, coming from Vern, doubled me up laughing, but Bobby barely smiled. And after he'd pushed his bike out of sight up the ditch, Vern and I waited long minutes. The cool breeze continued to gust.

"He'll never make it," Vern looked worried, watching up the ditch.

"He has to try, at least," I countered. "If he doesn't he'll be chickenshit to every guy in school."

Vern's head snapped around. "Oh, yeah? Just who's gonna tell?"

I couldn't believe my ears—this coming from the class daredevil and constant tease?

Bobby came into view, stomping those pedals, straining against the handlebars for every ounce of leverage. His rear wheel was kicking sand, but he wasn't up to speed. His face showed determination and, yes, fear.

Vern stepped into the ditch, forcing Bob to a skidding stop. "Something's wrong, Bobby," he said calmly. "Oh, I see…your back tire's soft," Vern continued, squeezing the bald tire.

Hell, the tire wasn't *that* soft!

"…tire like that would kill your speed and make your bike wander," Vern was saying. "Be suicide to ride the flume with a tire that soft, especially in this wind."

The unfairness was too much! We had risked it all; so should Bobby!

"Well, there's a tire pump at my place," I declared. Vern's glare was withering. "On second thought," I added, "maybe Dad loaned it out."

"Ours is in the car, and my folks drove into town," Vern said. "Guess the store's the closest place to get Bobby's tire pumped up."

Riding to Cooper's store took twenty minutes, plus more time at the "Free Air" hose. Then we checked the men's can for new dirty writing, and shared a strawberry pop that Vern bought. I was ready to return to the flume. But Vern insisted on a game of tag on the logs floating in the nearby mill pond, despite the watchman's yelling, "I'll call your folks!" All too soon, it was time to go our separate ways for Sunday dinners.

That evening at dusk, while I was pondering Vern's unnatural charity at the flume, our kitchen door banged open.

Bobby lurched in from the gloom, torn and bloody, cradling a crooked forearm. He must have hurt like hell, but he wasn't crying. While Mamma was after bandages and Daddy went to phone his folks, Bobby managed a little smile with his split, swollen lips.

"I went off the flume on my *second* ride," he mumbled proudly.

I gaped in wonder at this new Bobby. "You sonofagun!" I grinned, and faked a roundhouse right to his bloody head. "How's your bike?"

*   *   *

One of my bad bike spills was caused by a bottle of milk, which I had dangling in a cloth sack under my handlebars. While I was going at a goodly pace, the sack jammed between my front wheel and the handlebars, throwing down the bike and me instantly. Unfortunately, the glass milk bottle shattered under me, giving me some nasty cuts. Probably as regrettable for my folks was that the glass also lacerated a good pair of school pants. Against the rules, I had neglected to change them before my trip to the neighbors' for the milk.

The worst spill I experienced was on a spring night while returning home with a visiting friend, Verlan Moore, after evening roller skating at the Community Hall. We rode double on my bike, with Verlan pedaling and I seated sideways on the crossbar. The night was very dark. For most of the way, we could tell our location in the asphalt road only by the slightly lighter gravel berms.

We started down the steepest hill on our route, and Verlan had just finished pumping the pedals so we could coast a long way. I was enjoying the speed and the hum of the balloon tires on the asphalt when—bam!—an unseen barrier threw us through the blackness. We bounced and skidded and rolled down the roadway. Each new impact with the asphalt brought a jolt of pain. As I tumbled, I glimpsed sparks from my bouncing bike. In the blackness, I heard screams and groans, including my own.

Verlan and I found we could walk—sort of. We gathered ourselves and painfully made our way back to the "obstacle" in the road. It turned out to be a sobbing, moaning older schoolmate of mine, Jeanette "Tiny" Berg, being comforted by two other girls. The trio had been walking in the middle of the road, chatting, when Verlan and I crested the hill. Neither the girls nor we heard the others. When they finally realized we were speeding toward them in the blackness, they had no time to jump aside. Tiny had instinctively put her hands out and hit the handlebar, flipping our front wheel sideways and sending us tumbling. As her nickname implies, Tiny was a slender, small-boned girl, and the impact sent her flying, too. She suffered a broken collarbone and internal injuries which, fortunately, healed well. Daddy scraped together money to help pay her doctor bill.

Verlan crashed the hardest with the bike. He suffered a massive scrape on one shoulder blade, other cuts and bruises, and a nasty head wound with imbedded gravel. He was groggy for a day or two, but refused to be taken to a doctor.

I got off luckier. My sidesaddle position on the bike allowed me to instinctively curl and tumble, and also afforded protection between the bike frame and Verlan. Still, I too was bruised and skinned. And for weeks after that crash, when riding in our car after dark, I would cringe whenever Daddy gave the car a burst of speed.

As for my sturdy bike, it survived the crash with little apparent damage.

THE BIG FREEZE

Late October, 1935, was a crisis time for our family, a "tipping point" for the shaky ladder my folks had climbed to achieve what we had. A mass of sub-freezing air suddenly moved in and settled over the region.

In our valley, many apple crops—including most of ours and Grandma Lillian's—were still in the orchards.

If the weather had then warmed gradually, as usually happened after the first freeze of the fall, the apples could have thawed slowly and might have been marketable. Instead, the cold persisted and deepened. Overnight on October 30, temperatures dropped to single digits. Unprotected fruit froze solid.

Reporter Karl Stoffel of *The Daily World*, as the Wenatchee paper was then named, told the story in greater detail than I remember [Bracketed inserts are mine.]:

Young Entiat Couple Move Out Of Home, Move Apples In:
Weather Man Wins, Crop Lost, House is Worse For Wear
But Foxworthys Have What It Takes To Grin and Bear It

By Karl Stoffel

The Foxworthys, Mr. and Mrs. G. L. and young son, live up the Entiat Valley about nine miles. They have a small orchard, about half a dozen acres, mostly Delicious and Romes [Rome Beauty variety]. They recently made an unusual, but unsuccessful attempt to defeat the "Weather Man."

The Foxworthys live on the ranch, but during the summer and fall, they work out quite a bit, he hauling with his truck and she packing. In-as-much [sic] as their orchard is

—Daily World Photo

In the top photo are Mr. and Mrs. Foxworthy, standing on the porch of their Entiat valley home. Inside the house are 1600 boxes of frozen apples. Outside are various pieces of furniture, beds, tables, chairs, etc. When it got cold they attempted to protect their small crop by moving it in the house, the only available storage space.

The bottom picture is a general view of the house. It was partially destroyed by fire last summer and had to be rebuilt.

—Daily World Photo

Newspaper photos of my folks at the rebuilt house on the home place, in which they tried to thaw the apple crop after the Big Freeze.

in a sheltered canyon and considerably higher than those of the lower districts, their apples do not color or mature as early as others and they are able to work out longer in the fall than would otherwise be the case.

This year they had both worked enough to pay the entire harvesting cost of their crop. Whatever their fruit returned would be profit with exception of a small seed loan.

Late in October Foxworthy color-picked some Delicious, about 500 boxes, and sold them. Just before the 28th he brought in a crew and picked most of the rest. There were a few left on the trees but most of the rest of them were in boxes in the orchard.

Filled The House

It got cold. Then it got colder and for three days those apples were subjected to near-zero temperatures. Foxworthy had them covered up and came to Wenatchee to the Hort [Horticulture] office in an effort to find out how to handle them. On the fourth day, with no letup in the cold wave predicted, he and his wife decided to do something. They had no warehouse on the place, nor any sheds. The only available storage place was in the house, a four-room frame building that had been only recently restored on the top story from a fire of last summer. But once they had made the decision, it was easy. They moved out the furniture and moved in the apples. Beds, tables, chairs, everything that was loose and in the way was moved outside. Boxes were stacked in, as high as the ceiling, in the bathroom, in the closets, in the bedrooms, and in every corner.

The house was not new and the floors creaked and sagged, but that didn't matter. The saved fruit would pay for the damage.

Family Moved Out

In part of one day and a night, 1600 boxes of apples were stored in the house. Mr. and Mrs. Foxworthy and their son moved down the road a few miles [actually, less than a mile] to a small house owned by his mother.

At the end of the cold wave, the temperature inside the house was gradually raised. The Foxworthys watched the apples. In top boxes the fruit began to thaw. The Romes wrinkled, then grew soft and spongy. The Delicious didn't look so bad.

Day before yesterday [Nov. 20], having heard of their efforts, I went up to see how things were stacking up at the Foxworthy's. Charles W. Apley of the Wenatchee Seed Loan Division was also there.

Things weren't so good.

Despite the fact that the apples had been handled carefully and no heat had been near them, the Romes were nearly 100 percent soft and squishy and juice was running out of them onto the floor. About half of the Delicious were also wrinkling and getting soft, although some of the center boxes looked very good, both on the surface and inside the apples. Several hundred boxes had [not] yet thawed out completely.

To make it even worse the moisture from the frozen fruit was penetrating the walls of the house rooms, causing them to buckle and warp. The floor was also sagging as the foundation had never been intended to hold up that much weight.

You might imagine that Mr. and Mrs. Foxworthy were pretty discouraged with things in general. But that wasn't so. He grinned ruefully and said, 'It doesn't look good, does it, particularly for that seed loan.'

Mrs. Foxworthy also smiled. 'We don't mind the house so much,' she said. 'That can be fixed all right. But the thing that hurts the worst is that all that work goes for nothing.'

They started moving out the bad ones and sorting out the good ones yesterday. They hope that the government will buy some of the so-called distressed fruit of this district. They hope, too, that they will be able to figure out some way to pay back that seed loan in order that their credit will be good next year.

They Have It

Foxworthy had shaken all the frozen fruit off the trees but is a little afraid that a heavy snow would still break down a lot of limbs since leaves are still sticking tight.

In recent months, I have talked to a number of pioneers in this district. Their stories of obstacles overcome, privations endured and the spirit that was existent in the early days, sounded sometimes unbelievable. There's not so much of that sort of thing seen in this day and age. That's the reason this story about the Foxworthys was particularly interesting. They have provided an example in fortitude that stands out like a lighthouse on a mountain. A lot of people could learn things from this young couple.

(Karl Stoffel , *The Daily World*, November 22, 1935)

* * *

Thus, the entire 1935 crop was lost, both ours and Grandma Lillian's, except for about five hundred boxes that Dad had picked and sold early.

A new frantic effort ensued. My folks hurriedly carried all those leaking boxes out and stacked them in our yard. Daddy then had the further depressing chore of dumping all those boxes, the crop they had worked so hard for, out near the river bank below our outhouse. Mamma had the equally distressing task of cleaning up the mess left inside the house. No matter how much she cleaned, or the cleaning agents she used, the house always thereafter smelled a bit like vinegar, from the soaked-in apple juice.

One irony is that my folks came so very close to escaping the disaster. As the Stoffel story noted, nearly all our crop had been picked, just awaiting removal from the orchard. Dad would have needed only two more days—three at most—to haul the filled boxes out to the safety of a warehouse. But instead he had chosen to haul the fruit of his customers.

Grim but determined. The last family photo, in Mamma's beloved dahlia garden, before we had to leave the home place.

RIVER SKATING

The winter of 1935 was historic in its early arrival and severity, and a rare thing happened—the Entiat River froze solid and thick and stayed that way for weeks.

The river surface froze in a beautiful way, as a series of flat shelves of smooth ice with rounded "waterfalls" dropping a couple of inches or so to the next lower surface. The river became a sinuous band of white-blue ice perhaps a hundred feet wide, frozen solidly to the rocks that protruded above the surface. Through our part of the valley, the glistening ice extended for miles between the snow-topped river banks, and for days the ice remained free of snow. It was, of course, a magnet for skaters of all ages.

Naturally, we kids were the first on the river. We had been impatiently testing the ice, against our parents' admonitions, since it was still danger-ously thin. For once I was rising early and eager on weekends, making my bed and hauling in the first supply of firewood without bidding while Mamma cooked oatmeal for breakfast. After gulping down this hot, "stick-to-your-ribs" meal, I could bundle up, grab my skates, and rush to meet my buddies somewhere on the river.

While we rosy-cheeked, runny-nosed boys—and an occasional sister—were flailing around the ice, spraddle-legged with ankles bent in, the grownups were busy with daily chores such as thawing and priming pumps to get the water in, shoveling snow, cooking and cleaning and washing (to let the clothes freeze-dry on the lines), feeding stock, and starting stub-born vehicles for essential trips on the snowy road.

Winter evenings, especially in times so cold that even starting a car was a major challenge, were times when the valley adults needed all the recre-ation they could contrive. So I guess it was only natural that Daddy, Aunt Achsa, and some neighbors should come up with the idea of a nighttime skating party.

Arrangements were made, and the men stacked bonfire wood at stra-tegic places along the riverbanks. The evening of the party, kids were put down for naps so we could stay up late. I could barely eat supper, let alone wait for darkness.

When I was finally allowed to go to the river and clamp on my skates, the bonfires were flaring up along the riverbanks. Magically, neighbors began appearing on the ice, bundled up against the cold, skating with all manner of equipment, some pulling kids on sleds. They happily greeted each other, perhaps for the first time in months, and many clustered by the bonfires, talking.

I hadn't heard the term, "winter wonderland," but that is what it was. The darkness and the flickering fires transformed daytime's dull scene. Now we had mystery and adventure. The streamside trees, no longer ordinary, now reached out as shapes that made me veer away when I skated past. The dancing bonfire flames made flickering orange streaks on the ice, and threw long shadows of protruding rocks and bundled skaters. The air was still and very cold, scented only by the bonfires. Crispy sounds of our digging skate blades, and our high-pitched childish banter, echoed between the river banks as we stroked along the ribbon of ice. From the firesides came rumbling conversations of the grownups, punctuated by eruptions of laughter—and occasional ringing of dinner bells. At intervals through the evening, one or another of the neighbors rang these bells to call the skaters for riverside treats and beverages. Mamma went all out, offering cookies, cocoa, and coffee.

Some of us kids literally skated miles that night—up river to Packwood's bridge, down to Johnson's bridge, and back again, and then again. We raced, and rested, and circled around the protruding rocks, which showed clearly in contrast to the white ice, even in the dark reaches between the fires.

Most of the young skaters were boys, although an unusual number of girls showed up that night. One younger girl stuck close to me. She was cute, but I was at an age (not quite ten) when younger girls were about as attractive as dog scraps. Besides, she was constantly snuffling with a runny nose.

"Ooh!" I finally said, pointing. "Did you see that rock move? I've heard that some of the round ones are really the heads of river gnomes that come up from the underworld to kidnap girls."

The reaction to my ridiculous ploy was immediate.

"Mamma! Mammaaaa!" She flailed the ice frantically getting to the nearest fire, and disappeared for the evening. A couple of guys skated over and demanded to know what I'd said, so they could use it on their sisters.

I'm sure I was one of the loudest whiners when we kids were finally called in as the bonfires died down. The experience was just too good to leave, almost a magic tale come true, a night I shall never forget.

That evening was the more notable because it came after the early freeze in October of that year, when most of our apple crop and those of some neighbors were frozen and ruined. That night, while those folks drank coffee and chatted pleasantly around the fires, they knew that some of them faced financial ruin, with loss of ranches built up from nothing. Yet, then or later, I heard no bitter complaints, no railing against God or Nature, no wails of "Why me?" All I sensed that night was the warmth of neighbors gathered, the celebration of community, and the joy of living in our valley.

THE DOWNWARD SPIRAL

I had never seen Daddy in despair before, and I only saw it that once. I don't even remember exactly when, except that it was after we had lost our apple crop to the Big Freeze of October 1935.

Something woke me one night, and I noticed light coming from the living room. I slipped out of bed and peeked around the doorway.

Daddy was seated at our big table with his head in his hands. His whole posture spoke of tragedy. His ledger book with the green lines and black number columns lay on the table in front of him.

Shocked at the sight, I slipped back to bed, where I listened intently and wondered what it meant. Finally, the light went out and Daddy came through into his and Mamma's bedroom. Somehow, that reassured me enough so that I went back to sleep.

A day or two later, Daddy sat me down and began talking about land ownership, and buying on credit, and interest on borrowed money, and mortgages, and yearly payments to the bank. I think I understood most of it.

"Because of the hard times," Daddy said, "the bank's been letting us pay just the interest on our mortgage. But after we lost this year's crop, we can't pay even that. I talked to the bank, but they can't give us any more time. They're in trouble, too."

"But can't we get money from another bank, Daddy?"

"I wish we could, but we have no way to guarantee another loan. And we still owe for a government seed loan. We can't pay that off, either. We just have to wait and see what's going to happen."

I learned later that ours was far from the only fruit ranch in trouble. Other mortgages, like ours, had been assumed when interest rates were relatively high during the 1920s. Now that apple prices and consumer buying power were down, while packing and warehousing costs had climbed, those high mortgage payments were hard to meet. Several families in the valley were on the verge of losing homes and orchards.

But of course I didn't know all this when Daddy took me aside again.

"We've lost our home place, Son. The bank's foreclosing. We have to move."

"But where will we live, Daddy?" The enormity of it all was just sinking in.

"Your mother and I are looking for a place. We haven't found one yet. But we'll be okay—you'll see," Daddy added with a grin and a reassuring tousling of my hair.

The need to move should not have shocked me. Moves had been happening often on both sides of our family. On the Bedient side, Grandpa Albert had quit trying to find work in his printing profession, and had moved with Grandma and my uncle Max from one large orchard to another, where Grandpa did orchard work and Grandma cooked at company bunkhouses in exchange for their family's room and board. The families of Mamma's siblings were similarly moving around, following jobs and cheap housing.

On the Foxworthy side, Grandma Lillian had sold her little ranch to a single man named Stutzman, and had moved with Aunt Achsa into a small rental cabin just across the Entiat River, on the Johnson property. Shortly thereafter, Achsa married Frank Cook, and the couple first moved to a tiny house provided by the Harris mill, where Frank worked. But when the Gofinch's Zebra House became empty, Frank and Achsa moved there, across the road from our home place. They lived there for years, and frequently took care of me there, especially while my folks worked during harvest time.

In the meantime, Mr. Stutzman defaulted on his payments to Grandma Lillian, and she had to take back her little ranch. She moved back into her old house, this time by herself.

That was the situation when we lost the home place—Frank and Achsa in Zebra House, which was too small for my folks and me anyway, and Grandma Lillian back in her little house.

LIFE IN A BARN

My folks, having lost the home place, and without even seed-loan money which in former years had provided us with essentials until each harvest time, now could do no better than to move us into the empty hayloft of Grandma Lillian's old barn.

Unpainted and weathered brown like the rest of Grandma's outbuildings, the barn was larger than her house. Its dirt-floor lower level had once sheltered a team of horses and a cow, plus harness and assorted farm implements. Some pieces remained as disintegrating junk. Weeds grew abundantly outside the stone foundation. When considered as a home, that aging barn seemed a dismal prospect.

It was sturdily built, however, with a solid, open stairway to the empty loft. The lower landing of the stairs was near the wide, front door on the building's upstream side—the side facing the driveway to Grandma's house, some four hundred feet north. The ease of access helped greatly in moving our belongings up to the loft.

The loft was more expansive than the house we left, and unrestricted except for four timber posts that supported the roof trusses. One end, the end facing the valley road, had a large opening with swinging doors. The opposite end of the loft also had an opening, a horizontal, shutter-less "window" that overlooked the river and part of the Johnson property across the river. The sides of the loft floor extended all the way to the sloping roof rafters. Age had color-coordinated the loft's interior into shades of brown and gray.

Before moving in, we had to displace the previous tenants—a few families of swallows in roof niches, and a large family of gray rats. Even with the big loft doors swung shut, the swallows had free access through the opening in the opposite end. The rats ran through the place at will, up the walls and across the rafters as freely as on the floors and stairway. Poor Mamma jumped and shuddered every time she saw one of the fleeting gray shapes.

My dog Prince, an inveterate killer of rodents since he could waddle into the orchard after gophers, started hunting the moment he arrived. While Prince yapped and dug after the rats, Daddy brought up an orchard ladder and knocked down the mud nests of the swallows with a pole, and then swept off the rafters with Mamma's broom.

No one knew the dangers of rodent droppings then, and Mamma raised clouds of dust in her haste to sweep out the accumulation of dirt and animal waste from the loft floor. I was sent to the nearby river with a bucket to carry up water for her to scrub with. I lugged bucket after bucket of water up the stairs and splashed water where Mamma pointed, after which she chased the water vigorously with her broom across the bare wood. Trip after puffing trip I made, and yet she demanded more. As I struggled up the stairs with each heavy water bucket, Mamma's previous scrub water would still be raining down through cracks in the loft floor.

Just when I felt I could not make one more trip up those stairs, Mamma finally declared "That's clean enough for now." We got to rest a few minutes, sitting on the stairs, before Daddy arrived in his truck with the first load of our furniture.

Over the next few days, we gradually moved into the loft. We walked over to Grandma's house to wash up and eat our meals. Cooking there was a pleasure because Mr. Stutzman had installed an incredible luxury—an electric stove complete with oven. No longer did Grandma have to sweat through meal preparation over a hot wood stove.

As we hauled our belonging from the old house and yard, I asked Daddy what all we were going to take.

"Everything that isn't fastened down. That's what the law allows, and that's what we're going to do."

I wasn't much help with the heavy things. These included our kitchen stove and our bed-davenport, both of which we used as long as I can remember. From the house, things could be just carried or skidded onto the truck from our back porch, but at the barn, getting things up into the loft was sometimes a challenge. Fortunately, Daddy had a strong back and was clever with hoists and levers and skids, and Mamma and I helped as we could.

As we brought the fixtures of our life from the home place, my folks also worked long and hard to make the loft more livable. Using lumber salvaged from the rebuilding after our house fire, they erected free-standing walls that divided the loft into three spaces. A large room at the end overlooking the river was designated kitchen and living room. Next to that was a smaller space for my folks' bedroom.

"Do I get a room, too?" I asked tentatively.

"Son," Daddy answered with a smile, "You'll have the biggest room of all—the whole rest of the loft. We'll put up a rod over there to hang clothes on, and you can have all the rest."

That was not strictly true, because we always had storage boxes along the edges of the loft under the rafters, but I claimed most of the end nearest the valley road, which had the wide swinging doors overlooking an old corral. This was a fine arrangement for me. I could reach the stairs without going through the rooms. Also, I could stand in the loft doorway and sneak a pee out onto the corral ground below, being careful, of course, to watch for traffic on the adjacent road. Later, I got the idea to hang a rope from the big door frame and use that to slide down for quick exit to the ground, as for urgent trips to the outhouse. Fortunately, a crude one-holer was already there behind the barn when we moved in, and only needed the repair of a sagging door.

At first, the only privacy Mamma had to dress and use the chamber pot was afforded by sheets and bedspreads she hung on the bare 2 x 4 frame-work. Later, we got large cardboard boxes from Cooper's Store and Entiat businesses, opened them flat and tacked them up to separate the "rooms," leaving curtained doorways for access.

Daddy framed the opening in the "kitchen" wall to accept an old sash window, turned sideways so it would slide open horizontally. He also nailed up apple boxes for cupboards and built a counter, with shelves underneath, beneath the window. We had muscled our old kitchen stove up the stairs and into place, and Daddy sawed a hole in the barn wall to vent the stovepipe. Now we could heat that room, as well as cook and eat there. Later, to reduce air drafts into the kitchen (and also hamper the access of rats), Daddy framed an old, cream-colored door into the doorway he had made at the top stair landing. Mamma put up her old kitchen curtains to brighten the place.

Daddy somehow acquired an old, chipped enamel sink and mounted it into the counter top below the kitchen window, then hooked up a drain pipe that spilled out onto the sand at the base of the barn. In that dreary, makeshift kitchen, my mother had her first draining sink after eleven years of marriage. Never mind that our water for cooking and drinking was dipped from the same, familiar enameled bucket sitting on this makeshift counter. To Mamma, that draining sink was a precious gift.

We got our kitchen water from Grandma's well and kept it in a corner of the kitchen in a five-gallon, metal milk can. Daddy brought the filled water can in the car or on the truck. Our bath water was dipped from the river, mostly by me. We needed four or five bucketsful for baths in our big, round, galvanized tub.

The kitchen stove provided satisfactory heat for that room, even during the coldest weather, as I recall, and Mamma could open the curtains of the doorway to my folks' bedroom to "take the chill off" there. That surprises me in retrospect, because our cardboard-walled rooms had no ceilings, and we never installed our old heating stove. Bringing up the firewood was my chore, as it had been at the home place.

Of course, the stove's heat never extended to the part of the loft where I slept. I don't remember ever sleeping cold, however, and got used to the weight of several blankets pressing on me while in bed.

Fortunately, the barn had been connected for electric service, although when we moved in it had only one bare light bulb hanging high in the loft and another one down below. Daddy rewired enough to provide bright lights over the stairs and in the kitchen-living area, and installed a plug-in receptacle for our radio and Mamma's iron. Mamma ran an extension cord for a bedside lamp in their room. I don't remember having extra light in my space.

We cleaned out everything from our yard, barn, and old house that was not attached. In those days, one did not discard anything that might be useful later. Some of the stuff, like Dad's old cars and the salvaged lumber and metal scraps, went out of sight behind the barn. The produce and jars of canned food from our dirt cellar, of course, went into Grandma's cellar, below the old cellar house where we had once lived. Furniture, fixtures, and odds-and-ends that didn't immediately go into the loft were stored on the ground floor of the barn.

Among the things I brought were my collection of model airplanes. I remember setting them out on my bed and looking around the loft for places to put them. I think that was the first time, perhaps the only time, I actually cried about our forced move from the home place. Then I shut off the tears, wiped my eyes, and decided that my model planes would look silly hanging way up there among the dusty, brown barn rafters. The next time we visited my aunt and uncle Lanoue, I gave the planes to my young cousin, Gary, and helped to hang them in his bedroom.

I grew up a lot during our first months in the barn. I still rode my bike to Ardenvoir School, now nearly three miles one way, but I felt embarrassed among my schoolmates and teachers, and even with our neighbors. After the newspaper story about the loss of our apple crop to the Big Freeze, almost everyone in the valley knew of our bad luck, and word spread fast about the foreclosure and our move into the barn. Though never well off, we had been property owners at least, one of the valley's established families. Now we were reduced to living in a barn with spiders and flies and rats. For the first time, I could appreciate the plight of other valley families living a notch or two above squalor.

As ashamed as I felt at times about of our situation, I'm sure my parents must have felt greater discouragement. They showed me, however, that we all had to face up to the challenges of doing what was needed.

I had finally overcome my inherent shyness—at being small, at having been sickly, at being a "Brucie"—only to feel this new stigma of our fall from status. I felt it most when well-intentioned neighbors offered hand-me-down school clothes. Another blow came when the bank moved the

Morrow family onto our home place to care for the orchard, and the Morrow kids became ever-present reminders at my school. For a while I withdrew from all but my closest buddies. I retreated into books and daydreams and schoolwork, determined to do better with my future than risk it to the vagaries of fruit-ranching.

Prince was my great solace, the one companion I could confide in with complete safety. When I told him my secret feelings, he watched my face intently and tried so very hard to understand that sometimes I almost thought he could. And a boy can always hug a dog, when a hug is needed, without appearing sissified.

Prince also pleased Mamma with his marvelous job as rat eradicator. We only had to say "Rat, Prince. Rat!" and he would snap to attention, darting his eyes around the barn rafters and corners of the loft. If he saw no movement in the loft, he would dash down to the lower level and rummage around where he could smell the rats' presence, barking in his attempt to startle the rodents into showing themselves. I must admit that we took advantage of Prince's reaction to the "Rat!" command, showing it off to relatives and neighbors. I feel sure, however, that the dog enjoyed playing the game, even when he knew, better than we, whether potential prey was there.

The only part of Prince's success at killing rats that Mamma didn't like was his delivery of the carcasses. When the black-and-white dog brought up a dead rat to show us in the loft, we could do no less than heap on praise of "Good boy!" and petting. Prince, of course, basked in the praise, responding with panting, tail-wagging dog-laughs. But when we weren't around for the delivery, he left the carcasses on the top stair landing.

One morning while still in bed, I heard a shriek.

"Mamma! What's wrong?" I leaped from bed and dashed toward the sound. Mamma stood frozen in the doorway at the top of the stairs, with one hand over her mouth and the other pointing down. Where she pointed, on the top step, lay not one, but two dead rats.

"I-I almost stepped on them," she said with a shudder.

That time, I was the only one who praised my dog.

It was a relief to everyone except Prince when, after a few months of our move into the loft, we never again saw signs of rats.

Disposal of the dead rats was no problem. Grandma had two half-grown pigs. I think, like the electric stove, they had been left behind by Mr. Stutzman. Daddy simply fed the rat carcasses to the pigs which, of course, we later butchered for the meat.

Few non-farm people realize what valuable waste-disposal functions hogs provide, eating anything from vegetable peelings to the entrails of butchered small animals. Hogs also will clear out unwanted vegetation. They are one of the most effective eradicators of Poison Ivy, to which Mamma was especially susceptible. After the hogs eat the leaves and branches above ground, they will root out and pull up the rest. They seem to enjoy the activity. Daddy put the hogs in a movable pen and used them to eradicate Poison Ivy from a part of Grandma's riverbank where the plants had flourished, so that Mamma could safely pass by without getting a rash from just the sun-warmed vapors of the shrub's oily poison.

Not everything about our move into the barn was bad. Grandma welcomed our close presence, and we were able to help her a lot. Mamma and Grandma shared some of the cooking, most clothes washing, and the canning of Grandma's garden vegetables. Daddy was right there with more time to tend her orchard, instead of having to fit that work in between orchard tasks at the home place and his hauling jobs. And the barn had a big, sturdy workbench on the lower level, where Daddy and I could work on our projects under shelter and in the light of an electric bulb.

We had fun times, too, while living in the barn. Like having picnics in Grandma's front yard—the only patch of lawn remaining in the entire family. And we still had family fishing trips, and I got well acquainted with the fishing holes in the reach of the river skirting Grandma's place. Also, I was now much closer to a favorite swimming hole, just beyond one hill down the valley road.

The winter I turned eleven, I went on my first wood party into the National Forest with my Uncle Max and several family men. We found a nice fallen tree, which the men cut into moveable lengths and rolled up inclined planks onto Daddy's truck. In the loading, Grandpa Bedient strained so hard he suffered a hernia, which caused him to wear an abdominal truss the rest of his life. He refused to quit that day, though, and went back on a second trip for the rest of the tree.

In Grandma's back yard, Daddy unloaded our share—two log sections. I was given the task of cutting the logs into manageable "rounds" and splitting them for firewood to supply us and Grandma. I became proficient with our one-man crosscut saw, and truly enjoyed cutting each round from the log. Daddy taught me how to "read the wood" to split it. However, being small and poor at hitting the same spot twice with an axe, I did most of my splitting with a steel wedge and sledge hammer. That was slow, but it worked well for me, and I took great pride in our growing woodpiles.

Toward the end of the log-sawing, however, I got careless with the razor-sharp crosscut saw. I let it slip down and slice through the leather toe of new winter boots my folks had scrimped to buy for me. I tried to hide the accident, and the next day I walked to and from school in the snow, putting up with a wet, cold foot all day. Inevitably, my folks noticed the wet boot, and spotted the gash. As I confessed my carelessness, I expected doom, but they accepted it quite calmly. I wore some patched galoshes over tennis shoes for a couple of days, until Daddy took my boot to the saddle maker in Entiat for repair. My boot came back with a prominent patch of leather, not quite the same color, stitched onto the toe. I was ashamed of that patch, to me another badge of our decline, but had no choice but to wear the boots.

That and other experiences during our sojourn in the barn brought home to me the true value of money. Fortunately, Daddy still had his truck and could count on his hauling customers to keep him as busy as they could, and I feel sure they tried to pay him promptly because of our situation. Also, Mamma could count on her packing job in the fall. But until the harvest work, money was mighty tight. I don't remember ever going hungry, so I suppose we weren't really in poverty, although at times I wondered whether the word "poor" might apply to us.

After we had been in the barn loft for a while, Grandma Lillian traveled by train to visit her family in Indiana. While she was gone we moved to her house. We were staying there when her orchard received some unwanted nighttime visitors.

THE CAR COLLECTOR

Booze and automobiles mated during Prohibition, and this marriage remained strong after alcohol became legal again in 1933. During our up-valley days, a common occurrence was for folks to drink up their alcoholic beverage at a Community Hall dance and then make a night-time speed run down valley to replenish their supply. Occasionally, they didn't reach their goal.

The upstream end of Grandma Lillian's lower orchard adjoined the Entiat River Road at a tricky curve in the graveled roadway, a special nemesis for impaired drivers rushing to get more booze. Not surprisingly, the adjacent part of Grandma's orchard was something of a collecting ground for Saturday night wrecks.

The worst crash into the orchard happened while we were living on her property when I was about eleven. The crash woke us, and Dad guessed at once what it was. He grabbed his long-barreled flashlight and ran out the door in his gray long johns. I, in my pajamas, tore into the orchard after Dad's bobbing light, unmindful of the muddy dirt under my bare feet. Mamma followed in her robe and slippers.

When we arrived at the site, a late-model, yellow Chrysler sedan lay on its side with its steaming, crumpled nose against the trunk of a big Winesap tree. One of the wreck's headlights was still shining and a front wheel was still spinning. Dust covered everything. The smell of gasoline was strong.

Two young men were stumbling around, obviously drunk or in shock. Both of them had bloody heads and faces. Another guy was crawling from the wreck through a back window.

Mamma, bless her, was most concerned about injuries. We helped the bloody men sit down. Dad held the light while Mamma quickly examined their gory heads. "They're not as bad as they look," she said finally, mopping blood off with their shirttails.

The uninjured guy said friends were following in another car and could take them for treatment. He and Dad scrambled up the road bank and, when a car came along, Dad flagged it down with his flashlight. The three from the wreck quickly piled into that car and were driven away. My folks and I walked back to the house and relived the adventure until we got sleepy.

The next morning, we learned just how lucky the driver and front-seat passenger had been. When they showed up with two other men in a small truck, we saw only bruises and a scattering of black stitches on their heads and faces. What *they* saw was that Dad had chained the Chrysler to the Winesap tree and secured it with a padlock.

I kept a respectful distance from the confrontation but close enough to hear. The conversation went something like this:

"How come you chained up my car?" the driver demanded.

"It damaged my tree," Dad replied calmly. "You can have your car back when you pay for the damage."

"It's just a damn old apple tree. They ain't worth nothin' nowadays."

"Wrong," Dad countered. "That's a valuable tree in prime production— or was. No tellin' how much harm you caused. The car is mine until you pay the damages."

A stocky fellow who had not been in the wreck shouldered forward. "I say we just cut the chain and take your car back. Whataya say to that, Shorty?" he added, addressing Dad.

Dad shrugged. "Then it would be a job for the sheriff."

"Well, I do have insurance," the driver said.

Dad perked up like a cat spotting a field mouse. Most cars were not insured in those days.

"Fine," said Dad, with an amiable smile. "Send your insurance man around, and we'll get this settled quick. And you're welcome to take any tools and personal stuff from the wreck."

Next afternoon, a shiny, black Studebaker sedan drove into the back yard. The driver, a portly, sleek-looking man wearing a grey suit and tie and a grey, felt fedora, pushed himself out of the car. Dad stepped out the back door dressed in grubby overalls and shook hands with him. I stared at the heavy gold chain draped across the fellow's ample vest as he introduced himself. Then I noticed the pearl-grey spats over his shiny black shoes.

Spats? I had seen them before, but only in a city, certainly not in our dusty back yard.

The insurance man was affable, and Dad was polite too, but I already knew that this guy was in for a hard time. Dad did not like citified dandies, and this one defined the breed. He even reeked of Bay Rum.

"I see you are holding the automobile of one of my clients," the insurance man said with an excessive smile, offering Dad a fat cigar. "I looked over the scene from the road."

"Then you saw the damage that car did to one of my best apple trees," Dad said with a somber face as he waved off the cigar. "No doubt you saw how the tree is leaning, indicating broken roots and little chance that tree will survive. That means the cost of pulling the dead tree and replanting with a sapling that won't be in full bearing for ten-twelve years. You also must have seen the heavy load of fruit on the limbs—probably thirty boxes of fruit lost this year. And that tree was in the prime of its bearing, probably good for another twenty years. That's a lot of income your client cost us."

I'll give the insurance man credit. His smile hardly wavered as Dad piled on the damages. I had to look away when Dad mentioned the thirty boxes. A thirty-box crop from that tree would qualify as a miracle.

"Well, uh, I see," the insurance man said. Have you thought about your loss in terms of a cash amount?"

Dad looked down at the dirt and shook his head as if the next words were painful. "Yes, I figure the overall loss to be around twelve hundred dollars."

I gasped. That amount would buy two brand-new Fords!

The insurance man's smile vanished. "Surely, the loss can't be that much with the price of apples so low."

"But y'see," Dad said, shaking his head solemnly, "the big loss is in the future. The President says the economy is improving, and soon the fruit market will be back where it was. With apple trees, it's all about the future. Come on out to the wreck, and I'll show you the dyin' tree."

I looked away again to smile. Dad knew this dandy would never risk his spats to a walk through irrigation mud. He'd have to take Dad's word for the damage.

The insurance man suggested they talk in the house, instead.

"Sure, come on in," Dad agreed. "We'll get some lemonade goin' and we can talk it over."

I was dying to listen in, but I wasn't invited and I knew better than to impose myself. Instead, as soon as the two men entered the house I went over and studied every visible feature of the Studebaker, not touching anything, of course.

I had plenty of time, for the men didn't come out for maybe an hour. When they emerged, both wore smiles. The insurance man lit up another big cigar and again offered one to Dad. Again Dad declined before they shook hands amiably. As the insurance man approached his car, he reached into a vest pocket and flipped me a nickel. "This is for you, young man," he said with a smile as I plucked the nickel from the air.

"Th-thanks," I managed to stammer as he got into the shiny car and started it. He and Dad exchanged waves, and the Studebaker eased out down the driveway.

My head snapped around toward Dad. His grin had his gold tooth gleaming in the sun. "Did he pay, Daddy?"

"Oh yes, Son, he paid. Come on in, and I'll show you something."

Mamma, wearing a drab apron and a happy smile, was holding a bank check when we entered the kitchen. She handed it to Dad, who held it so I could see.

"Wow! Four hundred dollars! But you said twelve hundred earlier."

Dad ruffled my hair, a sure sign of his good mood. "Son, that was just to get the dickering started. I never expected that much in the end. You always want to start way high, so you can let the other fellow think he's beat you down. Then he'll be happier with the final deal."

Later, after the owner and his friends had towed the wreck away, I asked Dad just how little he would have settled for. Dad just smiled, and never did give me an answer.

The Winesap tree survived, although it was droopy for a while. Dad used his truck to pull it upright. He patched the gouged areas with grafting wax and pruning paint, and gave it extra fertilizer. It never produced the apple crops it had before, but it was very productive nonetheless.

You see, during the next two years, Dad "sold" that same Winesap tree twice more to errant drivers.

A MEMORABLE PICNIC

During the spring of 1937, when my buddy Dick Shumway had just graduated from the eighth grade at Ardenvoir School and I had finished the seventh, our teacher, Kenneth Long, rewarded us two boys for our good scholarship by leading us on a horseback ride. Other factors may have shaped his kindness, such as the fact that we were both only children in families that were living rough at the time.

For this exciting trek, we boys had to provide lunches for ourselves, and I had to borrow a horse. Our neighbor Art Johnson kindly loaned me his medium-size sorrel, named Duke. Dick used a horse from Mr. Long's family. Both horses came with saddles, although the one on Duke was more of a big leather perch than a decent fit for me. We assembled at the schoolyard and rode off walking the horses up valley along the shoulder of the graveled road.

The weather was beautiful and the ride up valley was great. In those days, traffic was light, and vehicle drivers had the courtesy to slow and give horses a wide path. Mr. Long relaxed from his classroom reserve and acted more like just an older kid. However, he was still teacher enough to point out interesting features along the way, and to give us some background about pioneer home sites as we passed. At some point, he led us off the main valley road to ride up a switch-back trail onto the southwest flank of the valley. There, we found an upland meadow where we stopped for lunch.

We released the horses to graze and sat in the warm grass to eat. Mr. Long surprised us by offering Dick and me each a can of delicious kippered herring (my first) and a block of Baker's milk chocolate. That kindness turned our plain lunches into small feasts.

With the last crumbs of lunches gone and everyone in a happy mood, Mr. Long decided it was time to hit the back trail. I hopped up and trotted over to where the horses were grazing. I kept on trotting around the back end of Duke to reach his left, or mounting side.

The startled horse kicked out with both rear legs precisely as I rounded his rear. He caught me with both hooves to my chest and sent me skyward. Dick estimated that I flew twelve feet before landing in a bush.

I remember being in the middle of that bush, down on my back. I knew I hadn't died but was sure I *was* dying.

Mr. Long dashed in and pulled me from the bush. He started rhythmically lifting on my belt to help me breathe. But I did not feel the help. Of all that air around me, I didn't seem to be getting any. I was smothering with nothing over my face.

Finally, aided by adrenalin of panic, I resumed breathing on my own. I never, since, had the breath knocked out of me for so agonizingly long.

We determined that I had no broken bones or other immobilizing injuries, but I was fighting back tears from abdominal pain. I could not rest for long, however. We had no choice but to mount up and ride back the way we came.

Needless to say, the ride back for me seemed endless. I sat clutching the saddle horn and reins, hunched forward and feeling every single step Duke took, tensing stomach muscles against the pain and taking only quick gasps when I had to breathe. Riding was a little easier after we got back down the trail to the valley road. From there, Dick said, we still had about seven miles to home. Fortunately, Duke walked along docilely with the other horses, so I didn't have to rein him much.

By the time we reached the schoolyard, I knew I would survive, and assured Mr. Long and Dick they needn't accompany me home. Good old Duke continued an easy homeward walk, and I had no problem riding on alone.

Unfortunately, nobody was home at the Johnson's when I arrived, so I rode Duke directly into his corral behind their barn.

Never was I so glad to slide down off a horse, and Duke seemed plenty happy to have the saddle off, after I'd walked him into the barn as close to the harness rack as I could. I tensed my battered muscles to hoist the heavy saddle up onto the rail where it was stored—then collapsed onto a nearby hay bale and cried like a baby from the pain.

Duke clomped close, reached his head out to me, and snorted.

"It's okay, boy," I told him. "It was my fault for running up behind you. I'll never do that again. But you're going to have to go without a rubdown."

Home at the time was the barn loft at Grandma Lillian's place, just across the river. As I hobbled across Johnson's wooden bridge, I could see that my folk's car was gone. Only my dog Prince was there to greet me.

The rigors of the day, topped off with the painful climb up the barn stairs, had exhausted me. I wrote a note saying I was going to bed early. To keep Mom from waking me as soon as she returned, I didn't mention being kicked.

When I took my shirt off to go to bed, two distinct imprints of horse-shoes showed in red on my chest, perfectly spaced on either side of my breastbone. If the hooves had struck me anywhere but over the strongest parts of my ribs, and if I hadn't been small and light enough to fly, the kicks could have killed me.

Surprisingly, I awoke the next morning with little pain, and had no lasting effects from that "adventure." I told my folks about the mishap the next morning at breakfast, and meekly accepted their scolding about being careful around large animals.

INCOME—ANY INCOME

My parents never passed up a chance to earn an honest dollar—or an honest penny, for that matter. I was brought up to believe that any job, no matter how menial or miserable, is an opportunity and not a hardship; that from every job we learn something which is useful later in life; and that we should finish every job on good terms with the boss. I still believe in these principles.

In this spirit, Dad worked at many jobs, some of them while trying to keep two small orchards afloat. Mamma and I, too, sought out various paying jobs, especially after the loss of our home place to foreclosure.

Dad's jobs included orchard work for other growers; short stints at the Harris mill; rebuilding and selling used cars and their parts; and making "puddle jumpers" (orchard tractors) from old cars in our back yard. He also worked briefly for the federal Public Works Administration (PWA) during construction of Ardenvoir School.

For a short time while we lived in the barn loft, Dad went on the road for Montgomery Ward, selling tires, batteries, and home appliances in the Methow Valley of north-central Washington. I remember that period well—Dad driving out in the old Pontiac after an early breakfast on Mondays, leaving me as "the man of the house" and Mamma without a car. Then his homecomings on Saturdays, hungry, with stories about his week and a suitcase of dirty clothes for Mamma to wash. He might also stop overnight at home during the week, if he had to visit the Ward's store in Wenatchee.

The Methow Valley, whose mouth lies nearly forty miles north of Entiat, is roughly seventy miles long. It was sparsely populated then, with farms and towns scattered through more than fifty miles of its length. Its sparse population and long driving distances made the Methow Valley an unpromising sales territory, but it was the company's only area available for a new salesman.

Dad got no base salary or travel expenses—just a ten-percent commission on what he sold. Because of the long drives involved, he probably would not have been able to even start the job had he not gotten his gasoline and oil on credit from Mamma's uncle, Ben Zesiger, who owned the Shell service station in Entiat.

From the start, Dad had no illusions about the job. "The few that are interested in buying always want to dicker on the price," he complained. "And with the store's fixed prices, I've got nothin' to dicker with, except my commission. And I'm sure not makin' enough to play with that."

Dad surely could not impress the public with his prosperity. Even his best clothes had seen better days, and all he had to drive was our road-worn 1928 Pontiac sedan, at least eight years old by then. Dad was vague about where he stayed while on the road, a fact I didn't think much about at the time. I learned later about a few low-cost hotels and tourist cabins in his territory, but I think Dad sometimes slept in his car, and bathed and shaved in the cold water of the Methow River.

About all that Dad had going for him while selling for Montgomery Ward was hard work and long hours, his knowledge about cars and trucks and what they needed, and being forthright with his customers.

"One fellow was mad at his old battery because it wouldn't hold a charge," Dad told us. "He'd taken it to the garage three times to get it charged up but, after he'd put it back in his rig, it would gradually run down. He was all set to buy a new battery from me when I noticed his fan belt was a little loose and probably slippin' in the generator pulley. His generator just wasn't spinnin' fast enough to keep his battery charged. All he needed was to tighten the fan belt.

"I didn't even get to sell him a new fan belt," Dad said ruefully. "But that's okay—he had two little kids and looked like he needed every nickel he could save."

As I recall, Dad lasted less than three months as a traveling salesman. It was our old Pontiac that did him in. Its front wheels got to shimmying so badly that even Dad, who was a master at breaking out of front-end shimmy, finally could no longer drive the Pontiac safely at anything near highway speed. He nursed the old car home, limping along the two-lane roads at very low speeds, stopping once to switch the front wheels to see if that would help. That last drive home consumed half a day from his territory to our barnyard. The Pontiac perched up on blocks for a couple of weeks before Dad could rebuild its front end, and he traded it away soon after. Fortunately, his truck was available for essential transport.

During those lean times, I'm not sure what kept us afloat, and Grandma Lillian too, unless it was money remaining from the insurance settlement for the crash into Grandma's Winesap tree. But before long, the fruit harvest, with its promise of better income, came along to lift us up.

Near the end of his sales career, Dad sold his only major appliance, a refrigerator. That sale not only netted his largest monthly commission—forty-some dollars, as I recall—but also resulted in a change to our lifestyle.

The purchasers, a young family near the town of Twisp, had outgrown their small refrigerator and wished to trade it in for a larger model. During arrangements for the sale, Dad noticed that the family had a pasture, but he didn't see any stock. His dickering alert clicked on.

"Nice pasture you've got there," Dad remarked. "Sure wish I had that in my back yard. We just lost our pasture, and now we have to get rid of our good old milk cow. No place to keep her."

Dad said he could tell exactly when the light went on in the other fellow's brain.

"That's too bad," the young husband said. . . . "Y' know, we've been hopin' to get a cow. Milk for the kids and all."

"What a coincidence," Dad said. "We've both got something we need to get rid of—me the cow, and you the old refrigerator, which probably isn't worth much to Wards as a trade-in. And I just happen to have a truck at home."

So, that's how we got our first electric refrigerator. Dad drove his truck to Wenatchee, picked up the customer's new refrigerator at the Montgomery Ward warehouse, and delivered it to Twisp, saving the customers a delivery charge. He hauled the little Coldspot fridge (Sears and Roebuck brand) home on the return trip. Then he and Mamma loaded Peggy onto the truck and delivered the cow to Twisp. It was one of those rare transactions that left all parties happy with the results. My folks and the Twisp family stayed in touch for years, and occasionally visited each other.

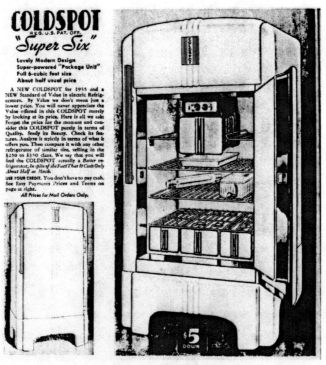

*Advertisement for the kind of refrigerator Dad acquired in trade
for our cow. It was Mamma's first electric refrigerator after
her years of challenge to preserve perishable foods.*

Mamma was delighted to have this first refrigerator we had owned. She would no longer have to struggle to preserve food in the cool river, the cellar, or the ice box. And she actually could make ice cubes and "refrigerator ice cream." A disappointment came, however, when we couldn't have the fridge with us in the barn loft. Dad didn't trust the wiring in the barn to handle the added load of a refrigerator, so we took the little fridge to Grandma's house. Consequently, I did a lot of running back and forth with food that needed to stay cold.

With Peggy gone, we had to buy milk from neighbors and butter from Cooper's store. But none of us regretted losing the chores of milking and tending the old cow.

*   *   *

Dad's greatest non-ranching income, by far, was from his trucking. He somehow always managed to have a truck, not only his beloved Model T Ford, which wouldn't carry much of a load, but also a succession of other trucks, none of which had a capacity rating larger than 1½ tons. During the leanest of times, he built one flat-bed truck from the wreckage of a large van (see "Peddling Apples").

Dad hauled almost everything imaginable for the local ranches and businesses—"custom draying," he called it—and I frequently got to ride with him. When the Interstate Commerce Commission (ICC) came into being in 1934 and required hauling permits, Dad was "grandfathered" in with an unlimited permit. He was permitted, literally, to transport everything from furniture to manure. Over the years he hauled both, and many other things. His main business, however, was ferrying freshly picked apples and pears from the valley orchards to packing sheds and warehouses in Entiat, and hauling packed boxes from the sheds to shipping points along the railroad. He prided himself on giving good service and taking excellent care of the fruit he hauled. Even so, much of the time his net income was meager.

Fruit harvest was a time of long, hard days for Dad. No mechanical loaders were available then for the loose fruit, and every box had to be stacked onto his truck by hand. Dad preferred to do this himself, to ensure that the load fit tightly and would ride securely. With loads comprising 112 boxes of loose apples, each box of which weighed about thirty-five pounds, Dad personally handled nearly four thousand pounds for each truck load. That might be repeated four or five times a day. Packed boxes and boxes of loose pears weighed more. Unloading could be easier, with more opportunities to use hand trucks for moving whole stacks of boxes at a time.

When Dad drove home from his last load of the day, after lifting all those tons of weight, he still had to service his truck and ready it for the following day. Still, no matter how exhausted he got, I'm sure Dad would have been quick to say that the harvest-time income made the tough days worthwhile.

Dad in one of his trucks.

*   *   *

Mother was mostly a stay-at-home mom. However, for as long as we lived in the valley, except for the first two years of my life and during my bad illness in 1932, she worked in packing sheds during the fruit harvests. The sheds started up in late August with the harvest of Bartlet pears, and operated through October, with the last of the "winter" apples. Mamma's harvest work brought much-needed income to the family, and also provided her with money of her own. During my early years while Mamma worked in the harvests, I stayed before and after school with relatives or with "Aunt Rachel" Johnson (see "Companions and Caregivers").

The first few years, Mamma worked as a sorter, culling out bad fruit and segregating the rest into different grades of quality. In later years, she packed the fruit. Mamma often packed fruit alongside my Aunt Achsa and Aunt Verna (Deed) Lanoue.

I don't remember when I first visited a sizeable packing shed in full operation, but I do remember being nearly overwhelmed by the sights, sounds, and smells. Men busily wheeled boxes of loose apples to the wet, loud, sloshing machine that washed the fruit, where one man methodically lifted each box and dumped it carefully into the maw of the machine. At the opposite end of the washer, in a quieter area, rows of ladies perched on stools alongside roller conveyors that carried the fruit past them for sorting. Beyond the sorters rose the noisy clatter of the long grading machine, which distributed the apples by their weight and rolled them into packing bins.

Alongside these bins of shiny apples, the packers stood balanced over carts that bore the wooden shipping boxes and trays of oilskin "apple wrap." Their rapid, rhythmic movements were almost hypnotic as they snatched and wrapped each apple and stacked it in their box. Each minute, it seemed, one of the packers would swing her cart around to an adjacent conveyor and slide a full box onto the rollers.

While that packer grabbed a new box from a supply nearby and quickly smoothed in a paper liner, the rollers carried the full box toward the lidder, a man who closed the box by nailing on a slatted, wooden top. The box then tipped onto another conveyor and disappeared into a storage area.

The whole busy, noisy place smelled of the steamy washing solution, the perfume of ripe fruit, and the piney tang of new apple boxes.

Few of the workers had time for a young boy ("Stay out of the way!" "Keep away from the machines!"). Exceptions were the sorter ladies, whose welcomes were embarrassingly effusive. But much was to be learned just by watching the panoply.

I was very proud of Mamma in her role as packer. The packers were key workers, whom I thought of as the "stars" of the packing sheds. Their proficiency had a lot to do with the quality and quantity of output from the packing shed.

Their skills included knowledge of the different "packs"—that is, the arrangements of the layers that fit tightly into each box according to the size of the fruit. Add to that the dexterity of grabbing each apple from a sorted bin, wrapping it in oilskin paper with a quick swipe of the hand and twist of the wrist, and quickly fitting the wrapped fruit into the wooden box. And not the least important was the stamina to do this eight or nine hours per day, six days a week.

Packers were paid according to the number of boxes they packed, in contrast to the other workers, who were paid an hourly wage. Thus, as packers gained experience and developed rhythm and speed, they could make excellent wages for the times. Mamma was never the fastest packer around, but she made very good money during a normal harvest season.

The packers were somewhat competitive, but operated under an established etiquette. For example, the packers rotated along the rows of fruit bins, packing from larger to smaller sizes, and then back around, but also making sure that no bin got overfull.

"Hogging the big sizes," which, of course, would increase the number of boxes packed per hour, was a sin ranking up there with the other "Thou Shalt Nots." At one shed, Mamma and Aunt Achsa shared the packing with a man named John, who tended to push his way to the large-size bins out of turn. Finally, at one lunch break, as the machinery was turned off and the shed went quiet, Aunt Achsa and an equally feisty gal named Gladys pinned John between the apple bins with their packing carts. Gladys told him, loud enough for all nearby to hear, that if he didn't mend his ways, the women packers were going to take him down and severely damage his manhood. The warning apparently worked. I never again heard my mother or aunt complain about John the greedy packer.

The long hours of standing slightly bent, and the repeated motions of handling and wrapping the fruit, made packing tough on hands, wrists and backs, especially at the beginning of the season. Mamma wore wrist bands, and said she tried to take it easy the first few days, but she often came home stiff and sore. After dinner dishes, she would soak her hands and wrists in cool water, and before bedtime she wrapped her fingers with white adhesive tape to take out some of the soreness overnight. (This really does help.) Even so, I remember Mamma's grimaces in the mornings when she stripped the tape off and first flexed her hands. But she was always up first in the mornings, starting the kitchen fire and cooking breakfast before she had to rush off to the packing shed again.

Mamma also worked at other outside jobs when they became available, especially as I grew older. One job that she and I worked together was picking strawberries, getting up in the dark and being in the strawberry field when it got light enough to see which berries were ripe. We worked bent-over until our backs rebelled, then on our knees, then bent over again to rest our knees. We stopped work in midday, not because the blazing sun had us wringing wet with sweat, not because our muscles ached for rest, but because the ripest berries were off, and the plants needed irrigation water. We were paid by the number of trays of berries we picked—I don't remember the rate. It was meager income, as I recall, but income nonetheless.

One job that all three of us worked was thinning apples in a small side-hill orchard that included some twenty-foot-high apple trees. Dad arranged the job with an orchardist friend, and took a low hourly wage to induce the rancher to hire Mom and me as well. The height of the trees meant that high limbs had to be thinned from sixteen-foot ladders, which Dad handled. I worked with Mother from shorter ladders. For all of us, though, wrestling the ladders around on that sloping, uneven ground was tough. At age twelve or so, and small for my age, I did a lot of my thinning by climbing up inside the trees, and Mamma did as much as she could from the ground. Even so, the work was exhausting, and I vowed to never work again in a sloping orchard with monster trees. We were always glad when a thunderstorm or sudden, cooling rain drove us to shelter and some rest, and we were especially happy to finish that thinning job.

Most of Mamma's earnings went in with Dad's to support us all. However, after some spirited "discussions" between my parents, Mamma began holding back some of her earnings to spend for religious purposes, such as buying bible tracts and traveling to nearby church assemblies.

I got dragged along to these church assemblies. I remember them mainly as interminable, boring sermons, endured like tortures while fighting my squirmy muscles to keep from fidgeting. They prepared me well for lectures and conferences in later years.

*   *   *

Like the rest of my family, I was always on the lookout for a chance to earn some cash. My first income I can remember was from collecting bottles in the roadside ditches between home and school, and turning them in at Cooper's Store for the deposits. As I recall, the rates during the mid-thirties were three cents for quart beer bottles and two cents for the smaller, brown "stubbies." Pop bottles, such as those for "Heep Good" or "Orange Crush," brought as much as five cents. Milk bottles, a rare find, brought a whopping eight cents. As today, bottles for whiskey or other liquors were not returnable.

Drink cans didn't exist at first. When the cans did come forth they were made of steel, and were considered worthless until World War II, when a concerted effort was made to salvage all metal.

Another way I made money was to detour through the Harris mill on my way home from Ardenvoir School. About once in every five times I came through, some mill worker would beckon to me and, over the noise of the zinging saws, he would ask me to buy him a candy bar at the nearby Cooper's Store. The deal was that I would get a nickel for the service.

I should confess here that the mill was strictly off-limits to kids. During non-working hours, however, my buddies and I regularly eluded the single watchman and prowled the mill pretty much as we wished. Therefore, I knew the locations of all the work stations and how to get in and out quickly past the bosses. I soon learned which guys might be needing an afternoon snack, and I always made sure to pass their work stations on my quick sweeps through the mill.

Only once did I get caught. A foreman nabbed me when I came back to deliver a candy bar. He ranted about all the dangers of the place, and made me promise to stay out of the mill—a promise which, alas, I soon broke. However, he said he would deliver the candy to my "client," so I went home that afternoon with a clear conscience.

I'm sure my folks never found out about that particular enterprise. The fact that I'm alive to write this is the proof.

While I was in my middle grades, Art Johnson gave me a job herding his cows after school. With my faithful dog Prince, I would hike up Morical Canyon behind Earl Fouch's orchard, where Art had released his three milk cows in the mornings. The main canyon contained a spring and plenty of shade and grass, so the cows were almost always easy to find. Prince and I would herd them back to their barn, at an unhurried pace so they would be calm for milking, and I would tally up ten cents for the trip. Having that steady, paying job made me the envy of my schoolmates.

Only a few times did the cows present problems. Once, when they wandered far up a side canyon, I was in panic before I found them. The other nervous times involved a place where the trail crossed a slope of loose, shifting rocks. A few times when we crossed this rock patch, our footsteps roused a rattlesnake or two.

Something about the buzzings of a rattlesnake among rock piles makes their locations hard to pinpoint and, if another rattlesnake happens to join in, the motivation to be someplace else grows quickly. At such times I wasn't above whacking the cows to hurry them along while I kept a sharp eye on the trailside rocks. Prince, indefatigable hunter that he was, almost had to be beaten to keep him from going after the varmints. Fortunately, these heart-speeding episodes were rare.

As I entered my upper grade-school years, the opportunities for earning money increased, and I hustled shamelessly for jobs. I also carved and painted wooden lawn ornaments and souvenir trinkets and tried peddling them door to door. I sold maybe two, and I'm sure those were sympathy sales.

Mamma helped by paying me fifteen cents a day when she was packing fruit, for after-school tasks of starting a cooking fire, peeling and boiling potatoes for dinner, making the beds, and sweeping the floors. When I was also herding the Johnson's cows, this netted me the grand total of twenty-five cents an afternoon—a princely sum indeed—for less than three hours of my time.

I did even better raising rabbits, starting with two does and a buck that Dad brought home, along with their hutches, after one of his swaps. I learned to kill, clean, and skin the rabbits with least damage to the meat and hides. Besides supplying us with tasty meat, I found buyers among the neighbors. I also learned to stretch and dry the pelts, and sold them by express freight to a hide dealer in Spokane.

To minimize the cost of rabbit feed, I picked armloads of greens from along alfalfa fields and ditch banks. My rabbits' favorite was wild water-cress.

A small part of my rabbit-related income would not have met the approval of my folks, had they known. I charged guys to watch the rabbits mate.

The mating of rabbits is a truly hilarious spectacle. The buck mounts the docile doe, jitters against her backside at blurring speed for about two seconds while he rapidly thumps the cage floor with a hind foot. Then he goes stiff as a board while he emits a loud groan, and falls over. The buck lies there panting for about three seconds, after which he mounts the patient doe for a repeat performance. I charged my buddies a nickel to watch one or two performances, or a dime to watch one pair throughout their mating session.

Summer vacations from school began during the height of the spraying season, which offered more opportunities. Although I was too small to drag the heavy spray hoses around, I got jobs tending spray machines during three summers. These jobs involved staying at the engine-driven machines while one or two men were at the ends of the long, high-pressure hoses, spraying the trees. When the tank of spray mixture went empty, I shut down the machine and waited for one of the men to walk back and mix another batch of spray. On one of these jobs, I also started water flowing to fill the spray tank, and even began mixing the pesticides while my boss walked back to restart the sprayer. I was not trained to handle those poisons, and my boss should have forbidden me from even touching the chemical containers. Instead, he praised me for saving his time.

I was a dismal failure at picking apples and pears, for several reasons. First, although I was tough enough, I was simply too small to efficiently handle the strapped-on picking bags when they were full of fruit. Second, I had been so thoroughly imbued by Dad to protect the fruit and the trees that my picking rate was slower than a snail on flypaper. Third, I have small hands, which limited my grasp to one piece of fruit per hand.

Small hands are a special handicap when picking pears. A person with small hands has difficulty securing a big pear when tipping its stem loose from the branch. And when a pear, with its tapered shape, starts to drop, you can seldom snap your hand closed fast enough to catch its diminishing top end. Dropping a lot of prime fruit does not make you a sought-after picker.

I did better at picking cherries. When climbing inside a big old cherry tree, being small and careful of the notably weak cherry limbs *does* endear you to the grower. And having nimble fingers is a further advantage. Unfortunately, I didn't have a chance to try cherry picking early enough in my orchard life to really cash in.

One of the easiest orchard jobs I ever had was "playing bee"—that is, pollinating trees by hand. When extended periods of cool or wet weather hampered the activities of bees to pollinate the fruit naturally, ranchers sometimes employed humans to do the bee's work. We used wooden dowels, or "wands," the tips of which had tied-on, gauze-enclosed balls containing fruit pollen. Working from ladders, we lightly touched the ball of pollen to each fruit blossom we could reach, then quickly moved on to the next ladder setting. For this kind of light work, the ranchers did not mind hiring kids, who would work for low wages and were agile at clamoring around the trees. If child-labor laws existed then, those laws probably were broken regularly, for ten-hour work days were not unusual. And goofing-off among the young workers was rare. We knew that, if we didn't produce, plenty of others were eager for our jobs.

*   *   *

The work that netted me the most income during those years was making apple boxes. Nailing together the wooden pieces, or "box shook," to form the standard apple box was a job that, like packing fruit, paid by the box—a half cent per box when I started. Therefore, the box maker controlled his own income, depending on the hours worked and his proficiency, which, of course, grew with practice. I got my start learning the trade from good old Art Johnson. He set up a box form in his barn loft and hired me to make several hundred boxes needed for his family orchard.

Like many skilled jobs, box making looked a lot easier than it was. First, the box ends were jammed into a cast-iron form, which held them squarely at the proper distance apart. Then, the wooden sides and bottom were nailed on in turn, using a special, checkered-faced hatchet, as the box-maker rotated the developing box in the form. Lastly, the completed box was pulled from the form and quickly stacked, and the operation repeated. Simple and straightforward. The challenge was to complete each box as quickly and smoothly as possible, and to repeat the operation for eight to ten hours a day.

The required speed and efficiency depended on having the setup and everything else just so. The box form had to be at just the right height and on solid footing to minimize the effort needed to drive the nails. The box shook had to be positioned so that each piece in turn could be pulled into place smoothly, without ever letting go of the hatchet. And the nails (5½ penny, cement-coated wire nails) had to be there to grab, snuggled and stacked so that each could be picked off by the hatchet's teeth and driven home in an instant.

An ingenious device called a "nail stripper" controlled the nail supply. Its upper part was a sloping hopper for the nails, and below that were wire

Upper: Early box-making equipment with box shook. Antique nail stripper is left of box form, which holds two box heads (end boards).
Lower: Key box-making equipment: nail stripper and checkered-faced hatchet.
Wenatchee Valley Museum and Cultural Center displays.

tracks, also sloping, into which the nails fell and hung with their heads neatly overlapped. When the box maker grabbed nails from the wire tracks (with practice getting exactly the eight needed for each side or bottom of the box), the overlapping nail heads were stacked perfectly for him to feed out under the hatchet. This allowed him to maintain a smooth and steady arm rhythm to start the nail with a tap of the hatchet and move the next nail into position while he sank the previous nail with a single blow. The steady "tap-BAM, tap-BAM, tap-BAM, tap-BAM" of the box-maker's hatchet was a signature sound of the fruit-packing industry in those days.

The key to productivity in box making was not hurrying, but instead establishing an efficient rhythm without unnecessary moves, and having the right equipment setup. I'm proud to say that I finally became one of the better box makers in the valley. By making six hundred boxes a day, I could earn as much as Mamma usually did in her day of packing apples, and that became my standard production goal. As I gained proficiency, I often made seven hundred a day. I even had a few days at eight-hundred boxes, when the yellow-pine box shook was especially good and I worked an extra hour.

The box-making craft diminished as machines gradually took over wooden-box making after World War II, and virtually died out when fruit packers later switched to cardboard boxes.

*　　*　　*

Rural folks soon learn that, if you can't buy something, maybe you can make it. And if other people might want the same thing, maybe you can also make money selling it. It was in this spirit that I decided to make and sell fireworks.

I was in seventh grade at Ardenvoir School, learning a little about the wonders of chemistry. The idea of mixing simple chemicals to make useful compounds inspired me to read all I could on the subject. About that time, I also received the gift of a small chemistry set, and I scrupulously followed the set's directions to make everything possible with the materials provided.

I didn't blow up anything with that set, although I managed to indelibly stain some clothing.

I don't remember where I learned the formula for gun powder, probably from my reading or from Uncle Max. The makeup is simple: sulfur, saltpeter, and charcoal mixed in the right proportions—and "pouf"—literally. I couldn't wait to make some.

My chemistry set came with a tin of powdered sulfur, so I had one ingredient. And any incompletely burned wood fire left plenty of charcoal to be pulverized. Only the saltpeter gave me pause. The dictionary told me that saltpeter is the common name for potassium nitrate, which gives gunpowder its "umph."

Where had I recently seen the word "nitrate?" Ah, yes! The chemical fertilizer that Dad was even then applying to Grandma Lillian's orchard.

I dashed to the cellar house, where Dad stored the bags of fertilizer. Sure enough, the contents listed on the bags included high percentages of potassium and nitrate. I grabbed a nearby coffee can and swiped a can full of the white beads from an open sack. To my astonished delight, I also found a bag of granular sulfur, the purpose of which, according to the label, was to "adjust soil acidity." I swiped some of that, too.

Rushing to Grandma's barn, I stashed my loot in a dark cranny on the ground floor. Then I found a paper bag and set about gathering charcoal bits from the ash pile where we burned brush. In no time, I had assembled all ingredients needed for gunpowder. I itched to make a batch and test it, but I sensed that I'd better not be caught doing it.

Finally, the opportunity came when no grownups would be around. I cleaned out a round-bottomed bowl we used to feed the cats, and measured in my ingredients. Because the fertilizer was in the form of beads, the charcoal in chunks and the sulfur in grains, I ground the mixture together, using an old Indian pestle to pulverize the pieces in the bowl. With trembling hands, I poured a sample out onto an old board and struck a wooden match. .

The result was better than I expected, except that the sudden "whoosh" of flame slightly burned my hand. Even as I shook that hand to cool it, I planned my next step—making firecrackers.

Years before, out of simple curiosity, I had unwrapped a firecracker to see how it was made, and found a long, tightly coiled fold of Chinese newspaper holding the gunpowder. That seemed simple enough to make. To my delight, the method worked with American newspaper, too. I sneaked some LePages mucilage to secure the end of my powder-filled coil.

I soon learned that the tighter I coiled the fold of powder-filled paper, the louder the bang. Also, the longer the folded trough of powder-laced newspaper, the bigger the finished firecracker and its explosion.

Fuses were a problem from the start. I couldn't duplicate the twisted-paper fuses of the store-bought firecrackers, so I finally packed finely ground black powder into hollow weed stems and put them into the centers of my firecrackers.

This whole process was very time-consuming, and I had difficulty finding the time for my project when the folks were not around. I quickly abandoned hopes of selling firecrackers for a profit, but persisted in plans to make my own supply.

After many hours of grinding up batches of gunpowder, rolling up the firecrackers and setting them off, I bragged about my experiments to Uncle Max. He seemed impressed, especially with my manufacture of the black powder.

"How did you dry the powder after you mixed it?" he finally asked.

"Huh? It was dry all the time. I just put the mix in the bowl and ground it up."

"You *idiot*! The factories keep the stuff wet while they mix it! Any little spark could've burned your stupid head to a cinder!"

I meekly dismantled my "laboratory" and disposed of my raw materials. Years later, I learned a description that fit perfectly: "Having just enough knowledge to be dangerous."

OUR LAST VALLEY HOME

After nearly two years of living in Grandma's barn loft, Dad somehow acquired a tiny cabin and moved it to a roadside spot a hundred yards or so down valley from Zebra House, where my Aunt Achsa and Uncle Frank Cook then lived.

I don't remember where the cabin came from or just how Dad got it to that site. I passed there daily on my bike trips to and from Ardenvoir School, and one afternoon the cabin just appeared, between two pine trees at the edge of that pine-and-sagebrush-dotted slope. Dad was jacking up one corner of the cabin to put a timber foundation underneath.

"This will be our home now," he told me, "until we can build a new house behind here."

It turned out to be our last home in the Entiat Valley.

It was a somber, shaggy looking little building, with brown-weathered wood shingles on the roof and sides. The interior walls and ceiling of the single room had been finished with painted wallboard and plywood, and the floor had a decent linoleum covering. At one end, under a window, a counter had been built, with shelves above and below. That was the extent of interior fixtures. The entire cabin was only slightly larger than the "kitchen"

View up Entiat River Road showing our last valley home (cabin under pine tree, behind leaning pole), with Zebra House beyond woodshed. Out of view on left is orchard we lost to forclosure.

space in the barn loft. My first reaction was: *It's awfully small, but should be better than living in the barn, especially in winter.*

The cabin was in the lowest corner of that bit of undeveloped land, less than a hundred feet from the up-valley end of an orchard owned by Mr. and Mrs. Earl Fouch. It was opposite part of our former orchard, separated from it only by the Entiat River Road, a barbed-wire fence, and the irrigation ditch which supplied our old orchard. Specifically, it faced the newer trees on our old home place, the trees Dad had worked so hard to plant. If that was a painful reminder to Dad of all we had lost, he never mentioned it.

My folks worked hard at preparing the cabin while we continued living in the barn. Mamma scrubbed the inside until the paint was thin, then started fitting things into the kitchen space. Dad dug a pit and built an outhouse so we wouldn't have to share the one at Zebra House. He also dug a cesspit, transferred Mamma's sink from the barn to the cabin's counter, and did the necessary plumbing for the drainage. We still had to bring in drinking water from a safe source, but at least we didn't have to throw waste water out onto the yard.

When Dad acquired the cabin it had only two windows, one on the kitchen end and one on the side near the cabin's door, away from the road. But Dad sawed an opening in the wall facing the road, and added a third window, which he made from two plate-glass car windshields.

Dad's major modification, however, was the addition of a lean-to bedroom on the up-valley end of the cabin. He built a framework and floor joists from the lumber we had used for walls in the barn loft, and bought plywood to cover the roof, walls and floor. He sawed through the cabin's back wall to make a doorway. My folks next bought some aluminum paint and brushed two coats of it onto the outside of the plywood roof and sides, as insulation against the sun's heat. On the back side of the lean-to, facing Zebra House, Dad framed in the window we had used in the barn loft.

The cabin had been wired for electricity before Dad acquired it, so, after the electric company added their meter and hooked us up, the place was ready for our occupancy.

The two parts of the building were a striking contrast—the rough, brown-weathered original cabin, and the smooth-surfaced, starkly silver addition. Even among the other makeshift dwellings in the valley, it was different enough to stand out. But I don't remember anyone, even other kids, ridiculing the "cabin with the silver lean-to." Of course, I explained at school that the place was only temporary, until we built our new house behind it. And it certainly was easy to describe to would-be visitors.

Not all our furniture fit into the cabin. Our kitchen stove fitted into a place where a previous stove had been, and Dad trimmed some of the kitchen shelves to make room for Mamma's little fridge. Our little old kitchen table, which Mamma now used as a work table, provided separation of her kitchen area from the "living room." That space barely held our round oak table, three chairs, and the bed-davenport. The latter, however, could not be opened into a bed for lack of space. Dad swapped some of our extra things for a newer radio, which he set up on an end table near the bedroom doorway. Another end table next to the davenport, holding a lamp, completed our living-room furniture.

In the lean-to bedroom, we set up our two beds at opposite sides of the room. Dad put up a hanger pole at the end behind my bed and, after Mamma hung curtains in front of that, it became our clothes closet. Two chests-of-drawers went against the bedroom walls. Mamma's treadle sewing machine sat under the bedroom window. Nothing but walk space separated the two beds. When Mamma hung a privacy curtain at the bedroom doorway, we were officially moved in.

Among the things we could not fit into the cabin were Mamma's washing machine and wash tubs. We left the washer outside, against the back of the cabin, with the tubs upended over it for weather protection.

The "overflow" item I remember with most regret was a nice ivory-colored vanity, or dressing table, which Mamma had used for as long as I remember. Dad removed the mirror from the vanity and hung it on a bedroom wall above Mamma's chest of drawers. He left the dressing table outside, against the cabin wall, and bolted a mechanic's vice onto the vanity's top. The once-beautiful dressing table became a little workbench, with its drawers thereafter holding tools instead of beauty aids. Watching how the weather gradually wrinkled, cracked and flaked the vanity's ivory paint saddened me. Once I saw Mamma staring at it, too.

"It's a shame, Mamma," I said.

"It doesn't matter," she answered. But the sadness in her smile spoke differently.

In those days, you used what you had and did with it what you had to.

* * *

After we fitted into the cabin as well as possible, Dad decided that the yard around our new home needed reshaping. As usual, he had a plan to minimize our work.

CLEAN FILL WANTED

My dad's ability to take advantage of opportunities certainly helped to get the family through the hard times in the Entiat Valley, but even the best of his plans sometimes went awry. Like the time, when I was twelve, that my folks decided to build up some low ground near our rude little depression-era cabin.

Dad didn't have a ready source of fill dirt, and paying good money for dirt was out of the question. So he painted a sign, "Clean Fill Wanted," and stuck it up near the valley road.

A couple of weeks went by without anyone showing up with dirt. But one day when we returned home after an absence, there was a big pile perfectly placed in the lowest spot. Unfortunately, it was a pile of trash, brush and rocks, with very little dirt.

Dad and I sweated most of the next day burying the rocks, burning the brush, and finally hauling the unburnable trash to the Ardenvoir dump. I seethed the whole time, muttering about finding those responsible and letting the air out of their truck tires. Dad, however, was philosophical: "At least they didn't leave rotten garbage."

But when another phantom load appeared a few days later, this time brush and broken concrete, Dad tore down the "wanted" sign and threw it on the burn pile. My chores for a while included stacking the concrete chunks to form a small retaining wall, which I liberally cemented with words that I wasn't supposed to know.

Only days later, Dad heard that the county had let a contract to straighten the roadway near our place. "I think we may have found our fill dirt," he said with a smile so broad that it showed his gold front tooth.

Our truck at the time was an old, stripped-down Model T Ford of a vintage unknown to me, which Dad loved and babied along to keep running. He had built a truck bed and low sideboards for it out of salvaged planks. The truck wasn't even licensed, but the local deputy understood that everyone was strapped for money.

The first day of the road work, Dad prepared the old truck while I hovered close. Finally, I dared the question that burns inside every young boy: "Can I drive some, Dad?"

"You're too young," he said, not lifting his eyes from the truck's engine.

I pressed my luck. "But I can reach all the pedals if I stretch, and I've been practicing—a lot."

Dad looked up then, and chuckled. "Yeah, but you've been practicing with the motor *off*."

I quit while I was even, and concentrated on helping to coddle the old engine to life. Soon, perched atop the hard, bare "under-seat" gas tank, we drove the old truck down to the work site, broadcasting the "kut-kut-kut" sound so distinctive of the Model T engine.

A billowing cloud of choking dust greeted us at the work site. A power shovel was excavating the old roadway and emptying the dirt into a dump truck that would have made five of our Model T. The dirt there was ideal; a nice, sandy consistency with hardly any rocks.

Dad waited to approach until the dump truck pulled away, at which time the shovel operator, a burly, Irish-looking guy, idled the power shovel and stepped down from his cab. While they talked, I got to slide over into Dad's place on the truck, holding down the foot brake and fingering the throttle to keep the engine alive. Finally, the shovel operator shrugged with his hands, and Dad came back all smiles.

Dad pushed the reverse pedal, edged the hand throttle down, twisted the steering wheel, and backed into the dump-truck's tracks. The shovel operator scooped up some loose dirt, eased the bucket down nearly touching our truck bed, and delicately released just enough dirt to make a full load. He even used the heel of the scoop to smooth the dirt for us. What an expert with that machine!

Dad gave the man a thank-you salute, revved the T's engine while he stood on the low-gear pedal, and we bounced out to the roadway and off to home.

We needed only minutes to shovel the dirt off the truck and get back on the road. Twice more that day we waited at the site to get our little truck filled, each time with just the right amount of dirt gently loaded by the light touch of the shovel operator.

The fourth time we arrived at the site, the burly operator was standing beside his power shovel, smoking a brown roll-your-own cigarette and cleaning the side of his machine with a broom. It may have been near quitting time, but the shovel engine was still idling.

"One more should do us," Dad called with a smile, and confidently backed the little truck into the loading tracks. The operator immediately tossed the broom aside and swung up into his cab.

I turned to watch the operator's artistry again, and was struck by the strange grin on his broad face. Then I saw the dirt scoop—heaped full. "Dad…!" I warned as it swung over our truck.

Dad's eyes bugged. "Hang on!" he yelled as the full scoop released from three feet up.

The dirt hit with a sickening "whump!" Brown dust engulfed us as the little truck squatted like a piddling pup. The front wheels bounced off the ground and the sideboards popped up. Stunned, I looked behind to see avalanches of dirt cascading off the sides of the truck and burying the rear wheels.

As the dust cleared, I stared in disbelief at the shovel operator, my former hero. He was rocking back and forth, laughing as hard as a man can laugh. How could he deliberately smash our truck and laugh about it?

Dad recovered first. "Come on!" he called, "We have to dig out the wheels!"

Hopping from the truck, Dad ripped a sideboard off and began digging frantically at the dirt beside a rear wheel. I went off the other side and got a board too.

That sideboard was plenty heavy, but somehow I mustered the strength to use it like a canoe paddle to get that wheel uncovered and free to move. Between digging efforts I glanced back at the shovel operator. He was leaned over the controls in front of him, his face on his arms, shoulders shaking. Then he raised his face, looked at us again and rocked back, once more roaring with mirth. He paused only long enough to pull out a blue bandana and wipe his eyes before dissolving again in roars of laughter. I could have killed him with my plank.

Dad interrupted my murder plans. "Let's try it now," he called.

We hopped aboard the truck and Dad began cautiously and deliberately rocking the truck forward. On the first surge, the front wheels bounced off the ground again, spilling dirt and sending the Judas shovel operator into renewed fits of laughter. Gradually, however, that poor, overloaded Model T worked its way free of the dirt pile, and we drove beyond the reach of the treacherous shovel arm. There we stopped, scrambled onto the heaping load of dirt, and spilled more off the sides until we could get the sideboards somewhat back in place.

The truck listed to one side, and had absolutely no springing action under the load. Surely, things underneath were badly broken. But Dad coaxed the old truck home.

With a sick heart I picked up my shovel. Was this the last trip for the poor old T?

But as we removed the dirt, a miracle! The truck bed began to rise off the rear axle housing. Hope lived!

While I shoveled off the last of the dirt, Dad crawled around the truck looking for damage. Finally he stood up, pushed back his cap, and scratched his sweating head.

"Well, I'll be blessed," he said. "I can't find anything *broken*. But those springs can't be what they were." He shook his head. "I s'pose both rear tires woulda blown, if the dirt at the site hadn't been so soft."

I whooped and threw my shovel. "That jerk couldn't kill the old gal after all!"

"He sure had a good time trying, though," Dad said. "Did you ever see anyone laugh so *hard*?" We laughed, too, in our relief.

"You know," Dad continued, wiping his eyes, "there's a lesson here, Son. When someone is doin' you a favor, don't take your benefactor for granted. I really shoulda bought that guy a carton of smokes or something."

"Does that mean you forgive him?"

Dad thought. "No," he said. "To punish me, he tried to smash an innocent old truck. That's not right."

"Now," Dad added casually, "why don't you see if you can crank her up and park her around behind the house."

"*Really? By myself?*"

And that evening I, too, fell in love with the old Model T.

Dad's little Model T Ford truck, star of Clean Fill Wanted.

* * *

When we moved into the little cabin we had no ready source of drinking water. Like my aunt and uncle living in the nearby Zebra House, we had to bring in safe water, usually from Grandma's well. Wash water was available during the irrigation season from major ditches passing above and below both houses, but that, too, had to be carried in by the bucketful. Digging a well became Dad's top priority.

With help from Mamma and me, Dad used pick and shovel to dig out a space where he planned to have a basement garage under the new house, and started the well there. He dug a hole four-by-four feet square, as deep as he could throw out the dirt, and lined it with wooden cribbing. He had to saw off the handles of a pick and a shovel so he could use them in the confined space. Next, he built a rope windlass over the hole and attached a sturdy, metal five-gallon pesticide bucket in which to bring up the dirt.

Dad also built a slender ladder for getting into and out of the well. He would slide the ladder into the hole, climb down, and Mamma and I would pull the ladder out while he dug. One of us would wait at the top, crank the windlass handle to raise the loaded bucket when Dad told us to, then drag the bucket a few yards away and dump the well diggings onto a growing pile.

After some experimenting with the cribbing boards, Dad pre-cut all the old lumber we had into the desired lengths and stacked them next to the windlass. He had to buy a small keg of nails. When he needed to extend the cribbing downward as he dug deeper, he would call out his needs, and Mamma or I lowered boards, hammer and nails in the dirt bucket.

Dad worked down there for hours at a time, filling the bucket to be hoisted, then continuing to loosen the dirt and square up the walls of the hole while I raised the bucket and disposed of the spoil.

"Don't get your hands in that bucketful," he called up occasionally. That warned me he had peed into that load of dirt.

When Dad needed to come up, I had a struggle to lower the ladder for him. Once, it slipped from my grip, and Dad was barely able to push the falling ladder past him without injury.

After that ladder fall, Mamma insisted on helping with the ladder, and she seemed nervous anytime Dad was in the hole, especially as he dug deeper. Danger hung over Dad's head with every hoisting of the heavy dirt bucket. If Mamma or I had ever let the windlass crank slip from our hands, the heavy bucket of dirt would have fallen freely, spinning the windlass wildly as the rope unwound, and almost certainly would have struck Dad, confined as he was in the hole. Dad had made a latch to lock the windlass, but it probably could not have stopped a falling bucket of dirt.

Another risk was the possibility of a cave-in. "Gerald, you're digging too far without adding boards," Mamma scolded once. "If that hole caves in, we'll never get you out."

"It doesn't show any signs of caving," Dad shouted back, "and I'm saving work this way. Nailing the cribbing together in this tight space is a lot easier when the boards are higher than my shoulders."

I never heard the matter discussed again. Fortunately, Dad's judgment about the firmness of the unsupported sand and gravel proved to be correct.

My folks let me go down the hole a few times, to my delight. I learned for myself the difficulties of digging in that small shaft. Yet, the confinement did not bother me, and I liked the smell of the damp soil and the actual digging down into the earth. I would happily have spent more time digging at the bottom of the shaft if my folks had let me.

We were very lucky about the rocks Dad encountered in the shaft. Despite having several granitic boulders on the property that Dad finally had to blast apart to move, I think he only found one boulder he could not dig out of the well shaft. Fortunately, that was at the side of the shaft, and he was able to build the cribbing around it. Other rocks he encountered were no bigger than a man's head, nothing we could not raise in the dirt bucket.

We had no assurance, of course, that Dad would be able to dig far enough to reach ground water.

"That's our bedrock here," Dad explained once, nodding toward the granite knobs on the hill above us. "We could hit that anytime. You never know how much sand and gravel there is above the bedrock at any one place in the valley."

"But we had a good well just over there," Mamma argued, looking across toward our former house. "Remember all that pumping during the fire?"

"Yeah, but the yard at the home place is at least fifteen feet lower than here, and it's closer to the river. That could make a lot of difference."

I was shocked. I had not realized that all of Dad's hard, patient effort might end with a dry hole, perhaps encountering the solid bedrock before reaching water.

By the second week of our laborious digging and hauling up the dirt, five gallons at a time, the spoil pile had grown into a long mound. In the shaft, Dad's feet now rested nearly twenty feet below the surface. Mamma and I kept asking whether the diggings seemed to be getting any wetter.

"No water yet," Dad would answer patiently, "but no sign of bedrock either."

Finally, Dad dug a shovel bite that filled with water. You could have heard his "Whoopee!" all the way to Cooper's Store. Mamma rushed to the windlass with me. "I hit water!" Dad exclaimed. "Send down a fruit jar and the flashlight."

I set a record cranking up the next bucketful of dirt. Mamma scurried into the cabin. Before I had emptied the bucket, she was back with the flashlight and a quart fruit jar. We lowered them in the bucket and waited anxiously, peering down the hole.

"Tastes fine," Dad called. You could hear the grin in his voice. "I'll send up a jar full."

The windlass fairly hummed as I cranked the bucket up. The fruit jar was two-thirds full of murky grey water. Mamma held it up, and we watched the silt settle to the bottom. The water cleared.

"Let me taste it," I begged. Mamma smiled and offered the jar.

I twisted off the lid and took a tentative sip. Then another. The water tasted good—cold and pure. "It's great!" I called down to Dad as I handed the jar to Mamma for her to taste.

"Lower the ladder," Dad replied. "I'm comin' up."

Dad rested until we finished a quick lunch, then donned his knee-high rubber boots and went back down the hole. He first extended the wooden cribbing down as far as he could, and then resumed deepening the shaft while I eagerly cranked up each bucket of dripping-wet sand and dumped it. I sensed urgency in Dad's work now, as he dug the wet grit from beneath his feet and sank deeper into the water. Finally he called up: "That's all I can do now. I'm freezing cold, and my boots are full."

Next morning, Dad hurried his breakfast to get down the well again. "Just pray we didn't get a cave-in overnight," he said.

Wearing the hip boots he used for fishing, Dad awkwardly descended the ladder. No cave-in had occurred, and he was able to deepen the well about two feet more. He ended by scooping the bottom deeper with a small bucket, immersing himself completely during the process. The bottom of the well then measured twenty-four feet below the top of the cribbing, with more than three feet of standing water.

Working from the ladder, Dad next built a sturdy wooden shelf, about four feet below the well top, to hold a pump. He shopped around Wenatchee for used equipment. Finally, though, he bought a new small electric pump and a pressure tank at the Montgomery Ward store, getting a good price from a salesman he knew. When Dad finished installing the pump and its drop pipe in the well, he pushed the power switch. The pump motor seemed to whir forever without anything happening. At last came a gulping sound, and water gushed out! I felt almost as if I were witnessing a miracle—a heavenly reward for all our hard work.

We borrowed a pipe-threading machine from my Uncle Jess Lanoue, and Dad began teaching me the rudiments of plumbing. From an assortment of used pipes Dad had been stock-piling, we cut and threaded and installed a short pipeline with a faucet near the cabin. Mamma still did not have running water in her kitchen, but she was thrilled with that handy faucet, yielding pressurized water, near the back door.

"Now we have another big job, Son," Dad said. "Now we're going to run a water line over to your aunt and uncle."

After we dug the trench, the actual installation of the pipe toward Zebra House went rather quickly, because we could use the long pipes without cutting them, merely cleaning and cementing the joints before twisting them together with our two big pipe wrenches. Dad estimated the least depth we had to dig the trench to bury the pipe below the frost zone. His guess apparently was good, for I don't remember that we ever had a frozen underground pipe.

We ran out of pipe before we reached the other house, and suspended operations while Dad scrounged more. I think he bartered for some of it but he finally had to buy some shiny new galvanized pipe. He got enough to reach the rest of the way with a little to spare. Near the door at Zebra House, Dad installed a standpipe with a faucet high enough for a water bucket. For the first time, Zebra House, too, had a ready source of good-quality water.

Dad and I had put another standpipe and faucet in the pipeline about a hundred feet from our cabin. There, near the road, my folks started a vegetable garden, watered from that spigot with a garden hose and a sprinkler.

Mamma insisted on first planting a double row of tall-growing dahlias on the road side of the garden. "I don't like people being able to see me while I'm bent over working in the garden," she explained to laughter from Dad and me.

The well always provided ample, good-tasting water, but during the first summer we learned that the pump was undersized for serving both houses plus the garden. Watering the garden required the pump to run for long hours. In the middle of a hot spell, the inevitable happened—the pump motor burned out.

Obviously, we needed a pump with a bigger motor. But when Dad checked the costs, he decided that we simply could not afford the next larger pump. He settled for buying a pump identical to the one we had, and getting the burned-out motor repaired. He also scrounged for cheap, used electric motors. Every summer thereafter, we simply accepted the occasional burn-out of pump motors, which Dad would quickly remove for repair and replacement with one of his back-ups.

With water readily available, living conditions in the cabin were better for all of us than they had been in the barn loft. We had the little refrigerator back from Grandma's, and the kitchen stove provided ample heat, even enough to take the chill off the bedroom in cold weather. Mamma still had to wash clothes outside, but at least we didn't have to carry wash water in buckets from an irrigation ditch.

*   *   *

The biggest problem with our cabin living was lack of privacy. This was a frequent embarrassment for me, then entering puberty. My folks, of course, had their own privacy problems. As a result, this was a period during which I did a lot of sleeping over at friends and relatives, including two-week summertime sojourns with my Bedient cousins who lived near Lake Chelan.

Dad's solution to our "togetherness" problems was characteristically ingenious.

Always on the lookout for a profitable car trade, Dad paid attention to car ownership throughout the valley. He not only knew who was driving what car at the time, but also where big old, gas-guzzling cars from the Roaring Twenties rested on blocks in barns or weed fields. I should not have been surprised, therefore, when Dad drove into our cabin's yard in a big, squarish sedan with weathered maroon paint and a wide, nickel-plated radiator cowl that bore the nameplate "FLINT."

"I got her for the value of the tires," Dad boasted. "She's sounder than the dollar, and just like new inside. And," he added with a smug smile, "the seats make into a bed."

That grand old car really was like new inside, and was luxurious in many ways. The thick, mohair upholstery showed little wear, and all the trim and fittings spoke of class. It even had an electric cigar lighter on a retractable cord, which could be pulled out from a rear-seat armrest. The four doors fit like they were on bank vaults. And the bench seats and seat-backs did, indeed, make into a bed, the flattest and smoothest I ever saw in a car.

Dad parked the Flint uphill from the cabin, with the car's nose pointed toward the valley road. We leveled it by digging holes for the rear wheels. It was handy to the outhouse and close to the cabin, yet not too close. I moved my blankets and pillow in immediately.

The Flint was my bedroom for the next few years during all but the coldest weather. I loved it from the first. The solitude was a blessing, and the setting fed my love of Nature. I would wind down a window of the car, lie back and gaze at the wonders of the Milky Way, dazzling in the clear skies of those times. I searched out constellations I knew and those I fantasized, until I fell asleep. Although I never felt confined in the Flint, I almost always slept with windows open, because when closed they silenced the soothing voice of the river. The patter of rain on the old car's roof was soothing too, even though I knew that, if the rain didn't stop before morning, I faced a "refreshing" dash to the outhouse and another to the cabin for breakfast.

With the Flint as my bedroom, I could again have guys sleeping over. My guest and I could stay awake talking for as long as we wished, discussing anything at all in total privacy. One year, my friend Verlan Moore stayed most of the summer.

Dad paid Verlan and me to dig dirt from the planned basement site. We shoveled it onto his little old Model T truck, drove the truck up the hill a ways, and shoveled the dirt off to form a terrace there. Dad paid each of us fifteen cents a truckload. We usually tried to do one load before lunch, another after lunch—before a quick trip on my bike for a swim in the river—and then a third load before Dad got home from whatever job he was working. When Dad paid us at the end of each week, we double-rode my bike up the road to Cooper's Store, where we bought candy, pop, "Big Little" books, and fireworks. We usually spent every cent of our wages. Verlan came from a larger family, and seldom before enjoyed that much pocket money. Under the influence of my wild-spending friend, I didn't save much that summer either. After a day or two of eating our goodies, and blowing tin cans skyward with our firecrackers, only the books remained to show for our previous hard work. We eagerly went back to digging to earn more for another buying spree. Ah, the power of capitalism.

✻   ✻   ✻

Shortly after we moved from her barn loft to the little cabin, Grandma Lillian became ill and was diagnosed as having Diabetes. She obviously needed closer care, so my aunt and uncle moved out of Zebra House and moved Grandma in. She had to leave behind her electric stove and oven and go back to a wood stove, but she now had running water at her doorstep. Uncle Frank already had installed a sink and made beautiful cabinets in the Zebra House kitchen. Also, the family pooled funds and bought Grandma a refrigerator, which was essential for storing the insulin she now had to inject. To Grandma, I think, the refrigerator and the handy water more than made up for the loss of her electric range.

267

The family also arranged for Otto Cook, a cousin of my uncle Frank, to take over Grandma's house and orchard. I don't remember the financial arrangements, if I ever knew them. For the first time in decades, all of Dad's family was out of apple ranching.

My Aunt Achsa and Uncle Frank moved into worker housing near the Harris Mill, where Frank was working on a new venture for the mill—an automatic box-making machine. The work paid well, and he seemed happy at that job. However, a labor strike developed, and in 1938 they moved to East Wenatchee, and Frank became a Chevrolet car salesman.

My folks and I thus became the sole guardians for Grandma. I benefited from this arrangement in several ways: I learned patience and responsibility in helping an old person. I learned the signs of diabetic coma, and how to give emergency injections. And I learned most of what I know about my Foxworthy and Denman forebears, as I sat in Grandma's kitchen, perhaps eating buttered biscuits hot from her oven, and asking questions about the past.

MORE CAR WOES FOR MAMMA

Mamma's most memorable grief with a car came in 1938, after we moved into the little cabin across the road from our former orchard.

In addition to our other vehicles, we had a big Flint luxury sedan of 1920's vintage, the seats of which folded down into a good bed. Our main use of the old Flint was as my warm-weather sleeping quarters during my pre-teen years. However, the old Flint was drivable, and we used it occasionally for short errands—somewhat nervous trips, because the Flint's license plates had long-since expired.

The Flint normally sat at the upper end of our dirt driveway, out of the way of other vehicles. To make the car level for sleeping quarters, Dad had dug little trenches for the rear wheels, deep enough that the car would not roll downhill on its own, but shallow enough that the car could easily pull out under power.

One fall afternoon, with Dad away hauling and I at school, Mamma decided she had to drive somewhere. Only the Flint and our old Model T truck were available. Mamma went out to the Flint, raised the front seat into its upright position, and prepared to start it. This time, she did not have a chance to flood the engine, as she often did, for the battery was too weak to crank it over.

In those days of manual transmissions, the usual response to a weak battery was to push the car or coast it down a hill to achieve momentum, shift into second gear, let out the clutch, and try to nurse the spinning engine to life. The Flint's location, headed down slope at the upper end of the driveway, was ideal for this kind of gravity start.

Dad and I had started the Flint several times this way. Usually, Dad would wait in the driver's seat while I shoveled dirt out from in front of the rear wheels until they were free to move forward. Sometimes, I then went to the back of the car and pushed to get it rolling. Dad could almost always get the engine to catch life before making the sharp turn out onto the valley road.

269

I don't really know what went wrong for Mamma that day. Perhaps she failed to set the hand brake before she dug out the rear wheels. Maybe she didn't dig quite enough and decided to get the car moving with a push. All I know is that the massive old Flint started rolling with Mamma outside the open driver's door.

I can only imagine the heavy Flint gathering speed down the driveway while poor Mamma tried frantically to catch up and get back in, her legs churning but never quite fast enough.

I give Mamma great credit—she stayed with it to the end. She steered the runaway to miss the cabin and an adjacent pine tree. And she hung on while the Flint continued across the highway and headed for the irrigation ditch beyond, where they both would have ended up if not for a sturdy barbed-wire fence at the ditch's edge.

The sight that greeted me when I got home from school was the Flint nosed down toward the irrigation ditch, with one rear wheel about two feet off the road's edge. I dropped my bike and rushed into the house. One look at Mamma told much of the story. She was in her robe and had a big bruise on one cheek. What I could see of her arms and legs were masses of scratches and cuts, which she was sponging with alcohol. A bloody dress thrown across a kitchen chair showed that she had torso wounds as well.

"I…I wrecked the car," she sobbed.

"How bad are you?" I asked.

"I'll live. Your dad will be mad."

"He'll be more worried about you. Besides, he's been mad before. Can I do anything?"

Mamma said none of her injuries was serious—that she could walk and move everything. Then she told me how the car had gotten away from her when she tried to start it, but skipped the details.

The worst part of the wreck for Mamma was that the sudden stop at the fence had pitched her into a thicket of poison ivy which flourished there along the irrigation ditch. Poor Mamma was highly susceptible to that plant's oily poison. So, on top of her scratches and cuts, she got a frightful rash and facial swelling that had her eyes swelled shut for days. Dad and

I sponged her rash with soda water and applied calamine lotion (the best treatments available then), and she finally recovered without visible scars. But she suffered mightily for the better part of a week.

The episode convinced Mother she needed a dependable car of her own. And one of her first purchases with her apple-packing income that fall was a brown 1935 Chevrolet sedan.

As for the Flint, Dad used his truck to pull it from the ditch that same day, and dragged it back up to the top of the driveway. However, the frame was twisted and the front seat was misaligned so that it no longer made into a bed. I had to move back into the cabin. Dad and I eventually modified the Flint into one of the orchard tractors called "puddle jumpers."

PUDDLE JUMPERS

After we lost the home place to bank foreclosure, Dad (and Mother when she could) supported us by any means available. One of Dad's enterprises that I'm most fond of, because we worked together, was making puddle jumpers.

Puddle jumpers were cars that were stripped, lowered, and shortened for use as orchard tractors. These innovative vehicles filled a niche market of the time. Before puddle jumpers, hauling within the orchard was usually done on "stone boats"—basically sledges dragged by horse or tractor—or on wagons, again drawn by horse or tractor. Both methods had disadvantages. The stone boats gave a rough ride to the boxes of ripe fruit, and also obliterated irrigation rills. As for tractors, most of those had cleated steel rear wheels which also tore up the rills, and they were high and wide enough to damage tree limbs. Wagons of the time usually were so high that they not only threatened the tree limbs but also caused extra effort in loading and unloading. Some enterprising ranchers had started building long, low-slung trailers with rubber-tired wheels, but towing those trailers through the orchards was still a problem.

Enter the puddle jumper—the chassis of a powerful old car, stripped of body and windshield, with frame and driveshaft shortened and spring shackles lowered. It was a perfect tractor for the low-slung orchard trailer, and a vehicle that also could be used for limited highway travel. Its rubber tires did little damage to the irrigation rills, and its short wheelbase allowed sharp turns between tree rows.

I don't think Dad invented the puddle jumper, and several ranchers built their own, but Dad was one of only two I knew who built them for sale. I think Dad built three. He started this particular enterprise while we lived in our tiny, makeshift cabin across the Entiat River Road from our old orchard.

Dad would buy or barter for a powerful old car, which usually was sitting on blocks somewhere because it was a gas guzzler or was disabled. If he could get it running there, we merely had to pump up the tires and drive it home. Other times he would have to tow the old car to our place, with Mom or me steering and using the brakes of the towed car to keep the tow chain tight. Dad acquired a variety of auto makes, including, I think, a Buick, an Overland, a Star, and a Flint. The only requirements were that the engines and drive trains had to be in reasonably good condition and, above all, they had to be dirt cheap.

After we got an old beast home, the next step was to tow it with his truck up to the back of our side-hill property, among the pine trees that would provide shade and serve as derricks for hoisting. (Unfortunately, the trees also provided pitch drippings and plummeting pinecones.)

We started with the Flint, which had been my bed for a few summers, until Mamma put it over the road bank while attempting a rolling start. Dad and I went to work with a hacksaw to cut the car body at the front door posts. Next, we unbolted the rest of the body from the frame, after which we hoisted the body and dragged the chassis out from under it. (Dad knew *everything* about pulleys and hoists, levers and winches.) Last to come off were the seats and the rear floorboards.

With the frame exposed, we went to work shortening it. First was removal of the driveshaft, which Dad stored. Then, we blocked up the frame. Dad measured everything six ways from Sunday, and made his final "blueprint." The trick was to cut a section from each side of the U-shaped steel frame so that the remaining ends could be telescoped and bolted together. Much to my disappointment, this required cutting each side of the frame twice.

"No use complaining, Son," Dad said, "we do whatever it takes."

Dad borrowed a second hacksaw so we could work together. I was slow at first, until he taught me to pace myself, to only put pressure on the cut during the downward stroke and, most importantly, to steady the hacksaw with my second hand to avoid breaking the blade. This last lesson didn't sink in until I had broken a blade.

"Son," Dad said, "that blade cost more than an hour of orchard wages."

After that, I became careful enough to do some of the frame sawing without Dad's close supervision.

After the frame was cut and telescoped, usually forced into place using a car jack and chains, we drilled holes for bolts to hold the frame sections together. Lacking electrical tools or even a breast drill (twist drill), we did all the drilling with an old-fashioned carpenter's brace with bits designed for drilling metal. This was mighty slow work, especially for me, as I could not apply much weight to the knob of the brace while I cranked it. Dad said I had a knack for quickly dulling every bit I used. Fortunately, he became proficient at sharpening those precious bits on his old treadle grindstone wheel. Still, augering our way through those layers of steel frame took forever, even for Dad.

With the frame bolted in place, Dad measured the precise distance that would be spanned by the shorter driveshaft. Shortening the driveshaft was the only part of the operation that we couldn't do ourselves. Dad relied on the E.T. Pybus company, a pioneer blacksmith and machine shop in Wenatchee, to shorten and re-weld those driveshafts. The bill from Pybus was sometimes more than Dad paid for an old car in the first place.

My greatest pleasure with the puddle-jumper work was the finishing touches, sometimes left to me while Dad did engine work, reconnected the shorter driveshaft, and rerouted the brake cables. I could smooth exposed saw cuts with a hand file, make neat wooden plugs to fill the gaps in sawed-off door posts, reinstall a seat for the driver, and generally spruce things up. If the front fenders had to go, unbolting those, using kerosene as a "de-ruster," was my job, too.

I don't recall that Dad had any trouble selling our puddle-jumpers; maybe he had buyers waiting. Part of the profits from the first sale went to the purchase of drills and hacksaw blades, and we started over.

I helped Dad convert another of the old cars into a puddle jumper, but we didn't work steadily on them after the first one. We both got busy with other things. The other junkers just languished on the hillside.

Mother hated the hulks and pieces left from the operation. As time dragged on, she would look at the hillside and say, "Gerald, I *wish* you would get rid of that junk."

Dad agreed that would be a good idea, and promised to keep the junk as far from the house as possible until he disposed of it. He never did get rid of the old cars and their pieces but, ironically, Dad's procrastination paid off. That junk pile was later mined for gold.

When our country entered World War II, all truck and car production was immediately directed to the military, so demands for used vehicles soon increased. Even though gasoline was rationed, a market quickly grew for any car that ran. Suddenly, Dad's junk pile became a treasure trove of parts for old cars being resurrected for wartime use. Dad didn't blink at charging hefty prices (enough, sometimes, to make me cringe) and the only guarantee was that the customer could return a part for a refund if it did not work or fit. Still, Dad had frequent customers, some from quite far. This unexpected income probably was not large in total, but it was enough to keep Mamma from complaining about Dad's junk.

But the products of war also doomed the puddle jumper. Surplus Jeeps were available to WW II veterans for ridiculously low prices, and these made fine orchard tractors. With their low bodies, short wheelbase, and fold-down windshields, they maneuvered easily between the trees, and their four-wheel drive provided traction impossible with puddle jumpers. Jeeps even came with a trailer hitch, and they were legal for highway use.

Taps for the labor-intensive puddle jumpers.

*　　*　　*

Besides youth programs sponsored by local churches, two secular youth programs became available in the valley during my last two years at Arden-voir School—the Boy Scouts and the 4-H.

I was immediately attracted to the Scouts because of its focus on outdoor skills and camping, both dear to my heart. I already owned a Boy Scout Handbook, acquired from my Uncle Max after he briefly tried the Scouts, and I had learned many interesting and useful things from that book.

275

However, three obstacles defeated my scouting plans: First, the scout meetings were held at night at the Community Hall, about two miles up valley from our cabin. Riding my bike alone to and from the meetings along the unlighted valley road was not attractive to me or my folks. Second, the cost of outfitting myself with scout uniform and equipment was formidable. Third, my pacifist mother was suspicious of the Boy Scouts' motives.

"They look too much like the German Hitler Youth and the Italian Black Shirt boys we see in the newsreels," she said sternly. "And those foreign groups openly admit they're preparing their boys for war."

I wasn't nearly as interested in the 4-H, but I wanted to be a part of something in addition to Mom's religious activities. The 4-H meetings started conveniently after school, and offered great flexibility in the projects one could undertake, including some that did not require much outlay of money. And neither of my parents objected to my participation. I joined the local 4-H group and chose as my project the cultivation of barren soil to raise a garden.

The "barren soil" part of the requirement was easy. Nothing but sagebrush and cheat grass grew between the pine trees on the sandy slope above our cabin. I finally spaded up a small plot just down slope from the Fouch Ditch, which passed through the upper part of our place. My intended water supply was that ditch.

After raking out the roots and rocks from my garden plot, I used our hoe to make zigzag or "switchback" grooves in the soil to spread water on the sloping plot, and began soaking the ground with bucketsful from the ditch. With the ground thoroughly damp, I planted a few short rows of radish, carrot, and onion seeds. Each afternoon, after rushing through my other chores, I dutifully dipped several bucketsful of water from the ditch and poured them into my irrigation rills.

I had chosen my garden plot for its sunny, southwest exposure, and before long the tiny plants broke the surface. One afternoon I was kneeling in my garden pulling weeds, when Mr. Fouch, our adjacent neighbor and manager of the ditch, approached from along the ditch bank.

"Hello, Mr. Fouch," I called. He was high on my friendly list at the time. He had just asked us to house-sit during the coming winter in his modern, roomy home while he and Mrs. Fouch wintered in California. He squatted down opposite me and smiled.

"I see you're starting a garden, Bruce."

"Yes, sir," I answered proudly. "It's a 4-H project."

"Oh. That's why it's up here, away from your folks' garden."

I nodded and pulled more weeds.

"And you're getting the water for it from the ditch here?"

"Y-yes, sir. Isn't that okay?" I had never before doubted that it would be.

Mr. Fouch smiled ruefully. "No, Bruce. Actually, it isn't okay. The only people who can legally get water from the ditch are the ditch shareholders. Your family has no shares in the ditch, now that your grandma's place has been sold."

"But-but people dip water from the ditch all the time—my aunt and uncle, the Albins—"

"Yes, but they take the water just for drinking, or for washing. All the ditches in the valley allow small amounts for those uses. But if I let you take ditch water for your irrigation, I'd have to let everyone else along the ditch water their gardens, too. And pretty soon, there wouldn't be enough water left for the orchards. Do you understand?"

"Yes, sir," I said grudgingly.

"Good boy!" He and patted me on the shoulder. "Say hello to your folks for me."

With that, Mr. Fouch stood up and walked back along the ditch bank toward his house.

For a while, I carried well water in buckets up the three hundred feet or so to my little vegetable plot. Each watering session soon became a burden, and I finally just gave up on the garden.

A handful of stubborn radishes survived to semi-maturity, but all my other plants withered and died. And with the demise of my garden, so died my participation in 4-H.

HIGH SCHOOL IN WARTIME

I entered Entiat High School in 1939 at age thirteen, riding the school bus about nine miles to and from the big town of Entiat (population 350). I remember well the intimidating first days: changing from a single teacher for all subjects to several different teachers and classrooms, and from fellow students I had grown up with to mostly new classmates. Making matters worse, during eighth grade I had developed a painful inflammation of my knee tendons, so my first persona at Entiat High was a small, underage freshman kid, wearing glasses and brand-new cream-colored corduroy pants, hobbling around the hallways and probably looking confused. That knee condition, which severely limited my running, lasted through my puberty and kept me from taking Physical Education, thereby further marking me as some kind of wimp.

Within days of the start of my freshman year, Adolf Hitler's German army invaded Poland, and two days later Great Britain and France declared war on Germany. Thus, my entire four years at Entiat High were shadowed by the specter of World War II.

*Entiat High School. Provided good academic and
social education, even during wartime.*

At first, we in the Entiat Valley felt only indirect effects of war in Europe. Although our government had officially declared neutrality, U.S. defense industries began sputtering to life. In the Puget Sound region, good jobs became available as military bases, shipyards, and aircraft manufacturing plants geared up. Local families were among the many rushing toward the new opportunities. It seemed family after family would be in the valley one week and suddenly gone the next. Several of our former neighbors, including the Schermerhorns, moved to Tacoma, sending back glowing reports about job opportunities there. Other neighbors followed, seeking a better life, taking more of my former schoolmates.

If any good can be said about World War II, it was that the war finally snuffed out the Great Depression.

For all of America, the war became a harsh reality when the Japanese attacked Pearl Harbor, Hawaii, on December 7, 1941. It was the middle of my junior year.

As with other momentous events in our lifetimes, survivors of that time remember exactly where they were when they heard of that sneak attack: I was in the yard at the Fouch's place, where we were house-sitting, washing my mother's recently acquired 1935 Chevy. Mom came to the door and, in a voice shaking with emotion, told me the news just announced on the radio. We perched around the radio as more and more of the terrible details came in. Then Mom hugged me, crying, and I knew she feared that I would be drawn into the fighting. But I, not quite sixteen, felt sure the U.S. would win the war before I reached conscription age.

The war quickly began to affect our lives at home and at school. Along with the rationing of commodities like sugar, butter, meat and shoes, auto tires and later gasoline were strictly rationed—a blow, indeed, to us new drivers. Furthermore, to conserve the precious tires and fuel, a nationwide speed limit of 35 mph was imposed, another perceived hardship for us teens. But there was "a war on," as we constantly heard and repeated, and trying to circumvent the wartime rules was patently unpatriotic.

❄   ❄   ❄

Entiat High School provided an introduction to new and interesting friends, both boys and girls. One of the girls, Cleo Buckley, and I had much in common. Both of us started high school young, she even younger than I. We were both burdened then with wearing glasses. And both families struggled through the depression, although her dad nearly always had a steady job, even at poor wages. We both were conscientious in trying to do what was right and not disappoint our mothers. I quickly recognized Cleo as a shy, kindred spirit. Even so, I was too timid at first to approach her except in the company of my best guy friend, Jerry Barnum, a red-headed transfer from Oklahoma.

In the spring of our sophomore year, the three of us were exploring an abandoned shed, where we found a treasure of 1920's magazines. While we laughed and joked about the contents of the magazine, Cleo mimicked the pose of one of the models. At that moment, I realized our classmate had transformed from a graceful, willowy girl into a shapely young woman—a very attractive young woman, indeed.

The next fall, near the beginning of our junior year, I walked Cleo home one evening along the dirt road leading to her house. At a bend in the road,

The author and Cleo Buckley,
high-school sweethearts.

still out of sight from her house, I put my hand on her arm and stopped her. She turned, our eyes locked, and we kissed. The thrill of that first kiss made me sag against her, and left an indelible mark on my heart. Only much later did I learn that Cleo had felt the same intense thrill.

Although both Cleo and I went out with other people too, most other girls I dated really made me appreciate Cleo all the more. We became engaged during our senior year.

CALIFORNIA CALLS

After the Japanese attacked Pearl Harbor, more and more young men volunteered or were drafted into the military, and families continued to move toward the defense industries. A severe labor shortage soon developed, not only for our local orchards and businesses, but in non-defense activities nationwide.

I easily expanded my summer box-making, and found other short-term jobs as well. In the early summer of 1942, I rode my bike home from a cherry-picking job and found my folks waiting for me.

"How long will your cherry picking last?" Dad asked the moment I walked in.

"Should be through tomorrow," I answered, puzzled. "There's only one more tree."

"Good!" Dad said, grinning. Mom smiled, too.

"Floyd McKeever telegraphed to offer jobs for all three of us for the summer," he said, "in California. They'll be there, too…and Harold."

Mr. and Mrs. McKeever were friends and former valley residents who had moved to North Seattle, and with whom we had stayed while Dad bought lumber for rebuilding our burned house. Harold, their son, was a year older than I and a favorite buddy. The prospect of working with our friends was inducement enough, but California? I had never been south of Washington. California was the land of gold and glamour!

"What will our jobs be in California, Dad?"

"We'll all be working in a soft-fruit packing shed," he replied. "Be sure to pack your box hatchet and apron—and your gloves."

"How soon can we go?" I asked.

My folks laughed, obviously excited too. "As soon as I can get your mother's car ready," Dad said, "and some extra tires."

"We're going to drive to California? What about gas?"

Strict gasoline rationing was in effect in East Coast states, and had been planned, then delayed, for the Pacific Northwest. But gasoline stations in our region were, by then, restricted in the hours they could sell gas and the amounts they received from suppliers.

"We'll just have to buy gas where and when we can, and hope gas-stamp rationing doesn't start while we're away from home. The paper says California doesn't have restrictions on gas."

Tires were a major concern, because all the tires on Mom's car were well used, and some probably had tread recaps. Dad went to the local Ration Board and requested a new tire. His justification was that our food-production jobs in California were essential to the war effort.

He returned shaking his head.

"The man said the whole state only got about a thousand new tires this month. He offered me a certificate for a recap, if I had a good, bald casing. But all our tires have a little tread left."

Tires, all made with natural rubber then, were among the first items to be rationed after the Pearl Harbor attack and remained closely regulated throughout World War II. Although the war spurred America's development of synthetic rubber, most raw rubber came from Southeast Asia, which the Japanese controlled through much of the war. It may be true that "an army travels on its stomach," but an army rolls on rubber.

Fortunately, Dad was experienced at evaluating and using second-hand tires and, as soon as war was declared, he began acquiring them like others hoarded sugar and booze. The difference was that Dad's hoard was legal, and proved to be a very sound investment. Not only could Dad thus ensure that his truck always had tires, but he acquired extras for Mom's car, too.

My folks arranged for Grandma Lillian to take care of the garden and feed Prince and our cats, and for neighbors to check on Grandma herself. After a hectic day or so of preparing clothes and packing, we finally loaded suitcases, bedding and assorted boxes into Mom's 1935 Chevy two-door sedan. In mid afternoon, with the car's gas tank full, the three of us crowded in alongside our belongings and headed south to U.S. Highway 97. It was "California or Bust."

Dad had made sure that our four best tires were on Mom's car. Four more used tires, one mounted on a wheel, were tied onto the back, looking like segments of a huge, black caterpillar hanging onto the brown car. All three of us, I'm sure, had our fingers crossed that the tires would last through the long trip.

Dad drove us over Blewett Pass and into sunset. At Ellensburg, he pulled over and stopped.

"Can I get you to drive for a while, Son?" Dad asked casually.

I almost injured myself scrambling out of the back seat.

Dad took my place in the rear seat, wedged alongside our suitcases and boxes. "Just stay on Highway 97," he told me. "We should be able to make Goldendale before we need gas, but watch the gauge."

I had not the slightest idea where Goldendale was but, at age sixteen, I wasn't going to let lack of knowledge keep me from a chance to drive. With Mom watching closely from the passenger seat beside me, I tried to make the smoothest take-off in history.

I must have done well enough, for I soon heard Dad snoring softly in the back, and Mom nodded off beside me. I had never driven the route before—had not even seen it—so the tension of the unexpected kept me alert. I did take a curve too fast in the twisty Yakima River canyon, eliciting sleepy complaints from my folks, and a reminder from Dad to "take it easy on the tires."

My folks woke when I stopped at the first traffic light in the Yakima. From then on, with occasional instructions from Dad, who knew all the roads from his hauling, I drove on through the city of Yakima and to the Indian town of Toppenish. Dad was asleep again when I followed the signs and turned onto the highway that led us onto a lonely, monotonous stretch of highway through the Yakima Indian Reservation and into Satus Pass. Driving up the pass, I again took a corner too fast, which woke my folks.

Dad watched the road until he recognized our location. "You're doin' fine," he said. "Just watch those sharp corners. Goldendale is just a short way on the other side of the pass."

We stopped in Goldendale for gas and sandwiches from our food box. While we ate and used the restrooms, the attendant pumped our gas, checked the water and oil levels and pressure in all four tires, and washed the bugs from our windshield. He even asked our destination and gave us a free road map. It was nothing special, just the normal treatment that we could expect at every gas stop along the way. That's why we called them "service stations" in those days.

We were able to fill the gas tank there, probably because the Goldendale station catered mostly to farmers, which were granted almost unlimited gasoline allotments.

With the car serviced, I made my pitch to continue driving. "I've been doing fine, haven't I? And you both look like you could use more rest. It's not real dark, and I feel great. There's hardly any traffic, and the car's running fine. I'll be sure to tell you if I get tired."

My passengers stayed watchful and offered advice while I drove carefully down a switch-back grade into the Columbia River gorge and over a bridge across the river. Then into Oregon, mostly through rolling, desolate reaches, where they faded to sleep again.

After nightfall, I could see little of the surroundings and met very few other cars or trucks. Even the towns we passed through had virtually shut down for the night. Town lights were subdued in "brown out" conditions, to conserve energy and also to avoid attracting enemy airplanes, a subject of paranoia at the time.

I continued following the shield-shaped "97" highway signs through the yellow cones of the headlights, and tried to stay alert while my folks slept fitfully. Eventually, however, the steady thrum of the faithful Chevy's six cylinders became hypnotic. The asphalt road seemed endless. The surges of adrenalin resulting from the occasional deer on the highway temporarily restored my watchfulness. Foolishly, I resisted waking one of my parents to take the wheel, feeling I had a duty to tough it out and let them sleep as long as possible.

To conserve precious rubber supplies, President Roosevelt had asked for a national speed limit of thirty-five miles per hour. Even though that limit was not yet mandatory (not until nationwide gasoline rationing began in autumn of 1942), our family generally tried to keep vehicle speeds below forty. However, during those dreary hours of driving through the blackness of central Oregon, with both of my passengers soundly asleep, slow speed became unbearable. With no one monitoring me, I held the speedometer at forty-five more often than not, unpatriotic though it was.

I cut back on speed, however, when I noticed the gas gauge. It showed less that one-fourth of a tank left, and I had no idea where the nearest gas station might be—or whether it would be open or have gasoline to sell.

I did some quick arithmetic: We had maybe four gallons of gas left. At fifteen miles per gallon, which we probably could count on even with our heavy load, that translated to about sixty miles of driving.

I pondered waking Dad, but I doubted that he knew the route this far from home. And what could he do anyway? Just tell me to press on and watch for an open gas station.

Just then, a speed-limit sign appeared and another that read "Entering Madras." My spirits rose until I reached the far end of the town without seeing lights at any of the town's service stations.

A highway sign told that the next towns down the road were Redmond and Bend. I don't remember the mileages shown on the sign, but I decided that we should be able to drive as far as Bend. Two more chances to find an open gas station.

Redmond was another disappointment. Only one gas station along the highway showed a dim light—just enough to read a sign, "Sorry—No Gas."

On to Bend. What's the worst that can happen? We might just have to wait in the car there until the stations open, and hope they'll sell us gas.

Still, I was mightily relieved when, in the surrounding blackness of early morning, I eased the Chevy alongside a gas pump at a dimly lit truck stop and diner in Bend, Oregon. We got out stiff-legged as a yawning attendant approached. He asked where we were headed.

"I can't fill you up," he said, "but I'll sell you enough to get you into California. They have plenty of gas there."

Thus assured, we went into the diner while the attendant serviced the car. Dad bought drinks—coffee for them, a root beer for me—from a sleepy-eyed young waitress in a striped uniform dress, who returned her attention to her dog-eared book as soon as she served us. While we, the diner's only customers, sipped our drinks, the silence of the night was punctuated by the "zzzt," "zap" of bugs electrocuting themselves on the diner's electrified screen door.

Dad took over the driving at Bend. I didn't argue this time, just crawled into the back-seat corner and promptly went to sleep.

The next thing I remember, the car was stopping. I looked into the pale dawn to see a uniformed man waving us to the edge of the road. What looked like sentry boxes sat on either side of the two-lane road.

Did we take a wrong turn? Is this a military base? Is there an enemy attack? All these questions flashed through my mind. As Dad and Mom got out of the car, I stumbled out behind them.

Dad, seeing my agitation, grinned. "Easy, Son. We're at the California line. This is an agricultural inspection station. They inspect for anything that might carry pests that could infest their crops."

He patted my shoulder. "You drove half way across Oregon and a fair piece of Washington. Good job." I felt much better.

We had to surrender a few apples from our food box, but were relieved that the uniformed inspector didn't make us unpack the car for a thorough search. Mom took over the wheel.

I tried to feel exuberant about being in the Golden State, but the scenery looked much like what we had passed through in parts of Oregon. The prominent volcanic mountains—Mount Shasta and Lassen Peak—loomed up grand and beautiful but, as I told my folks, we have lots of beautiful mountains in Washington, too.

The sun came up blistering hot. Somewhere in northern California, with me driving on asphalt near its melting temperature, our right-rear tire suddenly blew out. With the tire thumping and flopping and pulling us hard to the right, I managed to stop safely.

While Dad and I changed the tire, he lectured: "When the road's hot like this, it's a good idea to slow down, especially on the corners." I nodded meekly.

"Yep," Dad said as he examined the flat, "this one's a goner. See how the rubber parted company from its cotton fabric? Tube's shot, too, but we can still buy those."

I could only say how sorry I was. With that one ruined, we had only three extra tires left, and many hot miles to go.

I felt further chastened when Dad took over the driving. I smiled to myself, though, when he let the speedometer needle creep up to match my former speed.

At the town of Weed, where US-97 joined US-99, we stopped at a garage for gas and a new tire tube. Luckily, the garage had one last tube that fit our tires. Dad paid the attendant to mount another of our tires to replace the spare. While Mom and I fished bottles of pop from ice water in the garage's chest-type cooler, Dad hovered over the attendant.

"Careful not to pinch the tube," Dad cautioned as the young man worked with his tire irons. "You're getting it under the tire bead over here." I'm sure the attendant was glad to see us on our way.

We proceeded south on Highway 99, with Mom driving until the traffic gradually became heavy enough to bother her. That suited me just fine. I happily accepted the chance to get behind the steering wheel again. Dad stopped me at the outskirts of Sacramento and took over.

Our destination was a small town named Loomis, twenty-something miles northeast of Sacramento. None of us knew what to expect there. My folks just had two telephone numbers—one for the packing shed where the McKeevers would be during working hours, and another for the place they stayed.

For me, the uncertainty only added excitement to our adventure.

*   *   *

Loomis proved to be a small town strung out along a main highway (now beside Interstate 80) in the central Sacramento Valley agricultural region.

"It looks about the size of two Entiats," Dad remarked. "Maybe three."

We easily located the McKeevers at the motor lodge where they were staying. After the women hugged and the rest of us shook hands, Mrs. McKeever announced that she had paid a deposit for us on another cabin at the same motor lodge. We quickly got the key and unloaded the car.

Our home for the next few weeks was a two-room cabin just two doors away from the McKeevers, in a row of identical, wood-frame structures with covered carports in between. The place was cheap and looked it. Our front room held a brown, sagging, bed-daveno, a non-matching armchair, and an old floor-model radio. A kitchenette and dining area, with worn linoleum, occupied the other half of the room. My folks' bedroom and the bathroom (with shower, no tub) were in the back. I slept in the front room on the bed-daveno.

The place was not much larger than our cabin back home but, with hot-and-cold running water, a small gas range, refrigerator, and the bathroom, it was much better living. Mamma scrubbed what she could, resigned herself to what she couldn't clean, and we settled in.

The precious spare tires went into my folks' bedroom for safekeeping.

Mrs. McKeever directed us to a local market, where Mom used her food ration stamps from home to provision our kitchenette. She was too tired to cook, so we just stowed the groceries and ate from our food box for dinner. Getting into the shower and the beds was more pressing.

Next morning, we followed the McKeevers to the packing shed, an easy walk from our motel. In comparison to the packing sheds in Entiat, it was a relatively small building, extending to a covered loading dock alongside a railroad siding. The sorting and packing lines, with simple, rather primitive equipment, were in the main building. Two box-making stands stood on the loading dock, near a stack of box shook.

While Mr. McKeever showed us around, I heard for the first time the full reason we were there. The packing shed was owned by a family of Japanese-American (Nisei) folks who, in earlier years, had been friendly neighbors of the McKeevers in Seattle. Several weeks earlier, federal marshals had forced the Nisei family into a detention camp. Somehow, the family had gotten a message to the McKeevers, appealing for help in meeting the shed's contracts with local growers to pack and sell their fruit. Defaulting on those contracts would ruin the family's business. Mr. McKeever said he approached several of his friends to help, but we were the only ones to respond.

"What did they do to get thrown into prison camp?" I asked Dad later.

"Probably nothing, Son," Dad said. "The McKeevers said they're good people who love America. Folks are running scared, about spies and sabotage. The marshals just rounded up a bunch of people with a Japanese background and put 'em all into camps. As soon as they figure out these people are okay, they'll probably release them." Mom thought so, too.

Not everyone in Loomis agreed with our efforts. Mr. McKeever had trouble hiring enough help because several former employees now declined further work "at that Jap shed." He had to settle for a skeleton crew that included several Hispanic ladies, some with little or no experience and some who spoke little English.

Mom encountered the prevailing negative attitude at the local food market.

"You're one of them northerners come down to work at that Jap packin' shed, ain't you," a woman clerk said while Mom was checking out. "Why would a good American want to work there?" she added haughtily.

"Probably to help the local ranchers get their fruit packed and sold instead of rotting on the trees," Mom answered coolly.

The clerk said not another word, just bagged Mom's groceries and accepted her cash and ration stamps. I could have hugged Mom right there in the store.

Most people in Loomis, however, were not that confrontational. Generally, the locals seemed reasonably polite, if reserved. One exception was the owner of the local ice-cream store, who warmed to us over the weeks as we kept buying his outstanding maple-nut-flavored ice cream, our dessert of choice throughout our stay.

Dad mentioned only one interaction with a local who might have had malicious intent. One evening, Dad was at the motel changing a tire on the Chevy, the second tire to go bad of the eight we started with. A man came up and told Dad he "knew a guy" who might sell Dad a new tire "for a price." Dad just smiled and said, "No thanks."

"I didn't like his looks," Dad explained. "I thought he might be an undercover federal marshal, or someone else trying to get us into trouble. Besides, I'd have to be mighty desperate to buy on the black market with the war goin' on."

We actually had little time for interaction with the folks of Loomis. The shed began operation the afternoon following our arrival, and the pace of processing all the contracted fruit with a skeleton crew over the next several weeks allowed little time for social life.

When we walked back to the shed after lunch on our first day, two trucks carrying boxes of apricots were waiting at the shed to unload. We saw Mr. McKeever and Harold hurriedly unloading the first truck, stacking boxes on the loading dock and then wheeling them into the shed on hand trucks. Dad sprinted ahead to help them.

Within a few more steps, I heard the unmistakable sounds of a box maker—an unsteady, slow box maker. Mom and I also picked up our pace, and entered the shed just as clickity-clacking noises of grading equipment started up. The packing shed had come to life for the season.

While Mom stayed inside to help Mrs. McKeever train the inexperienced ladies who would be sorting and packing the fruit, I hurried through to the loading dock. There, I found a smallish Hispanic boy fumbling away at one of the two box forms. I watched while he drove a nail that made a "shiner"—a nail protruding out of the box head—and then approached.

"Hi. I'm going to be working alongside you. My name's Bruce."

He gave me a shy smile, showing perfect, white teeth and quick, dark eyes. "I'm Chico. Mr. McKeever hire me last week to make the boxes. I think I am the only one he can find." He spoke English fairly well, though shyly.

I nodded, looking at the meager stack of made-up boxes. Unless the packers were mighty slow, those boxes wouldn't last long.

While we talked, I checked out the other box-making form. It was misaligned and infirm on its base.

"It bounces," Chico said, "so I took this one." I told him I would have done the same.

The pressure was on to get myself into operation and turn out a batch of boxes before the packers used up those few Chico had made. Yet, crooked boxes wouldn't do. I trotted back to our motel for Dad's wrenches and a big screwdriver and, of course, my hatchet and leather apron. Back at the loading dock, I began squaring up the box form, adjusting three pairs of steel nuts on spacer bars. It was a careful, give-and-take series of adjustments and, without the use of a carpenter's square, I had only the box shook itself to guide the adjustments. The squaring-up process took more than an hour, during which Mr. McKeever popped out of the shed several times to check my progress. Even in the shade, I was sweating heavily from the pressure and the California heat. My work clothes, old corduroy pants and a short-sleeved shirt, were too heavy for the summer weather, but I had no others. I soon shed my shirt. Chico seemed unaffected by the heat.

By mid-afternoon, I had aligned the form and moved it to a solid part of the loading dock. Awkwardly, I began nailing together this different breed of wooden box. It was "squattier" than an apple box, had thinner box heads, took smaller nails, and the slatted box bottom went on first, before the sides. Still, by the end of that first day, I had made up enough 'cot boxes to win the approval of Mr. McKeever and the awe of Chico.

For the next several days, Chico and I worked steadily side by side. He was fourteen, and lived in Loomis with his mother. His father was in Mexico. I showed Chico the fine points of box making and he shyly taught me a few basic Spanish phrases, like *Yo tengo mucho hambre* (I am very hungry) and *Tengo sed por agua* (I am thirsty for water).

Mom soon had her packers trained and then became their cheerleader and champion. Similarly, Mrs. McKeever settled into her role as head sorter and forelady of the shed. The women along the sorting and packing lines were picking up speed, and the output of packed apricots increased steadily.

Dad worked wherever he was needed, including nailing lids onto the packed boxes, then hand-trucking stacks of those boxes into the shed's cold-storage room to await shipment. Soon, I was splitting my time between making boxes with Chico on the loading dock and rushing inside to nail lids on accumulated packed boxes, while Dad worked elsewhere and Chico continued making the boxes and wheeling stacks of them in for the packers' use. Mr. McKeever seemed to be everywhere, not only supervising and giving orders, but also lending a hand wherever needed. Harold worked with two Hispanic men, receiving the loose fruit and feeding the sorting machine. It was, as Dad said, a three-ring circus with a few performers wearing six different hats.

Because the little warehouse had a small cold-storage room, the packed fruit had to be shipped out every couple of days. Mr. McKeever arranged for boxcars to be moved in along the railroad siding to our loading dock. I don't know which of the men—Dad or Mr. McKeever, or maybe both—knew how to load the boxcars. I didn't wonder then. I just followed orders.

When a shipment had to go out, we Washingtonians went back to the shed after supper and loaded the fruit, often into a partially filled boxcar that had been moved down the track from one of the other packing sheds in Loomis. If we left the boxcar partly filled, we moved it along the level railroad tracks to an adjacent packing shed, where other workers would later fill out the car with that shed's fruit.

We moved a boxcar by all of us men pushing, after we got the car started using special levers, called car jacks, between the massive steel wheels and the rails. Near the destination shed, one of us would jump aboard the slowly moving car and twist a big, spoked brake wheel to stop. Although moving those boxcars was hard work, I loved the feeling of power it gave me, as if I could shout "Shazam!" and turn into Captain Marvel to move trains at will.

One morning, Mr. McKeever came to Chico and me and told us to stop making 'cot boxes and start making plum boxes. He pointed to the far end of the stacks of box shook and went back into the packing shed. The order caught me by surprise, although I vaguely remembered that we would be changing varieties of fruit.

Chico and I trucked some of the shook over to our box-making stands and looked it over. To my relief, the bottoms and sides were the same length as the 'cot boxes, so we wouldn't need to readjust our box forms. Only the height of the plum boxes was different—higher than the apricot boxes but not so high that we needed to change our sequence of nailing the parts together. By the time the plums started arriving by truck that afternoon, Chico and I had several hundred new boxes ready.

Our work-filled days with the apricots merely prepared us for the higher volume, longer work with the plums—making boxes, hand-trucking fruit, nailing lids, loading boxcars—all blurring together as the days raced past. Cold-cereal breakfasts; sack lunches; quick, simple suppers (lots of macaroni and little meat) by Mom at the motel; waiting turns for the shower, perhaps while listening to war news on the radio, and then to bed.

Finally, Mr. McKeever announced that we would be working half-days while the last of the plums dribbled in from the orchards. He called Chico inside the shed, and I never saw my young friend again.

In a few days, the shed closed down and this big adventure was over for me.

When Mr. McKeever issued our last checks, I was astounded at how much money I had earned. Even though my folks and I had been on hourly wages because of our varied tasks, my hourly rate was a generous sixty-five cents per hour, and we had worked long hours. The three of us went to the Loomis bank and then the post office, traded most of our wages for money orders, and sent those home to Grandma Lillian.

I kept out enough money for clothes to get me started in school and, as soon as we could, Harold and I rode the bus into Sacramento for our shopping. I bought a pair of dress slacks and a beautiful teal-blue shirt, and splurged on a pair of top-brand dress shoes.

Back in Loomis, Mr. McKeever took us all to a restaurant for dinner, where he made a little speech. He thanked us for our hard work and congratulated us on getting all the shed's contracts fulfilled.

"We sold all the fruit at good prices for the growers, and made a tidy profit for the shed owners, our poor friends in the camp. May they be out soon." The rest of us clapped in agreement.

Mr. McKeever also said he had learned that the pear harvest was starting in nearby Auburn, and that packing sheds there were desperate for experienced help.

"The wages they're offering are unbelievable," he said. "I think we should send the boys home by bus, and the rest of us should go up there to cash in on the bonanza."

After only brief discussion, we all agreed. Mom had about two weeks before she was to start work at a packing shed back home, and Dad had a similar time before his fruit-hauling started. Harold and I delighted in the prospect of riding a bus, without our parents, all the way to Seattle and, for me, on to Wenatchee and Entiat.

Two days later, waiting in Loomis for the bus that would start Harold and me on our next adventure, I was eager to leave, but a little self conscious that my belongings were in a cardboard box tied with twine, while Harold's were in a suitcase. We got the usual admonitions from Mom.

"Now you two watch out for strangers, and keep your wallets safe, and be good boys."

"Mom! I *am* sixteen…and Hal's almost seventeen. We'll be *fine!*"

Our mothers waved, smiling but dabbing their eyes with hankies, as the bus pulled out. We had said goodbye to our dads back at the motel, where they had been packing for the move to Auburn.

At the Sacramento bus station, we changed to the bus that would carry us through to Seattle. I was surprised that only about half of the seats were occupied, and that few people got on at the small towns along the route.

One passenger who joined us somewhere in northern California was a pretty, dark-haired girl, dressed in slacks and a sweater, apprehensively clutching a small handbag. She went past us and chose an empty seat several rows behind us, across the aisle. I nudged Hal.

"Why don't you go talk to her?" I urged.

"You go. She looks too young for me."

"Too young? She has a great figure."

"So does my cousin, and she's only twelve." He showed his dismissal by staring out the window.

The dark-haired girl occupied my thoughts for the next hour or so, while the bus rolled northward. From my seat on the aisle, I could turn my head and catch glimpses of her. Suddenly I saw a guy behind me leaning across the aisle, talking to her. He must have been in his twenties. He was grinning—leering at her! His talking went on and on.

By the time we reached a rest stop, I was more than agitated. I moved to let Hal out and told him to go ahead, that I would be in the lunchroom in a minute. Then I waited, tight as a drumhead, watching the two behind me.

Finally, the old lecher rose and came past me to leave the bus. I shot to my feet and went back to the girl's seat. As I stood there blocking her way out, my rehearsed spiel tumbled out.

"Hi. I'm Bruce. Uh…I couldn't help but notice that old guy trying to pick you up. I-I could come back and sit with you if you'd like. Would you like to go inside and have a Coke or something?"

Her surprised look turned to a smile. "Sure," she said. "Both, I mean. Would be nice, I mean. I'm Beth." She slid from her seat and preceded me out the door.

Hal didn't look enthused when I introduced Beth. He declined to join us at the counter for a Coke, choosing to scan the magazines instead.

When Beth and I reboarded the bus, Hal was already in his seat. When I told him I was going to sit with Beth, he didn't look pleased but said okay, flipping pages of his new magazine.

A moment after I slipped into the seat beside Beth, the driver started the engine and closed the bus door. The guy who had been opposite Beth was not in his seat. I looked around the bus for him, but he had not returned. I would not get to protect Beth from the old lecher after all. Still, I felt proud that I had made the effort.

Hal was right. Beth was too young for us—thirteen, she said.

This was her first long trip, Beth said, and she was scared of traveling alone. "But the bus driver is watching out for me, and now I have another friend." Her smile made me feel like her knight-protector against the world's dragons. But I also became aware that the driver was watching us in his rear-view mirror.

"I *hate* the war," Beth continued. "Dad's been sent to San Diego, and Mom is moving down there to be close to him and work in some defense plant. I have to go to my grandmother's in Portland and go to school there. And they already sent my brother to Phoenix to live with our aunt and uncle. I *hate* it!" She turned her face toward the window.

This was my first realization of how badly the war was upsetting lives and disrupting families. I didn't know what to do, so I patted Beth's hand. Instantly, she clasped mine. We would hold hands much of the way to her destination.

That night we slept together, with her head on my shoulder, part of the time with my arm around her. And always under the watchful eyes in the bus driver's mirror. I slept fitfully, not only because my right arm kept going numb, but because my feelings about this girl puzzled me. Pretty though Beth was, I felt little sexual interest in her, mainly sympathy and protectiveness. Of course, she was just a kid—three whole years younger.

Is this how guys feel about their sisters? I wondered.

The next morning, as the bus rolled steadily north along Highway 99 through Oregon, Beth and I talked of many things, but nothing intimate. I told her about my classmate Cleo Buckley, whom even then I considered my girlfriend although we weren't "going steady." Beth said she hoped the boys in her new school would be nice.

When we neared Portland, Beth took a note card from her purse and wrote her grandmother's address. "Write me," she said. I told her I would, but I never did.

I was relieved when Beth began waving frantically at a well-dressed lady waiting outside the Portland bus station. Beth would be in good hands. My "brotherly" duty was fulfilled. I smiled when Beth paused in her eager exit to thank the fatherly bus driver.

I rejoined Hal to go into the Portland bus station, where we lunched on hamburgers and discussed Beth's situation and the war in general. Our talks of the war continued after we re-boarded the bus. Hal, who was about a year short of eighteen, the age of draft registration, admitted he was nervous about going into military service. I confessed that I was, too. The war news, censored or not, was not encouraging. Radio news reported that German submarines were sinking our tankers and cargo ships by the dozens off the Atlantic Coast. In the Pacific, the Japanese not only controlled most of the Orient, but had captured U.S. bases in Midway and Wake Islands, as well as the Philippines and some Alaskan (Aleutian) islands. Obviously, the war would not be over soon. At the end of our discussion, though, Hal and I agreed that, when the time came, we would do our duties.

The rest of my long bus trip passed uneventfully. From the Seattle terminal, Hal led the way via streetcars to the McKeever house in North Seattle, where I stayed overnight and enjoyed a soaking bath in a real tub. Hal made a surprisingly good supper of canned beans, Spam, and crackers. The next morning, after a breakfast of canned peaches and fried Spam, he accompanied me back to the bus station and saw me off on the bus for Wenatchee.

The subsequent bus ride from Wenatchee north to Entiat seemed interminable. From Entiat, I had no trouble hitching a ride up valley to our little cabin.

Grandma Lillian hugged me warmly and assured me that everything had been fine there, and that she had received our postal money orders. I told her about my folks' plan to stay and find more work in California, and that I didn't know exactly when they would come home.

After we chatted a little more, Grandma said, "You're just in time to help me look for your dog. He didn't show up last night for his supper, and I haven't seen him at all today. He's probably just on one of his hunting trips, but you know better than I do where he might be."

My heart chilled. Prince did spend hours in the hills hunting groundhogs, but he had always returned by sundown. A dread foreboding twisted my gut. I ran across to our cabin and, without even changing from my good clothes, grabbed my bike. I raced up and down the valley road scanning the roadsides, the usual recovery sites for missing pets. But even though I biked back and forth farther than Prince had ever roamed, I found no sign of him.

Only a little relieved, I returned to our cabin, opened it up to dispel the stuffiness, and changed out of my good clothes. All the time my mind reviewed Prince's favorite hunting places. I hurried up the hillside behind our cabin to the nearest cluster of boulders where a family of groundhogs had often enticed Prince with their shrill whistles.

With no luck at the first groundhog den, I roamed on to others, scanning the deer trails as I crossed them for his footprints. I whistled and shouted, "Here, Prince! Here, Prince!" until my throat hurt. Alas, I found neither Prince nor recent dog tracks in the hillside dirt. At dusk, I dragged back to Grandma's and submitted to a scolding for not telling her where I went.

After another day of futile searches, and queries among the neighbors about Prince, my folks drove in. The extra California jobs had not worked out. I choked out the news that my beloved dog was missing.

It was not until another day or so had passed that the odor of death led us to Prince's body, in the crawl space under our cabin. His distended right jowl showed the fang punctures of a rattlesnake. Poor Prince never could resist those varmints—and this time I wasn't there to call him off.

As a country boy, I certainly was no stranger to the death of animals, but I couldn't handle the burial of Prince. He had been my companion and protector since my early grade-school years at the home place. Dad buried him someplace on the hillside where he used to roam. I begged off from helping, and didn't even want to know the grave location.

*   *   *

Our local region faced the same wartime worker shortages we had found in California. One result was that we high-school boys no longer had to scrounge for jobs—they were thrust at us. And many of us were eager to respond, not only for the chance to earn money, but also because it was the patriotic thing to do, to help the war effort.

301

*Prince and friends: Dad, Grandma Lillian, Mamma,
and Uncle Frank Cook's mother, "Cookie."*

I shall never forget one job, resulting from an announcement at school that a rancher in the lower part of the valley needed three boys to pick up brush in his orchard. Three of us fellows decided to apply for the job. We sent home word to our parents that we would be working late, rode the school bus three miles up valley to the rancher's place, and presented ourselves. The rancher said he could put us to work immediately, and would pay us each fifteen cents an hour.

"Fifteen cents?" one of my buddies said "That's way low for orchard work nowadays."

"But you're kids," the rancher said. "I don't pay kids the goin' wages for men.... Look, it's a good way to make some extra money. You can take it or leave it."

After huddling for a couple of minutes, we agreed to accept the job. Although the pay was an insult, we had already committed ourselves to a six- or seven-mile walk farther up valley to our respective homes. We might as well get something for our trouble.

The rancher set us to work on three adjacent tree rows, then ranged back and forth behind us like a sheepdog barking at reluctant strays.

"Pick it clean, now...and don't lag back. We have to clear these rows and three more before dark.... Hey there, I'm not payin' you to stretch and rest."

After three hours of that, the blessing of darkness emancipated us slaves.

"We'd like our forty-five cents now," my older buddy told the rancher.

"Nah. I don't pay by the day, only when the job's done. See you tomorrow, boys."

With that, the rancher turned and strode off toward his house, leaving us looking at each others' open mouths.

During the long walk home along the unlit road, we cursed and derided the rancher in every term possible. When I complained to my folks over my reheated plate of supper, Dad laughed.

"That old buzzard would sell his mother into slavery for an extra buck," he said, clapping me on a shoulder. "You boys got snookered by an expert."

"But, what can we do?"

Even Mom smiled. "Simple," Dad said with a grin. "You can give up the forty-five cents he owes you, or you can finish out the job and learn from the experience—to always get a clear agreement about wages and paydays before you start a job."

That brush-picking job lasted six more back-breaking hours, with the rancher driving us most of the time. The grand sum of $1.35 that I earned lasted a lot less time than that life lesson.

*   *   *

In response to the labor shortages, the Entiat schools suspended classes during the peak of the local harvests so that students and teachers could help fill the labor gaps. Saturday classes were added afterward to make up the lost school time. In deference to female students and teachers who might have weekend social plans, they were allowed to attend Saturday classes in slacks, instead of the usual dresses or skirts. Also on Saturdays only, the young women could attend with their hair in rollers or pin curls, under a neat head-scarf, of course.

During the school break in 1942, I got a job at the Entiat Warehouse, where Wilbur (Buck) Buckley, father of my girlfriend Cleo, was a foreman. I'm not sure why Buck hired me, an undersized lightweight at the time. I know he recognized my eagerness to work, and my diligence. And perhaps he thought I might be part of his family one day. Or maybe he thought that, since I always seemed to be hanging around, he might as well get some work out of me.

As a warehouse worker, my tasks included stacking and un-stacking boxes of apples, wheeling them from place to place on hand trucks, and transferring them to waist-high conveyors. Along with other young men facing military duty, I worked both in the cold storage and the so-called "common storage" facilities, and also helped receive and store the boxes of loose fruit hauled in from the orchards. Occasionally, I helped load the packed fruit into boxcars, where my California experience helped greatly. I think my pay was sixty cents an hour, or roughly four times what my Grandpa Bedient had earned in the orchards during the worst of the depression.

*   *   *

At school, the war limited uses of school buses and heating oil, among other things. Classroom temperatures were lowered slightly during cold weather (not a real hardship, as I recall), and nighttime school events were curtailed. Certain ordinary supplies became hard to get; for example, the paper we finally were using for writing and duplicating was only a slight grade above newsprint.

Very few bus trips took players to sporting events, and then only to the closest rival schools. This was a personal blow to me, because by then my knees had healed, and I looked forward to turning out for sports, with my eye on baseball. I made the school tennis team instead, and we played a couple of the nearby schools, traveling in private cars loaded with teammates. Besides earning two letters in tennis, I also got a letter for being manager for the basketball team. Playing quarterback on a six-man intramural football team during my senior year rounded out my high-school sports career. During that last year, our teams diminished as older boys decided to forego graduation and enlist in the military services.

My senior year also saw the beginning of my writing for publication. Under pressure from the faculty, I took on the job of sports reporter for our school paper. Actually, this was just a few pages of mimeographed newsletter, named *E-Hi Breeze*. Under wartime restrictions on games, travel, and printing supplies, this was not an inspiring job. I regret to say that I did little beyond the basics, turning out meager articles to fit restricted page space.

Activities not greatly curtailed by the war included drama performances, carnivals and mixer dances, and the essential proms. All these activities helped familiarize us bussed-in "valley kids" with the local "town kids." Being a poor dancer at the time, I did best with the drama, and performed in four plays during my high-school years.

Academically, I did better than in sports, after a memorable tussle with freshman algebra. One of the most inspiring teachers I've ever known saw me through that and other high-school math and science courses. Her name was Helen Kinzel, and she also gave us wise advice on social values and personal goals—not that we always welcomed it at the time. She had been a rising young chemist who, while visiting friends in Entiat, fell for a young apple rancher there. Industry's loss was a mighty gain for generations of Entiat High students after Mrs. Kinzel turned to teaching. She was so loved and respected that a new gymnasium was named for her, and a scholarship fund established in her memory at Wenatchee Valley College.

Another teacher who stands out among the many good teachers at Entiat High was Mrs. McCain, a bright, no-nonsense lady who taught the "commercial" courses such as typing, shorthand and bookkeeping. I took her Typing I class, learning on a heavy old Remington manual typewriter. I'm sure Mrs. McCain was generous in giving me a "C" grade. Near the end of that school term, she came to my typing desk and asked if I intended to sign up for Typing II. When I said "No," she nodded wisely and said, "It's probably just as well."

Despite my struggles with algebra and typing, I managed to graduate from high school as valedictorian of our eighteen-member class, squeaking past two deserving, bright young women, Barbara Meredith and my sweetheart Cleo Buckley. As I gave my graduation speech before the assembly, three chairs on the stage were empty, representing classmates who already were in military service.

At graduation, I was about seven months short of my eighteenth birthday, when I would need to register for the draft. By my sophomore year in high school, I was sure I would be in the war, described by recruiters as a high-technology war needing technically trained people. To prepare myself, I took all the math and science I could at Entiat High, and even took an aviation pre-flight course the military provided to local schools. And when I graduated in June 1943, I was already working on my strongly pacifist mother to let me enlist.

Graduating seniors at Entiat High School followed a tradition of painting the numbers of their class year onto a high rock cliff, known locally as "Numeral Rock," near the mouth of the Entiat River. This was a hallowed tradition, going back to the graduating class of 1923. It also was a competition of sorts between the junior and senior classes. The seniors would plan the painting expedition and assemble the paint and climbing equipment in secret. At dusk on the designated evening, they climbed the hill, sometimes anchoring safety ropes from above, and finished the painting before dawn. The challenge to the junior class was to learn about the plans or keep close watch on the cliff for painting activities, then storm up the mountain to disrupt the painting, sometimes battling seniors left at the cliff top to defend the painters. Once the class number was on the cliff, the juniors could not deface the painting, and another graduating class had literally left its mark.

I would like to say that Cleo and I took part in an exciting rock-painting expedition that year, but we did not. We were as surprised as anyone else when our class number appeared one spring morning on Numeral Rock. Our class number, "43," is still clearly visible on the cliff. Beneath that number, our classmates had added three dots and a dash, the international Morse code for the letter "V"—V for the longed-for victory of allied forces in World War II.

A CAR OF MY OWN

During the fall of 1942, with the prospect of a warehouse job in Entiat, I needed transportation. At the time, our operating vehicles were limited to Dad's truck and Mom's 1935 Chevy, which she needed to drive to her packing job. But about that time, and perhaps in anticipation of my need, Dad made some kind of trade and acquired a 1928 Model A Ford two-door sedan.

The Ford certainly was no beauty. It had been painted a rather garish shade of green. The black fabric roofing was torn and peeled, and resultant leaks had left ugly brown stains in the cloth headliner. The seats were hemorrhaging their cotton batting. And the front wooden floorboards were so worn and weak that a cat could have dug through them just about anywhere.

Still, the engine ran, the body was generally sound, the front end wasn't too loose, all the glass was intact and—vitally important in wartime—it had five decent tires and a light thirst for gasoline.

As the Ford sat in our yard, it began to look better by the day. My interest in the car became a lust, heated, no doubt, by the friction of my recent driver's license rubbing against my new checkbook showing California savings. After discussions with friends and family about how the car's cosmetic problems might be fixed, I told Dad I wanted to buy the Ford.

"Ninety dollars," he said.

"I'll write a check," I answered.

The next time we drove to Wenatchee, Dad and I went to the courthouse, transferred the title and got new license plates.

A car of my own! My pride and enthusiasm were boundless. On the drive home, Dad listened to me bubble over about my plans to fix up the Ford. Finally he said quietly, "You paid too much for your car, you know."

I could scarcely believe my ears. My heart sank.

"But you said—"

"I didn't say it was *worth* ninety bucks. I just gave you a price. You should've come back with a counter offer, way below ninety. I was lookin' forward to a few days of friendly dickering before we settled on a price.

"You didn't even check 'er out real good," Dad continued, as I sat beside him in deflated shock. "How good are the brakes? You made sure the car runs, but how about stoppin'?"

"Well, the brakes stopped it when I drove it around home."

"Yeah, driving slow. But how well would they stop when you're out on the road? You should'a pulled the wheels and checked the brake drums and shoes. I'd have showed you how. Bad brakes would'a been a strong dickering point for you. And believe me, your mother won't let you out on the road unless those brakes are good."

I had to defend my car. "Well, at least she starts easy."

Dad smiled patronizingly. "Sometimes when an engine cranks up real easy it's because everything's loose inside."

When Dad and I drove into the yard, I saw the old Ford through newly unfettered eyes. I don't think the term, "buyer's remorse" had been invented yet, but that's what I had—in spades.

I jacked up the rear end of the Ford and put it on blocks so Dad could show me how to pull the rear wheels and check the brakes. As Dad suspected, the brake linings were badly worn, and one was glazed with grease leaking through a rear wheel-bearing seal. It was a dismal sight for me but an eye-opener about Dad's diagnostic skills.

Restoring brakes wasn't as easy then as it is now. Instead of the modern way of trading old brake shoes for refurbished ones with new linings cemented on, I had to drill out the rivets that held the old brake lining onto the curved brake shoe, buy a roll of lining material of the correct size, cut and fit the lining to the shoe, and secure the new lining with rivets. Adjusting my brakes was similar to the way it's done today, except that all the linkage and adjustments were mechanical. No hydraulic system was there to multiply, many times over, my force on the brake pedal (not on Fords until the 1939 models). So when I had to stop quickly, I pushed on that brake pedal as if my life depended on it—which it may have.

The 1928 Model A had been advertised as being able to go sixty-five miles per hour and, with the weak mechanical brakes, the wisecrack of the day was that the Model A was built to go but not to stop. Still, the '28 Model A was innovative in ways other than speed. The 1928 was the first Ford model to have safety glass and the first to come with an electric self-starter. Of course, the car had a hand crank too, and a front-end crank socket. When my car battery got too low to run the starter, I had options of coasting the car downhill to start it on compression, or hand-crank it to life like earlier cars.

Relining the brakes, buying and installing the wheel seal, polishing the brake drums by hand with steel wool, re-mounting the wheels and adjusting the brakes were only the first of my expenditures of money and time on my old Ford. Dad's trained ears had detected "piston slap," due to excessive cylinder wear, and he helped me open up the four-cylinder engine and install oversized piston rings and new connecting-rod bearings. On the body's interior, I rebuilt the floorboards and sewed twine across the bulging stuffing of the seat cushions. Dear Mom made new covers for my fold-down front seats. Mom also helped me install a new fabric roof. Rebuilding the front end with new bushings completed my main work on the car.

My little, green Model A served me well for commuting to work, special trips to and from school and, of course, dating. The latter use was mostly restricted to the warmer seasons, for the car had no type of heater. I soon found that traveling or "parking" in the freezing cold was not conducive to romance—or to getting second dates.

I used the Model A until the winter of 1943, selling it just before I enlisted in the Navy. Despite Dad's prediction that I would never recover the ninety dollars I had paid for the car, I sold it for one hundred forty dollars. The fifty-dollar "profit" probably just about covered the cost of all the parts I had bought to upgrade the car, but I was delighted to have proved Dad wrong for once.

LEAVING THE VALLEY

While I was in the Navy and events of unimaginable importance unfolded around the world, four events of lesser magnitude impacted my personal future.

Cleo's breaking off our engagement hit me hardest. She watched local marriages split apart in wartime, and decided she wanted more than the traditional small-town marriage with a passel of kids. She entered nurses training and later had a series of office jobs. I took the breakup rather hard, but Cleo was sweet enough to write to me all through my time overseas. By the time I returned from the Navy, she had married a handsome, newly discharged marine. During my subsequent times away from home, we lost track of one another.

The second event impacting my life was the enactment of the "GI Bill of Rights," which provided many of us veterans from poor circumstances with our only practical chance at a college education.

The third major personal change was my folks' move out of the Entiat Valley, although just barely out. They bought a strip of rocky, sandy shore land between the Columbia River and the highway (now U.S. 97A) extending southward from the mouth of the Entiat River, opposite the town of Entiat. In this new location, less than ten miles from where we had spent most of our lives, they still lived with river voices, just different ones.

Their reasons for moving from the valley cabin had to do with wartime shortages and support of my grandparents. Grandma Lillian had died, eliminating the need to stay near Zebra House. And plans to build the new house there had been stifled by wartime restrictions on building materials. Also, most of Dad's hauling customers and Mom's packing work were closer to Entiat than to the cabin, so the move conserved precious gasoline. And finally, Grandma and Grandpa Bedient, by then living alone in Entiat, needed frequent supporting visits from my folks.

The property they bought had two houses on it, both of them rustic and weathered. My folks moved into the larger one, beside the highway

The author in May 1946, shortly after discharge from the Navy.

about one-quarter mile southward from the Entiat River's mouth. The other house, smaller and closer to both rivers, was occupied by two elderly pensioners, who apparently had just built their little cabin there and had been "squatting" on the property for years. My folks not only allowed the old couple to stay, but Dad even ran a water line to their cabin after he dug a well near the mouth of the Entiat River and ditched a pipeline to my folks' house.

With their water supply secured, my folks remodeled the "new" house. Despite wartime shortages, they managed to upgrade the plumbing so that Mom finally had a kitchen sink with hot and cold running water, and an indoor bathroom with a toilet and shower. They acquired an oil-fired stove for heating but still kept Mom's old wood-fired kitchen range. For cooking in hot weather, though, Mom used electric fry pans and hot plates. Other amenities the new house provided were a screened sleeping porch (in addition to an inside bedroom) and a crude basement that held Dad's workbench and tools.

*Our house on the shore of the Columbia River south
of Entiat, fronting busy U.S. highway.*

315

A fourth change during my absence was that Mom had directed her love of pets into a new enterprise—dog breeding.

THE SCRUB

My blessed mother had a sweet-tempered little Cocker Spaniel female named Rusty, really more reddish blonde than rust in color. Rusty, when mated appropriately, produced beautiful puppies. Although perhaps not world class for the show ring, Rusty's pups were always sought after by local spaniel lovers. The "mated appropriately" part was sometimes a challenge, because Rusty had a personal preference for big, black dogs instead of the beribboned blonde male cockers that Mom chose for her. But that's another story.

My folks were living then in a small, brown-weathered house on the west shore of the Columbia River, south of the mouth of the Entiat River, opposite the town of Entiat. The back door opened onto the sand-and-rock beach of the massive, free-flowing, blue Columbia, over which the moon rose with a brilliance possible only in clear desert air. In front of the house, across Highway 97, cliffs of green-gray metamorphic rock had been steepened by highway construction and sculpted by flash floods, which left steep gullies lined with blocky talus. In a few of those miniature canyons, enough ground water seeped to the surface to support a variety of shrubs and bushes that harbored chattering flocks of Chukar partridge—and the occasional rattlesnake.

Rusty's latest litter was about three weeks old when I visited my folks for a Thanksgiving break from the University. Five of the pups were beautiful: blonde, chubby and active—just what Mom needed to please the waiting customers. But there was a sixth pup, too. He shared the blondeness, and he was at least as aggressive at pushing his way to Rusty's milk supply, but he was noticeably different from the others. He was bigger yet slimmer, and if you looked closely you could see a difference in his nose. He obviously was not going to be a poster boy for modern Cocker Spaniels.

"That scrub has to go," Mom said one day at breakfast. "He's a disgrace to the breed, and he'll ruin our—Rusty's reputation." Her eyes fixed on Dad.

"Don't look at me," Dad said around a mouthful of eggs. "Breedin' dogs is your business."

Mom's eyes shifted to me. "Son—"

"Hey, no way. I'm not killing a perfectly healthy pup." And that closed the subject.

I was pretty sure that soft-hearted Mom could not bring herself to put the odd pup down, but she might get someone else to do it. That threat put me squarely in the scrub's corner, yet I didn't feel it was my place to interfere with Mom's business. Each time I called home from school I asked about the odd pup, and was always pleased when they told me he was still around, although his future remained in doubt.

When Mom had the other pups' tails docked, she refused to spend the money on the scrub; he retained his embarrassing, God-given conformation. "He won't be around that long," Mom said.

He was still around, though, when the time came for the pups to go home with their new families. Mom tried to keep the scrub out of sight; to those who saw him, she explained that the "mixed breed" pup was her son's, and that she and Dad were keeping him for me.

This was the first I'd heard that the scrub was mine, although I didn't take it seriously. I still had to finish school and find some kind of job, so we all knew that my folks would have to keep "my dog" indefinitely. The fable apparently worked with the townsfolk, Dad said. By then the scrub not only was larger than his siblings, but was looking more different all the time.

When I arrived home on summer break, stubby-legged, floppy-eared Rusty came out in the yard to greet me. And she had with her this waggly, exuberant, long-tailed golden pup that already was almost as large as his mother.

Mom came to the door as I unloaded my stuff from the car. The pup bounced and charged around me, getting dangerously near the highway. "Boyzy!" Mom called with exasperation in her voice, patting her leg, "Boyzy, come home!"

"What a name for a dog," I teased after I had hugged Mom and was greeting Rusty and the pup. "Who came up with that?"

"It just happened, I guess," Mom said with a shrug. "I didn't want to name him because, you know, we didn't plan to keep him. But we had to call him something. We began to call him 'Boy,' and when I called him and his mother it became 'Rusty and Boyzy.' Now he kind of knows that name, and I guess it's too late to change."

I was watching the pup as I laughed at her explanation. He responded to my laugh by waggling all over, giving a little bark and his own dog laugh, and jumping up against me. That quick, as our eyes locked and I scratched his neck, abiding love was born.

"I hope you can train some manners into him," Mom was saying. "I'm not doing too well at it. He knows his name and 'come home,' but that's about all. Don't get him excited on the rug—he's been slow to house-break. And *do not* leave your shoes out, or he'll chew them."

My summer job that year was at a fruit warehouse in Entiat, close enough to ride my old bike to and from, and even to ride home for lunch. So I had plenty of time with Boyzy, and before my October classes started he was thoroughly house-broken and responded fairly well to commands of "down" and "sit." He was still growing out of his puppy stage, no longer chewing shoes, but eating Friskies like he was still competing with siblings. I used part of my summer earnings to get him all his shots and to leave a giant bag of dog food before I climbed aboard the Greyhound bus for school.

Because of a murderous class schedule and also avalanche problems in the Cascade highway passes, I did not get home during that winter. When I finally made it home in the spring, Boyzy muscled his mother aside to greet me.

His transformation during my six-month absence was astounding. He had reached his full size and developed a confident poise. He bore some resemblance to his classic Cocker Spaniel mother, but he was really more like a sleek, miniature Golden Retriever. Mom called him a "sport," but I've always thought of Boyzy as a kind of throwback to an earlier stage of spaniel development. Anyway, the result was beautiful to me: a proud, alert, happy guy whose eager eyes and dog-laugh said, "Isn't life fun? What shall we play?"

Boyzy's playground was my folks' entire six acres of rock-and-sagebrush land that lay between the Columbia River and the highway, and calling him home from a distance was often a vocal challenge. He had long-since given up trying to get his stubby legged mother to roam with him, so when I was not available to partner with him, Boyzy was a free-ranging loner.

Boyzy, "The Scrub," most resembled a miniature golden retriever.

Among his favorite playmates through the summer were the "dipper birds" that made their living along the fluctuating fringes of the Columbia River. Boyzy spent hours chasing those birds, barking and whining his frustration whenever he almost, but not quite, nabbed one. The birds, too, seemed to relish the game. They watched Boyzy creep near while they continued their rhythmic dipping and search for food at the water's edge. Then, with impeccable timing, they leaped and flew barely out of reach when Boyzy pounced, scolding him with shrill screeches before landing again near enough to encourage another chase. We never saw Boyzy catch one, yet he could not resist the game.

Boyzy never liked the baths I gave him in an old wash tub after his encounters with dead fish and such. Yet, he would unhesitatingly jump into the river and swim powerfully after a paddling duck, which of course would either fly or simply paddle farther out. Boyzy learned about swift water that way, following ducks out into the current—which was about seven miles per hour there during low flow.

The first time I saw him charge into the swift water and get swept downstream I was frantic. I yelled myself hoarse calling, "Boyzy, come home!" But I guess by then he had learned his limits, and when I raced downstream along the river bank, stumbling on the loose cobbles, crashing through the shoreline vegetation, and gasping my anxiety and lack of wind, I met Boyzy walking back, wet and tired, but seeming unconcerned. After that, whenever I saw him swim out too far and get swept out of sight, I gritted my teeth and kept myself from distracting him with a call, trusting Boyzy to know when he should swim out of danger.

Mom would just frown and shake her head. "That dog will either die in the river or on the highway out front. He doesn't have proper respect for either one," she said.

The highway worried me the most, because Boyzy had little fear of vehicles. He loved the sound of engines, in fact, because they meant that he might get to ride in either Mom's car or one of the trucks Dad used in his small trucking business. The folks lived beside a long, straight stretch of US 97, where the speed limit was fifty mph but cars regularly passed the yard doing sixty or so, and Boyzy grew up nonchalant about those speeding cars.

Boyzy's kinship with Dad's large truck, in fact, got us in trouble. It all had to do with Boyzy learning how to swing.

Behind the house, dangling from a pine tree near where Dad parked his trucks, hung a hefty rope with a knot at the lower end. Dad used the rope to hoist engines and other heavy parts while working on them, and afterward left it hanging there, with the frayed, knotted end about three feet off the ground. Boyzy probably was first attracted to the sway of the rope in the wind. Like a kitten, he could not resist anything that moved.

Mom called me to the kitchen window one morning. "Now I've seen it all," she said, chuckling and pointing.

There was Boyzy, hanging from the rope knot by his teeth, swinging back and forth. Only when the canine pendulum stopped did he drop back to earth. He immediately ran to the uphill side of the tree, took a running start before launching into the air and snapped onto the knot in mid-leap. He was able to achieve marvelous amplitude to his swings this way, and as the swinging slowed he would sometimes throw his hind legs as if he were a child learning to pump a playground swing. We all thought this was extremely cute, and could hardly wait to show Mom's younger brother, Max, who was single then and had a way of showing up for weekend breakfasts.

Much of the charm of Boyzy's swinging died the day Dad stomped into the house scowling and waved a traffic ticket under my nose. "Your dog just cost me seventy-five bucks! Seems he's been swingin' on the wiring under my truck…and the State Patrol frowns on trucks out there without clearance lights!"

I rushed out to check Dad's truck and, sure enough, some wires were ripped loose under the flat bed. Tell-tale teeth marks showed on the insulation. All I could do was apologize for Boyzy, offer to reimburse Dad when I got paid, and help rewire the truck. But Dad had simmered down by then and said, no, never mind.

Boyzy, of course, could not figure the reason for all the glares directed at him, but he soon forgave us. Dad wisely judged that we'd probably never train the dog to stop swinging on things, so he rewired the truck lights with snap connectors, and soon he was taking Boyzy with him again on hauling jobs. We just had to remember to never take the truck out of the yard without reconnecting the back light wires.

The next thing that got Boyzy in trouble was his unusual appetite.

Along with Dad's small trucking business, he had a little ranch that yielded a few cherries and apricots. The crops of each were too small for the warehouses, so Dad and Mom sold some of the fruit from their front yard beside the highway. During the summer, at least one box of either cherries or apricots was often on display in the shade of their big locust tree. Because of my summer job, I didn't get involved in that enterprise except to sometimes sell a box or two when I relieved the folks.

One summer afternoon, after I'd been in charge during their absence, Dad sought me out. "If you wanted cherries, why didn't you get some from the bowls inside, instead of eatin' from the box out front?"

"What?" I followed him out to his display box propped up on the lawn. The level of fruit was down a couple of inches from the top.

"Yeah," I said. "The cherries in the box I sold had settled, too. I had to top it off from a box in the basement."

Just then, Boyzy came around the house to investigate our voices. He stood watching us, munching calmly with a cherry stem protruding from his mouth. His chin was streaked with red, and a cherry pit fell from his lips as he chewed.

I made sure that Dad was laughing before I let myself join in.

"My fault, I guess," Dad said when he got his breath and wiped his eyes on his bandana, "for bein' too lazy to make some kinda stand for the boxes."

Boyzy liked the apricots, too, but by the time they were ripe the display boxes were on a sturdy wooden stand, and the dog had to settle for the culls Dad brought home for him.

Rock islands in the formerly free-flowing Columbia River created the channels and rapids which Boyzy and I enjoyed in our canoe.

Boyzy and I shared glorious times that summer. I found a canoe for sale so cheap I couldn't resist buying it with some of my summer wages. From the first Boyzy loved that canoe as much as I did. After a few spills into the water for him, and several near spills for both of us, Boyzy learned to stand in place at the bow, savoring the breeze and occasionally looking back and wagging his tail as if to share his enjoyment of the ride. With that canoe, we were companion explorers of all the rocky islands in that part of the Columbia River, and we learned to navigate the short rapids that ran between quiet backwater pools existing at low river stage. Boyzy exulted in these adventures.

As summer wound toward fall, Boyzy showed more of a quiet nature. One clear, moonless night, I found him standing on a grassy hummock near the house, just staring out above the horizon, scanning the starry sky, occasionally lifting his head to sniff the breeze or perking his ears as if to sense some cosmic sound inaudible to mere humans. The sight tingled my spine, and I wish I could have recorded it by some means other than memory. That night Boyzy stayed there even after I went in, and thereafter we often saw him on that same hummock, night or day, looking intently into the distance, listening and sampling the breeze. If he received communications of some kind, he never answered back. By some unspoken agreement, the whole family respected Boyzy's mystic vigils.

After I left for school that fall, Dad decided to put Boyzy's abilities to use by taking him hunting for Chukars in the little canyons across the highway. The family told the details this way:

Boyzy led while Dad picked his way uphill among the talus blocks toward a cluster of spring-fed bushes, holding his shotgun at the ready. Suddenly, the buzz of a nearby rattlesnake startled Dad just as he was stepping. He fell hard, with a leg between two rocks. He heard the snap, and felt the stab of pain. Then he felt a new pain—a sickening chest ache that dimmed his sight. *Heart attack!* Dad realized. He drifted toward unconsciousness.

The next thing Dad remembered was Boyzy whining and licking his face. The chest pain had lessened. Dad roused himself to pull his twisted leg free. He crawled, dragging his throbbing leg, to the shotgun he had flung away so his hands could break his fall. But when he tried to fire the gun to bring help, he found it was disabled. He was too far from the house to call for help. And he knew he could not get there on his own.

Dad's despair brought panic, which may have saved his life. He began to hyperventilate, and the extra oxygen just may have made the difference. He realized that his only hope was Boyzy, the irresponsible, headstrong scrub of Rusty's litter.

"Boyzy, come home!" Dad ordered, as calmly as he could. He repeated the command when Boyzy cocked his head and whined uncertainly. At the third command, Boyzy whirled. Without a backward look, the dog raced down the hill and across the highway, barking as he neared the house. Mom knew that something bad had happened. Fortunately, my Uncle Max was with her, and he led the way. They followed Boyzy charging up the hill to Dad. Max, whom his buddies had dubbed "The Bear," carried Dad down in his arms. Mom was stumbling alongside, encouraging Dad to take deep breaths, when they heard the screech of sliding tires—and then a thump.

Boyzy lay in the middle of the road, three feet in front of a black Packard. Blood stained his golden head.

"He just stood there in the way," the driver wailed, jumping from the car. "I tried to swerve but he moved in front of me. I just couldn't stop in time."

Then the man saw Dad's condition, and in moments Dad and Mom were in the car, speeding toward Wenatchee. They made the twenty miles to the hospital in eighteen minutes, and Dad survived that first evidence he'd ever had of a bad heart.

By the time I got home, Dad was there too, looking pale and suddenly old and tired, lying on the couch with his leg cast stretched out. All the doctors could do in those days for his heart was to give him nitroglycerin pills and advice to "take things easy."

Max walked me out to Boyzy's favorite grassy knoll. "I buried him right under there," Max said, pointing, "right where he used to stand and watch."

I couldn't talk just then, and after a pause Max continued. "Y'know, it was as if he deliberately tried to stop that car. Maybe to get more help, or maybe to block the road until we got your dad across."

Again I didn't answer.

"Well, thank God he picked a fast car to challenge," Max went on. "Who knows if we'd used your Mom's...."

"If only its brakes had been a little better," I managed to say before I turned away.

I stayed home long enough to make sure the folks were all right on their own, then headed back to school. Before I left I sold the canoe to Max. He never finished paying for it, but that's okay. I didn't want it any more.

Dad was incapable of following the doctor's orders to take it easy—he just couldn't live that way. Within three years, at age fifty-four, he got the Big One. I made it to the hospital in time for him to know that I was there, and to grip his hand at the end while Mom kept pleading for him to breathe—"just one more time."

Mom sold out to the power district and moved into a house trailer that was to be her last home. The town of Entiat, the highway and the railroad were moved to higher ground, and the old weathered house and other buildings in the way of a new, permanent flooding were demolished. Lake Entiat, the engineered lake behind Rocky Reach Dam, now covers everything that was so familiar—the shore lands, the rapids and the quiet pools, even the nearby islands in the old, free-flowing river.

For years after Mom moved—even after she died—when I drove along that part of the new highway, I found myself looking out to where that grassy knoll lies under the murky water and murmuring, "Good Boyzy."

Sometimes I still do.

THE END

Gerald and Alma Foxworthy, shortly before his fatal heart attack in 1955.

EPILOGUE

After one of my public readings of "Popcorn Odyssey," a young woman in the audience muttered, "Nobody could be *that* broke!" Believe me, we and many of our neighbors *were* that broke at times during the Great Depression, when the nation's economic structure had all but shattered, jobs had disappeared, and families had used up their reserve resources. Even with all the frugality, ingenuity, and toughness we could muster, bleak times came when there was no money and no way for decent, law-abiding folks to *get* money.

As an example, my wife's father, Wilbur "Buck" Buckley, told of his and an Entiat neighbor family pooling their meager cash to buy a ten-cent bag of salt. The worst part for Buck was that he had to pitch in three Indian Head pennies he had saved for years.

*   *   *

The "seed loan" of 1935, which my folks could not pay off because that apple crop was lost to the Big Freeze, remained an obligation and a debt of honor to my mother, if not to Dad. After Dad died, Mom tracked down an agency that would accept the few hundreds owed and paid off the debt from Dad's estate.

*   *   *

Our hard work in 1942 at Loomis, California, to save the fruit-packing business of the Nisei family was ultimately in vain. Dad's prediction, that the family would soon be released from the internment camp, was overly optimistic. While the family remained confined, some unscrupulous locals managed to swindle them out of their business, their packing shed, and even the business bank account that Mr. McKeever had so carefully protected.

*   *   *

In early June of 1948, a flood of historic proportions forever changed the Entiat River of my childhood. That flood took out the dam at the Ardenvoir mill of C. A. Harris and Son, and also removed the big rocks sheltering my favorite swimming hole downstream from Grandma Lillian's orchard. The flood changed the course of the river in many places, straightening curved reaches and removing many of the best fishing holes.

A further insult to my beloved river has been the "mudding in" of the lowermost part, below Numeral Rock, including filling of the favorite swimming hole of Entiat kids of my generation. This degradation has resulted from the creation of Lake Entiat, the reservoir behind Rocky Reach Dam. Before this engineered lake, the sediment load of the Entiat was swept away each year by the rushing waters of the free-flowing Columbia River. Now, with the Columbia raised and drastically slowed by the dam, the sediment of the Entiat drainage has no natural disposal. Instead, the sediment has built a delta into the lake and also backs upstream in the Entiat's lower channel.

*   *   *

Good fortune allowed me to eventually find my high-school sweetheart, Cleo, at a school reunion. While we chatted pleasantly, catching up about our recent lives, the band started playing a 1940's ballad. Of course, I asked her to dance. The moment she came into my arms, decades dropped away. A swell of emotion stunned me—as if my arms had been programmed long ago to thrill at holding this one, special lady.

330

Cleo snapped me back to awareness. "We're not dancing," she whispered against my ear as couples moved around us. Somehow, I made it through that dance, moving in a kind of unbelieving trance.

I didn't tell Cleo then how I felt, and didn't learn until later that she, too, had felt the thrill. But this time I managed to not lose her, and within two years we were settled together in this region of our youth.

ACKNOWLEDGMENTS

Circumstances of my childhood favored the compilation of these memoirs. A great deal of help allowed them to see the light of day.

My Aunt Achsa Foxworthy Cook was an invaluable source of remembrances and verifications. That sweet lady lived to the ripe old age of ninety-two and retained a sharp mind almost to the end. I also have Aunt Achsa to thank for many of the early photographs. She was a photography buff who, as a self-sufficient young woman, somehow managed the costs of photo film and processing when those were unjustifiable expenditures to most of the family.

I am also indebted to scores of other relatives, friends, neighbors, classmates and teachers, living and past, who shaped my early history and contributed to these memoirs. Some you have met in these pages by their real identities; others you have met only by their roles in the stories. Some, alas, did not make their way into these pages.

For local details of those times, I have relied on microfiche archives of *The Wenatchee Daily World* (now *The Wenatchee World*) and the former *Entiat Times*. My memories also were helped, and in some cases modified, by three significant books about early times in the Entiat Valley: *Entiat Remembers: An Anthology of Pioneer Strengths,* by Ginger Sage (1997); *First*

Schools in the Entiat Valley, by Rachel Stanaway Sines (2001); and *Under the Guard of Old Tyee—A Reflection of the Early Days in the Entiat Valley,* by Albert Long (2001). These books are listed with other references that follow.

Members of my Wenatchee Valley Writers Group provided invaluable reviews and suggestions throughout this compilation. A more talented, kind and diligent group of writers and reviewers would be hard to find, and their unselfish advice has greatly improved the quality of these presentations.

REFERENCES

Brinkley, Douglas, 2003, Wheels for the World: Penguin, New York, 858 p., illustrated.

Cheatham, James T., 1990, The Atlantic Turkey Shoot—U-boats off the Outer Banks in World War II: (self-published), 61 p., illustrated.

Harden, Blaine, 1996, A River Lost—The Life and Death of the Columbia: W.W. Norton, New York, 271 p.

Layman, William D., 2002, Native River—The Columbia Remembered: Washington State University Press, Pullman, Wash., 195 p., illustrated.

Lewis, David L. and others, 2003, 100 Years of Ford: Publications International, Chicago, 480 p., illustrated.

Long, Albert, 2001, Under the Guard of Old Tyee—a Reflection of the Early Days in the Entiat Valley: Cascade Graphics & Printing, Wenatchee, Wash., 166 p., illustrated.

Nostalgia, Inc., 1978, Sears Roebuck Catalogues of the 1930's—A Journey Back to Hard Times and High Hopes: Nostalgia, Inc., New York, illustrated.

Sage, Virginia Lee, 1997, Entiat Remembers—An Anthology of Pioneer Strengths: Cascade Graphics, Wenatchee, Wash., 204 p., illustrated.

Sines, Rachel Stanaway, 2001, First Schools in the Entiat Valley: (self-published), 142 p., illustrated.

Stick, David, 1952, Graveyard of the Atlantic: Univ. of North Carolina Press, Chapel Hill.

Sulzberger, C. L., and others, 1966, The American Heritage Picture History of World War II: American Heritage Publishing Co., 640 p.

Watkins, T. H., 1999, The Hungry Years: Henry Holt and Co., New York, 587 p.

The Wenatchee Daily World, archives (microfiche), various years: The World Publishing Co., Wenatchee, Wash.

*   *   *

Printed in the United States
139434LV00003B/2/P